Praise for *The Misunderstood Jew*:

"This is precisely the book we have long needed, abundant in scholarship and leavened by gentle humor. I hope it finds its way into the hands of those who need it most."
— Rabbi Harold Kushner, author of *When Bad Things Happen to Good People*

"Full of the usual vim, vigor, and vitality that so characterizes Levine's lectures and writings, *The Misunderstood Jew* is quite simply the best book ever written about the Jewishness of Jesus and his earliest followers and the sad and ironically contrasting misunderstanding of Jews, and indeed of Jesus himself, by his own mostly Gentile followers in subsequent generations. This book is such a seminal work that it makes us all reexamine what it really means to be a Jew or a Christian and to examine the New Testament documents in a fair way."
— Dr. Ben Witherington, III, Prof. of New Testament, Asbury Theological Seminary

"This book is a searing challenge from the heart of Judaism to the conscience of Christianity. It is a very delicate but very definite *j'accuse* that requires Christians to rethink not only the accuracy of our history but the integrity of our theology. It reminds us that Judaism and Christianity are twin-children of the same mother and calls us beyond a sibling rivalry that has been too often dismissive at best and savage at worst. Finally, it compels us to see that God has proclaimed a covenant for all and challenges us to take our place in that destiny."
— Dr. John Dominic Crossan, author of *Jesus: A Revolutionary Biography*

"Levine combines brilliant scholarship with a keen historic consciousness, calling Christians and Jews alike to move beyond their shallow and distorting stereotypes of each other, *The Misunderstood Jew* will open a new chapter in both religious understanding and mutual appreciation."
— John Shelby Spong, author of *Liberating the Gospels: Reading the Bible with Jewish Eyes.*

"Levine is learned by scholarly standards, a wonderful writer by literary standards, and a sensitive, witty, and wise teacher by human standards. She is one of those scholars whose life and scholarship are obviously not two separate things. Reading this book, one feels her passion, appreciates her experience, enjoys her humor, and still learns from her. Easy to read, easy to understand, hard to ignore. I learned from this book. So will everyone."
— Richard Elliott Friedman, author of *Who Wrote the Bible?* and *Commentary on the Torah*

"In this slim volume, Levine has literally carried out a revolution in biblical studies. In passage after passage she exposes anti-Jewish bias and provides rabbinic alternatives that are not only more sound exegetically but more fun. In short, this book delivers us from a monism of method and a dogmatism of conclusions, all served up by a spicy autobiographical approach that makes the text accessible to readers of every kind."

— Walter Wink, author of *The Human Being: Jesus and the Enigma of the Son of the Man*

"With insight and erudition—and the blessed leaven of humor—Levine challenges both Jews and Christians to move past their mutual misconceptions without ceding what is essential to both. Firmly rooted in her Jewish tradition, yet deeply conversant with Christianity, Levine is uniquely poised to show how Jesus of Nazareth is a Jew who can unite, rather than divide, Christians and Jews. Judaism and Christianity could be described as two faiths divided by a common religious language, and Amy-Jill Levine is the perfect interpreter for these communities that, even today, seem to be talking past each other. *The Misunderstood Jew* is an indispensable guidebook to future Jewish-Christian dialogue."

— David Gibson, author of *The Rule of Benedict: Pope Benedict XVI and His Battle with the Modern World.*

"Levine brings us irrefutable textual and historical evidence of how the frailties of human suspicion and misunderstanding have harmed us for centuries, and how we can now affirm that we are all children of God, with common roots in faith and love. This book is compelling statement of the hope for harmony, and the promise that 'the Lord will be with you—and also with you.'"

— Rabbi Wayne Dosick, Ph.D., author of *Living Judaism: The Complete Guide to Jewish Belief, Tradition and Practice*

"Levine characteristically writes with learning, passion, humor, and insight. *The Misunderstood Jew*, a stellar example of her scholarship, offers Jews and Christians a significant resource for deepened conversation."

— Mary C. Boys, author of *Has God Only One Blessing?: Judaism As a Source of Christian Self-Understanding*

"Levine has written an immensely valuable book both Jews and Christians. For Jews, she gives an expanded and deeper understanding of Jesus as a Jew. For Christians, she offers new understandings of Jewish stereotypes and anti-Judaism that have sullied the Christian theological world for generations. Everyone needs to read this important book."

— Rabbi Leonard A. Schoolman, Director, Center for Religious Inquiry

THE
MISUNDERSTOOD
JEW

*The Church
and the Scandal of
the Jewish Jesus*

AMY-JILL LEVINE

HarperOne
A Division of HarperCollinsPublishers

For Jay, Sarah Elizabeth, and Alexander David

HarperOne

All biblical quotations are taken from the New Revised Standard Version or are the author's own translation, unless otherwise noted.

HarperCollins books may be purchased for educational, business, or sales promotional use. For information please write: Special Markets Department, HarperCollins Publishers, 10 East 53rd Street, New York, NY 10022.

HarperCollins Web site: http://www.harpercollins.com
HarperCollins®, ■®, and HarperOne™ are
trademarks of HarperCollins Publishers.

FIRST EDITION
Designed by Joseph Rutt

Library of Congress Cataloging-in-Publication Data is available.
ISBN: 978–0–06–078966–4

07 08 09 10 11 RRD(H) 10 9 8 7 6

Contents

Introduction

When I was a child, my ambition was to be pope. I remember watching the funeral of John XXIII and asking my mother, "Who was that man?" I understood very little about him, but I did learn from the television coverage that he lived in Italy, had a very nice white suit and a great hat, and everyone seemed to love him. My mother responded, "That's Pope John XXIII." She, like most Jewish parents, was familiar with then cardinal Roncalli's efforts to save Jews during World War II as well as with his convening of Vatican II, the gathering that finally condemned the teaching that all Jews, everywhere, were responsible for the crucifixion of Jesus. Thus she added, "He was good for the Jews." I immediately decided I would be pope: it meant lots of spaghetti, great accessories, and the job was good for the Jews. "I want to be pope," I announced to my mother. "You can't," she replied. "You're not Italian." Clearly, for a variety of reasons, I was in desperate need of instruction regarding the relationship between church and synagogue.

My parents explained to me that the church (in my neighborhood, there were no Protestants, so "the church" meant "the Catholic Church") used the same Bible that we did, but whereas we in the synagogue read our texts in Hebrew and used scrolls, in the church Christians read their texts in English and used books. Further, they told me that Christians thought a Jewish man named Jesus was extremely important. I only later, and painfully, learned that because of these distinctions, and others, the separation between Jews and Christians was much more complicated.

I was raised in North Dartmouth, Massachusetts, a suburb of New Bedford, in a neighborhood that was predominantly Roman Catholic and Portuguese. Thus my introduction to the church was through ethnic Catholicism, and it was marvelous: feast days and festivals, pageantry and mystery, food and more food. I loved Christmas trees and Easter bunnies; I sang Christmas carols in the school choir (although like a number of Jews in similar settings I typically only mouthed words like "Christ" and "Jesus," and although hesitant to admit it, I found "Silent Night" a much prettier song than "I Had a Little Dreidel"). My favorite movie was, appropriately, *The Miracle of Our Lady of Fatima*, a 1952 production starring Gilbert Roland and, as Lucia, the girl who had the vision of the Blessed Virgin, Susan Whitney. I couldn't decide which would be more exciting: to have a vision and become a nun, like Sister Lucia, or to elope with Gilbert Roland.

When I was seven, this early fascination with Christianity came to a head with two events. First, I became insistent upon making my First Communion. All my friends were preparing for this special event, and I didn't want to be left out. My desire was not motivated by religious fervor or even religious understanding; I lacked both. Rather, I wanted the dress with the matching white patent-leather shoes. To provide me some consolation, my mother bought me a wedding gown for my Barbie doll. I'd dress Ken in his groom suit, with the jacket on backwards and with white construction paper for the clerical collar. Then, practicing what I learned from my friends, I'd have Barbie, in her bride dress, take Communion from Ken every morning before school.

Second, that year a friend on the school bus said to me, "You killed our Lord." "I did not," I responded with some indignation. Deicide would be the sort of thing I would have recalled. "Yes, you did," the girl insisted. "Our priest said so." Apparently, she had been taught that "the Jews" were responsible for the death of Jesus. Since I was the only one she knew, I must be guilty. But at the time I did not understand the reasons for the charge or have the means to address it.

I was convinced that priests wore special collars to keep them from lying. Since the priest wasn't dead, the charge had to be true. When that horrible trip from school was finally over—and thank heaven these were the 1960s, when mommies met their kids at the bus stop—I was in hysterics. Calming me down, my mother learned what had so traumatized me. She assured me that my friend had misspoken. Calls were made, and—to the enormous credit of the local diocese—this hateful teaching was stopped.

But I had become obsessed. I initially concluded that the priest had misinterpreted his Bible. It must have been a translation error, I thought, since even in second grade I knew from Hebrew school that it was easy to make a translation error. So I decided I'd learn to read the Christian Bible (no one told me it was in Greek), find the problem, solve it, and then go on to do other things, like learn how to knit or to establish world peace. That was forty-three years ago; I'm still working. The following year, by the way, was the publication of *Nostra Aetate*, the Vatican document stating that all Jews are not directly responsible for Jesus's death.

I also asked my parents if I might attend catechism with my friends. I had Hebrew school two days a week after school; my friends had catechism the other two days. So my parents agreed. "As long as you remember who you are," they said, "go learn." On occasion I'd go, and I loved it! When I couldn't go, I'd pump my friends for the stories they were learning, and I'd listen to Sunday morning Mass on television (whenever I could skip Sunday school) to get more details. My general reaction to Gospel stories was one of familiarity.

Jesus meets a woman at a well and concerns about marriage emerge, just as with Abraham's servant and Rebekah, Jacob and Rachel, Moses and Zipporah. Jesus is a good shepherd, just like David. Jesus fusses at priests, just like Amos. Jesus tells parables, just like the prophet Nathan and a number of rabbis whose stories appear in postbiblical Jewish sources. Jesus heals and raises the dead; so too Elijah and Elisha. Jesus survives when children around him are slaughtered, just like Moses. I didn't have to read Matthew 2–7 to know that the rescued baby would take a trip to Egypt, cross water in a life-changing experience, face temptation in the wilderness, ascend a mountain, and deliver comments on the Law—the pattern was already established in *Shemot*, the book of Exodus.[1]

Nor was the cross strange. The story resembled that of the deaths of the Maccabean martyrs, the mother and her seven sons, whom we recall at Hanukkah. Making the connection even closer, these Jewish martyrs also anticipated vindication and resurrection. Second Maccabees states, "The King of the universe will raise us up to an everlasting renewal of life, because we have died for his Laws" (7:9). Written by Greek-speaking Jews, the books of the Maccabees were preserved by the church; they are found today in the collection known either as the Deuterocanonical Writings (the Catholic designation) or the Old Testament Apocrypha (the Protestant designation). Later Jewish texts would retell the stories of the Maccabees, and the synagogue would continue to celebrate the holiday of

Hanukkah; both church and synagogue recognize the exemplary mother and her seven sons. The irony is we Jews celebrate the holiday of Hanukkah, but the church preserved the earliest records of the events that form the basis for the holiday.

The description of Jesus's suffering recalled for me the accounts in the Yom Kippur martyrology of the rabbis executed in the second revolt against Rome (132–35 CE). They also faced the power of the empire and did not falter in their faith. The death of the innocent was, moreover, part of my understanding of the Shoah, the deaths of millions of Jews at the hands of the Nazis. Jesus even complains about those who want the best seats in the synagogue (Matt. 23:6)—I have been known to do the same.

I don't recall hearing anything negative about Jews per se, save that I didn't like the fact that the Levite in the parable of the good Samaritan was a bad guy. I am a Levite; I took that parable personally. But my initial impression of the New Testament was that it was a collection of good Jewish stories told by a good Jewish storyteller. And my initial impression of Christianity bolstered this positive impression. My parents had told me that the church was like a cousin to the synagogue: we worshiped the same God, we both believed in the Golden Rule. Christians and Jews also shared many books of the Bible in common, although I believed at the time that Christians had to work harder, because their Bible was longer than ours. My friends had welcomed me into their homes, and they answered as best they could the questions I asked. They took me to Mass with them (usually on Saturday, after skating at the now-defunct Lincoln Park roller rink, to the 5:00 PM service at St. Julie Billiart Church on Slocum Road in North Dartmouth).

It was not until I was in high school that I actually read the New Testament. The Gospel of Matthew started off just fine: a genealogy with five women, Tamar, Rahab, Ruth, Bathsheba, and Mary. Nothing wrong here. Then came the virgin birth, the magi, the temptation, and the Sermon on the Mount. But as I continued to read, I began to see all too clearly where that priest had found his hateful teaching. Verses such as Matthew 27:25, the cry of "the people as a whole" that Jesus should be crucified and that "his blood be on us and on our children," provided the rationale for branding all Jews at all times "Christ killers" and therefore for killing them. The Gospel of John, with its repeated use of the word "Jew," seemed a litany of hate. Peter's sermons in Acts about the responsibility of the Jews for Jesus's death (2:23; 4:10) ... Paul's statement in Romans that the Jews are "enemies of God" for the sake of the Gentiles (11:28) ... First Thessalonians' comments about "the Jews, who killed both the Lord Jesus and the prophets ... and displease God, and oppose all everyone" (2:15) ... The list went on, and the pain continued.

Yet I had, fortunately, been inoculated against seeing only hate. My Christian friends had modeled for me the grace and friendship that are at the heart of the church; my parents had told me that Jesus was a Jew speaking to other Jews, and that his basic message was exactly the same as that of Judaism: to "love the Lord your God" and to "love your neighbor as yourself." So I knew that, although the New Testament could be read as being anti-Jewish, it did not have to be read that way.

Unless we Jews understand the beliefs and practices and histories of our Christian neighbors and unless Christians understand Jews and Judaism—we'll never achieve the *shalom* ("peace") that the children of Abraham (including Muslims) all claim to be seeking. Thus I write not only as an academic who teaches New Testament in a predominantly Protestant divinity school but also as a Jew—and a member of an Orthodox synagogue—who recognizes the beauty of the Christian tradition, the harm that has been perpetrated in its name, and the several means by which its basic, important messages of justice and peace can be heard anew. Further, I am convinced that interfaith conversation is essential if we are to break down the prejudices that have kept synagogue and church in enmity, or at best tolerance, for the past two millennia. In other words, I am placing my scholarship in service to personal, pastoral, and even political ends. That, of course, makes me biased. But being biased is not the same thing as being wrong.

Jews and Christians can, and must, talk to each other. Although all interfaith dialogue is educational and salutary, Jews and Christians have a number of special reasons for engaging each other. It is sometimes said that Judaism is the mother religion and Christianity the daughter, but church and synagogue are better seen as siblings fighting over the parents' legacy. Who are the true children of Abraham and the heirs to the books of the Bible, the Law, and the Prophets? Who followed the correct path, and who veered off? Christians must engage with Jews, since Jews are explicitly mentioned in the Scriptures of the church, and those references have had substantial repercussions throughout history, most of them bad.

Jews should engage with Christians, not only because the early history of the church is the history of Jews as well, but also because the synagogue and the church developed in dialogue, and debate, with each other. The break between the two traditions began not at the cross or the tomb but centuries later.

Looking back, behind the culture wars of today, behind the death camps and the Crusades, behind Constantine and Judah the Prince, to the first century allows Jews and Christians to recover shared roots with Jesus of Nazareth and his immediate followers. The effort does not forget the past two thousand years, but neither does it allow those years to abort the conversation. For far too long Jesus has been the wedge that drives Christians and Jews apart. I suggest that we can also see him as a bridge between us. The image is not meant to indicate that either of us cedes our own views of Jesus—the bridge spans two separate lands—and it does not mean we need to find common ground on everything. I do not envision Jews and Christians standing over a wide chasm and reciting the Lord's Prayer or the Kaddish or singing "Kumbaya." Conversations across religions need not, and should not, end with all participants proclaiming an ultimate unity of belief. Such an exercise only waters down both traditions into a bland universalism that, in an attempt to be inoffensive, winds up offending everyone.

Understanding of and appreciation for our neighbor's tradition are not the same thing as agreement with it. Jews and Christians will disagree. Jews will also disagree with other Jews, and Christians with other Christians. The day that Jews and Christians agree on everything is the day the messiah comes, or comes back. The point of interfaith conversation is not to convert the person across the table, but it is also not to abdicate one's own theology for the sake of reaching agreement. Put another way: there is no reason for Jews and Christians to sacrifice their particular beliefs on the altar of interfaith sensitivity. The former bishop of Sweden and dean of Harvard Divinity School Krister Stendahl speaks appropriately of "holy envy," that is, the appreciation of the beliefs and practices of another.[2]

By seeing Jesus as a Jew with regard to both belief and practice, Christians can develop a deeper appreciation for the teachings of the church. To be sure, anyone engaged in biblical study, whether in the privacy of a living room or retreat center, reading with a church group, listening to tapes, or taking a class, can develop an impression of Jesus. Those who study the text for spiritual reasons will find a Jesus who speaks to them personally. As my students sometimes say, "I read the text, and the Holy Spirit guides me." Yet even more can be done, or, as I am wont to reply, "Give the Holy Spirit something to work with."

In particular, I think the Spirit would appreciate a bit of historical investigation. Today Jesus's words are too familiar, too domesticated, too stripped of their initial edginess and urgency. Only when heard through first-century Jewish ears can their original edginess and urgency be recovered. Consequently, to understand the man from Nazareth, it is necessary to understand Judaism. More, it is necessary to see Jesus as firmly within Judaism rather than as standing apart from it, and it is essential that the picture of Judaism not be distorted through the filter of centuries of Christian stereotypes; a distorted picture of first-century Judaism inevitably leads to a distorted picture of Jesus. Just as bad: if we get Judaism wrong, we'll wind up perpetuating anti-Jewish or anti-Semitic teachings, and thus the mission of the church—to spread a gospel of love rather than a gospel of hate—will be undermined. For Christians, this concern for historical setting should have theological import as well. If one takes the incarnation—that is, the claim that the "Word became flesh and lived among us" (John 1:14)—seriously, then one should take seriously the time when, place where, and people among whom this event occurred.

Christians obtain yet another benefit in seeing Jesus in his Jewish context, for the recognition of Jesus's Jewishness and of his speaking in a Jewish idiom can also restore faith in the New Testament. Doing just a bit of historical investigation provides a much-needed correction to America's Christ-saturated, albeit biblically ignorant, culture. For example, those who prefer the fiction of *The Da Vinci Code* over the facts of history because the novel seems to enhance the role of women in early Christianity will find that studies of the Jewish Jesus reveal the leadership roles and economic freedoms women had at the time. Moreover, such studies yield more options to women than the relegation of Mary Magdalene to the role of "Mrs. Jesus." Those who prefer the *Gospel of Judas* over the Gospels of Matthew, Mark, Luke, and John because they see it as eliminating anti-Jewish views from Christian origins would do well, instead, to see how

Jesus fits into his Jewish context, and that includes the notice that Judas does not, in the Gospels, represent "the Jews."

Jews too can learn much from appreciating Jesus within his Jewish context, for the New Testament texts preserve for Jews part of our own history. The stories of Jesus tell us a great deal about Jewish life in Galilee and Judea in the first century, and the only uncontested Pharisee from whom we have extant written sources is Paul of Tarsus. I find that the more I study Jesus, Mary Magdalene, James, Peter, and Paul in their own historical contexts, the more I come to appreciate my own Judaism: the diversity of its teachings, the richness of its encounter with the divine, the struggles it faced in accommodating to the Roman world. I appreciate, even find inspirational, the message of the kingdom of heaven, a message that spoke of the time when all debts are forgiven and when those who have willingly give, without thought of reciprocity, to those who need; a time when we no longer ask, "Who is my neighbor?" but "Who acts as neighbor?"; a time when we prioritize serving rather than being served. ... But as much as I admire much of the message, I do not worship the messenger. Instead, I find Jesus reflects back to me my own tradition, but in a new key. I also have to admit to a bit of pride in thinking about him— he's one of ours.

If on the popular level we Jews are willing not only to acknowledge but also to take pride in the Jewishness of such generally nonobservant Jews as Sigmund Freud, Albert Einstein, the Marxes (Karl and Groucho, although Karl was baptized as a child), and Jerry Seinfeld, why not acknowledge the quite observant Jesus? Such recognition need not entail citing the Gospels in a bar mitzvah talk or in a *d'var Torah*, an interpretation of the biblical reading for the week, although I have heard rabbis in Reform and Conservative synagogues cite Homer (both the Greek poet and Bart's father), Plato, the Buddha, Muhammad, Gandhi, Martin Luther King Jr., the Dalai Lama, and even Madonna (the Kabbalah-besotted singer, not the mother of Jesus). At least Jesus is Jewish with regard to family, practice, and belief.

A critically aware, historically informed study of Jesus in his Jewish context does more than provide benefits to Christians and Jews alike; it aids in preventing the anti-Semitism that tends to arise when the history is not known. The concern to recover Jesus's Jewishness is these days particularly urgent. In churches and in the academy, in pronouncements made by Mexican Americans and Palestinians, women from Benin and men from Korea, the World Council of Churches and Catholic liberation theologians, Jesus's Jewishness is frequently erased. In the churches, as Jesus continues to be the symbol for all that is socially good, Christian ministers and laity alike depict his Jewish background as the epitome of all that is wrong with the world. If Jesus preaches good news to the poor, so the common impression goes, "the Jews" must be preaching good news to the rich. If Jesus welcomes sinners, "the Jews" must have pushed them away. If Jesus speaks to or heals women, "the Jews" must have set up a patriarchal society that makes the Taliban look progressive.

In the academy, certain schools of thought have managed to distinguish Jesus, whether implicitly or explicitly, from any sort of "Judaism." The popular push to depict Jesus as a Galilean and see Galilee as religiously and ethnically distinct from Judea winds up conveying the impression that "Judaism," with its Temple and its leadership, is quite distinct from the Galilean Jesus. The popular image of Jesus as a "peasant" often serves not to connect him to his fellow Jews but to distinguish him from them, since "the Jews" remain in the popular imagination not peasants but Pharisees and Sadducees or, in academic terms, members of the retainer and elite classes. Worse, the lingering view that Jesus dismissed basic Jewish practices, such as the Laws concerning Sabbath observance and ritual purity, turns Jesus away from his Jewish identity and makes him into a liberal Protestant.

In liberation theology—that form of religious thought proclaiming that God has a "preferential option for the poor" and seeking to put biblical pronouncement in service to political and economic ends—Jesus is the pedagogue of the oppressed, the redeemer of the underclass, the hero of the masses. The problem is not the use of Jesus for political ends; the biblical material has always been (and should continue to be) used to promote a more just society. The problem is that the language of liberation all too often veers off into anti-Jewish rants. Jesus becomes the Palestinian martyr crucified once again by the Jews; he is the one killed by the "patriarchal god of Judaism"; he breaks down the barriers "Judaism" erects between Jew and Gentile, rich and poor, male and female, slave and free and so can liberate all today. The intent is well meaning, but the history is dreadful, and the impression given of Judaism is obscene.

All of this appalling material results in good measure from the fact that Jews and Christians are ignorant of both their own history and the history of the other. The level of religious illiteracy is staggering. Jews and Christians share a common history (not all of it pleasant), as two recent books, James Carroll's *Constantine's Sword* and David Klinghoffer's *Why the Jews Rejected Jesus*, make abundantly clear.[3] Yet common history is not the same as common knowledge. In years of teaching about Jesus and the origins of Christianity, first at Duke University, then at Swarthmore College, and now at Vanderbilt University Divinity School, I have seen both the extent of the ignorance Jews and Christians have of each other and the unfortunate results of that ignorance. A substantial number of my Christian students view Jesus as opposed to Judaism rather than as a Jew himself. They see Judaism as a religion of law as opposed to Jesus's religion of grace; they believe that Jews follow the commandments to earn a place in heaven; they suggest that Jews rejected Jesus because he proclaimed peace and love instead of violence against the Roman occupiers of Jerusalem. Comments from my Christians students typically begin, "Why do the Jews think ..." as if all Jews think alike.

Christians tend to know even less of Judaism's legacy following the time of Jesus. A number of students assume that all Jews strictly follow every single letter of Torah (the Pentateuch, the first five books of the Bible). I've even been asked where Jews in urban areas keep animals needed for Temple sacrifice; one young man inquired whether we needed to get a zoning variance for the practice. It came as no small disappointment to him to learn that animal sacrifice stopped with the destruction of the Second Temple in the mid-first century CE. I have met Christian congregants who are stunned when I tell them that many, if not most, American Jews are not fluent in Hebrew, do not know intimately the plot lines of the Bible after the book of Exodus, do not keep kosher, and do not observe the Laws of family purity, such as going to the *miqveh* (ritual bath). Some Christian students, and even a few Jews, are surprised to learn that Judaism has a very long and robust acknowledgment not only of an afterlife, but also of resurrection of the dead. Comparably few Christians have heard of the great Rabbi Hillel (unless they happened to stumble into a Hillel House on a college campus), Rabbi Akiva, and Rabbi Judah ha-Nasi, let alone Rashi, Maimonides, and the Baal Shem Tov. That many Jews don't recognize these names either just makes matters worse, since Jews who don't know who Judah ha-Nasi, also known as Judah the Prince, is (he is the man responsible for the codification of the

Mishnah, the major early book of Jewish Law, ca. 200 CE) have surely heard of the Virgin Mary, St. Augustine, and Martin Luther.

Numerous Christians (even nice ones) think that all Jews are smart and rich (we should be so lucky); that all Jews stand against the establishment of a Palestinian state, since God gave the land of Israel to our ancestors (wrong again; Jewish views on the Middle East range from the idea of "Greater Israel" to support for a two-state resolution to the view that there should be no Jewish state until the messiah comes); and that all Jewish mothers are domineering, neurotic, and overprotective (a depiction that fits neither my mother nor my mother-in-law; as for me, you'll have to ask my children).

But this level of ignorance is not surprising, for there are few mechanisms whereby Christians might become informed about Jews and Judaism. Despite the efforts of Vatican II and a steady stream of documents produced by the Roman Catholic Church as well as numerous Protestant churches, Christian teaching from the pulpit continues to present a negative picture of Judaism to the faithful, and select readings of New Testament passages confirm the negative impressions.

Popular culture exacerbates the problem. The major elements of "Judaism" on the Christian radar are the Shoah, the Holocaust, which is primarily a racial rather than a religious issue (a Jew who converted to Christianity was just as much a Jew to the National Socialists as a rabbi), and the State of Israel, which, although formally a "Jewish" state, is substantially a secular culture. Therefore, Christians from Tanzania to Tennessee gain their dominant impressions of Jews and Judaism by combining selective readings from the church's Scriptures with *Fiddler on the Roof,* current Israeli policies, and an occasional episode of *South Park.* As for Judaism more narrowly defined—its practices, liturgies, holidays, history of biblical interpretation—most of that is unknown or ignored. I emphasize here the "religious" aspects of Judaism, for a secular Judaism does exist in America's popular culture. Adam Sandler's "The Hanukkah Song" introduced some non-Jews to Jewish practice. Sustaining Jewish identity in the United States are such lines as:

When you felt like the only kid in town without a Christmas tree,
Here's a list of people who are Jewish just like you and me....
David Lee Roth lights the menorah
So do James Caan, Kirk Douglas, and the late Dinah Shore-ah.

The message is that Hanukkah is the most important holiday on the Jewish calendar. Wrong again.

Nor are matters much better on the Jewish side, for ignorance cuts both ways. Just as some Christians distort Judaism by seeing it as a tradition of law without grace, so some Jews distort Christianity by seeing it as a tradition of belief without action. Both Judaism and Christianity would agree with the Letter of James's insistence that "faith without works is dead" (2:26). Others think of Christians as polytheists, since the church proclaims a Father, Son, and Holy Spirit, although Christians themselves are quite explicit in being monotheists.

Most Jews do have a general familiarity with the stories of Jesus's birth and death: from postage stamps to mall decorations to the annual fight somewhere in the country about displaying a crèche or a cross on public property. Knowledge of Christian teaching comes from the occasional pronouncement of someone claiming to be, and recognized by the media as, a spokesperson for the church writ large. Such speakers range from the pope to Billy Graham to Pat Robertson, James Dobson, and Jerry Falwell. Jews who attended U.S. public schools before 1962 may well have recited the Lord's Prayer (also referred to as the Our Father) every day before or after saying the Pledge of Allegiance. Jews have exclaimed, and in some parts of the country are still expected to exclaim, in song every December, "Born is the king of Is-ra-el"; we continue to get the message that the "faithful, joyful, and triumphant" are those who worship "Christ the Lord."

When the topic turns to postbiblical Christian history, most Jews know the great figures and events of Christianity, although the knowledge is selective. The familiar figures include the Spanish Inquisition's Torquemada and the Protestant Reformation's Martin Luther. The former convinced Queen Isabella and her husband, King Ferdinand, to expel all Jews (and Muslims) from Spain; Columbus was not the only one who sailed in 1492. The latter is remembered for his 1543 treatise "The Jews and Their Lies," which begins by citing Gospel texts:

He [Jesus] did not call them Abraham's children, but a "brood of vipers" [Matt. 3:7]. Oh, that was too insulting for the noble blood and race of Israel, and they declared, "He has a demon" [Matt. 11:18]. Our Lord also calls them a "brood of vipers"; furthermore in

John 8 he states: "If you were Abraham's children ye would do what Abraham did.... You are of your father the devil" [vv. 39, 44]. It was intolerable to them to hear that they were not Abraham's but the devil's children, nor can they bear to hear this today.

He then advises that these "truly stupid fools" who "lie and blaspheme so monstrously" should have their synagogues burned to the ground, their houses razed, their prayer books and Talmuds taken from them, their rabbis forbidden to teach, and a host of other concerns that cannot help but remind one of Nazi laws. The Vatican has renounced Torquemada's intolerance; the Evangelical Lutheran Church of America and a number of other Lutheran groups have denounced Luther's anti-Jewish invectives. But the memory remains. Many Jews will recall the erstwhile president of the Southern Baptist Convention, the Reverend Bailey Smith, who announced at a 1980 Religious Roundtable national affairs briefing in Dallas, "God Almighty does not hear the prayer of a Jew." He also noted that he is "pro-Jew" because "they are God's special people, but without Jesus Christ, they are lost." Jews were not much comforted by this notice.

However, Jews are often unaware of the enormous diversity in practice, polity, theology, and biblical interpretation within the Christian communion between Baptist and Orthodox, Amish and Episcopalian, and the popular culture is of little help. "Baptist" too easily becomes equated with "Southern Baptist Convention" and then with the convention's most conservative voices. Jews (and a number of Christians) are unaware of the Cooperative Baptist Fellowship, Free Will Baptists, Primitive Baptists, American Baptists, National Baptists, and so on. Nor is there much familiarity with those in the churches who sit uneasily in the pew; just as not all Jews agree with everything their rabbi says, so too disagreement with the priest or pastor or the church teaching is far from uncommon. For some Jews, the Christian default is Roman Catholicism, with the attendant erroneous views that all Catholics think alike and that Catholic teaching never changes.

On Yom Kippur, the Day of Atonement and the holiest day of the Jewish year, Jews remember those who died for *kiddush ha-Shem,* "sanctification of the Name" [of God], that is, by forfeiting their life rather than abandoning their Jewish identity and belief. Included are victims of the Crusades and of Christian states whose call was "convert or die." We recall blood libels, the accusations—still repeated in twenty-first-century Saudi newspapers—that Jews use the blood of children to bake matzo for Passover. We recall pogroms, attacks on our communities, by Christians seeking to avenge the death of Jesus on his killers. We know that the church established the first ghetto, a section in Venice to which Jews were restricted, lest our very presence infect the pure Christian city. For every "righteous Gentile" honored by the Jewish community for saving Jewish lives during World War II, we know that hundreds of thousands of so-called good Christians stood by during, or participated in, the planned extermination of the Jewish people. Historical memory is selective, and tragedy is not forgotten.

Although forced baptisms, ghettoes, and pogroms sponsored or tacitly permitted by the church are things of the past, their effects continue to impact Jewish-Christian conversation today. Some Jews adopt the role of victim and expect Christians to come to the table only with abject apologies. Guilt thereby replaces dialogue. But victimization at one period of history does not accord any group the moral high ground. If Jews come to the table with a sense of victimization and Christians come with a sense of guilt, nothing will be accomplished. Conversation cannot begin with either entitlement or apology. Christians are not in the position to apologize for the sins of the past: regret them, yes; swear not to repeat them, yes. But one group of Christians or one Christian cannot speak for all Christians or the church universal. The individual can only speak for the individual. In like manner, the Jew is not in the position to receive the forgiveness, let alone to grant absolution.[4] That is the role of the victim, or of God. One comes to the interfaith table not with guilt and not with entitlement, but with humility and interest. The conversation will not be between "church" and "synagogue" but between Ari and Christine, Worthington Wentworth Smyth-Jones-Windsor VIII and Frima-Sarah.

Moreover, no tradition is pristine. As a Jew, I am appalled by the sanctioned genocide suggested by passages in Deuteronomy and Joshua. I take no comfort in such passages as Deuteronomy 20:16–18: "But as for the towns of these peoples that the Lord your God is giving you as an inheritance, you must not let anything that breathes remain alive. You shall annihilate them—the Hittites and the Amorites, the Canaanites and the Perizzites, the Hivites and the Jebusites—just as the Lord your God has commanded, so that they may not teach you to do all the abhorrent things that they do for their gods, and you thus sin against the Lord your God." I find horrific the description of holy war in the book of Joshua, where the Israelites, in the taking of the city of Jericho, "devoted to destruction by the edge of the sword all in the city, both men and women, young and old, oxen, sheep, and donkeys" (6:21).

I am disgusted by Ezekiel's misogynistic images:

> Thus says the Lord God, because your lust was poured out and your nakedness uncovered in your whoring with your lovers ... therefore I will gather all your lovers, with whom you took pleasure, all those you loved and all those you hated; I will gather them against you from all around, and will uncover your nakedness to them, so that they may see all your nakedness.... I will deliver you into their hands ... they shall strip you of your clothes and take your beautiful objects and leave you naked and bare. They shall bring up a mob against you, and they shall stone you and cut you to pieces with their swords.... So I will satisfy my fury on you, and my jealousy shall turn away from you; I will be calm, and will be angry no longer. (16:36–42)

The rabbinic tradition and subsequent Jewish interpretations of these verses and others denounce the violence. But the texts are still there, just as the history of the relationship between church and synagogue cannot, and should not, be forgotten. The passages and the past should serve as perpetual reminders of the evils that humans perpetrate on each other in the name of religion.

Given this history, it should not be surprising that a number of Jews have never read the New Testament (the same can, alas, be said for a number of those who call themselves Christians). I recall one relative asking me years ago, when I was working on my Ph.D. on the Gospel of Matthew at Duke, "Why would you want to read such anti-Semitic stuff?"

"Have you ever read it?" I asked.

"No, why would I want to read such anti-Semitic stuff?"

When Jews and Christians study Scripture together—both the texts we share and the texts distinct to each group—we discover *both* what we share *and* how we come to define ourselves over and against each other. More, we see that invective does not always poison the interpretation. Jews, for example, need to know that many, if not most, Christians do not read the New Testament texts traditionally seen as anti-Jewish in an anti-Jewish manner. Nor do we Jews associate the evil Egyptians of the Passover story with Omar Sharif or Hosni Mubarak. And it is always salutary to hear with each other's ears.

After two thousand years of ignorance, the time has come for church and synagogue, Jews and Christians, to understand our intertwined histories, to see Jesus as a Jew who made sense to other Jews in a Jewish context, to learn how our two traditions came to a parting of the ways, to recognize how misunderstandings of Jesus and Judaism continue even today to foster negative stereotypes and feed hate, and to explore how the gains in interfaith relations made over the past several decades can be nurtured and expanded.

Jesus and Judaism

Belief in Jesus as the Christ—the Messiah—separates church and synagogue, Christians and Jews. It is not the only distinction, but it is the basic one. For Christians, the claim that Jesus is the way, the truth, and the life is obvious: it is proved by Jesus's resurrection, confirmed by the Bible, and experienced by the soul. For Jews, claims of Jesus's divine sonship and fulfillment of the messianic prophecies are false. Since we live in a world of cancer and AIDS, war and genocide, earthquakes and hurricanes, the messianic age cannot be here yet. Since there is no messianic age, obviously the messiah has not yet come. "How could anyone believe in Jesus?" ask Jews, while Christians wonder, "How could anyone not believe in Jesus?" What is self-evident to one is incomprehensible to the other.

Differences between Jews and Christians derive not only from different sacred Scriptures, historical memories, and lived experience; they derive also from belief, from faith. Christians "believe" in Jesus because Jesus fills Christian hearts and souls. In Christian terms, belief comes through "grace." Once the belief is in place, then the various arguments from the Bible, from nature, or from personal testimony about Jesus's lordship serve to bolster that belief. In other words, belief is like love: it cannot be compelled. It does not rest on logical argument or historical proof.

The same argument holds for Judaism. For Jews, the system is complete: there is no need for a New Testament, for the Torah and its interpretations within the Jewish community already offer revelation of the divine. Although the analogy is a tad strained, the Torah functions for the synagogue as Jesus does for the church: it is the "word" of the divine present in the congregation. Thus to ask Jews why they don't believe in Jesus is tantamount to asking Christians why they don't follow Muhammad. For

Jews, Jesus is unnecessary or a redundancy; he is not needed to save from sin or from death, since Judaism proclaims a deity ready to forgive repentant sinners and since it asserts that "all Israel has a share in the world to come" (Mishnah *Sanhedrin* 10:1).

And yet some Jews do convert to Christianity, and some Christians convert to Judaism. Again, conversion is not a matter of whose teaching is "better" or "true" in any sort of objective sense; it is prompted by the teaching that provides the best personal sense of truth and fulfillment to the individual.

Where we can agree, however, is in Jesus's own connection to Judaism.

Jewish Context and Content

The fact that Jesus was a Jew has not gone unrecognized. Libraries and bookstores are replete with volumes bearing such titles as *Jesus the Jew, The Galilean Jewishness of Jesus, Jesus and the World of Judaism, The Religion of Jesus the Jew, Jesus in His Jewish Context, The Jewish Reclamation of Jesus,* and three volumes and counting of *A Marginal Jew*.[1] The point is more than simply a historical observation. Numerous churches today acknowledge their intimate connection to Judaism: connections born from Scripture, history, theology, and, as Paul puts it, Christ "according to the flesh" (Rom. 9:5). Nevertheless, when it comes to the pew, the pulpit, and often the classroom, even when Christian congregants, ministers, and professors do acknowledge that Jesus was Jewish, they often provide no content for the label. The claim that "Jesus was a Jew" may be historically true, but it is not central to the teaching of the church.

The Nicene Creed, composed in the fourth century, proclaims:

> We believe in ... one Lord, Jesus Christ, the only Son of God, eternally begotten of the Father, God from God, Light from Light, true God from true God, begotten, not made, of one Being with the Father; through him all things were made. For us and for our salvation, he came down from heaven, was incarnate by the Holy Spirit of the Virgin Mary and became truly human. For our sake he was crucified under Pontius Pilate; he suffered death and was buried. On the third day he rose again in accordance with the Scriptures. He ascended into heaven and is seated at the right hand of the Father.

He will come again in glory to judge the living and the dead, and his kingdom will have no end.

The Apostles' Creed, likely dating a bit earlier, acknowledges

Jesus Christ, his only Son, our Lord, who was conceived by the Holy Spirit, born of the Virgin Mary, suffered under Pontius Pilate, was crucified, died, and was buried. He descended into hell. The third day he arose again from the dead. He ascended into heaven and sits at the right hand of God, the Father Almighty, whence he shall come to judge the living and the dead.

On the one hand, the creeds do not speak of "the Jews" as responsible for the death of Jesus; he "suffered under" and "was crucified under" Pontius Pilate. On the other hand, the creeds do not mention Jesus's Judaism at all. With the stress in some churches on Jesus's divine sonship, the cross, the resurrection, and the redemptory role of saving humanity from sin and death, his historical connection to Judaism gets lost along with his very Jewish message of the kingdom of heaven.

The problem is more than one of silence. In the popular Christian imagination, Jesus still remains defined, incorrectly and unfortunately, as "against" the Law, or at least against how it was understood at the time; as "against" the Temple as an institution and not simply against its first-century leadership; as "against" the people Israel but in favor of the Gentiles. Jesus becomes the rebel who, unlike every other Jew, practices social justice. He is the only one to speak with women; he is the only one who teaches nonviolent responses to oppression; he is the only one who cares about the "poor and the marginalized" (that phrase has become a litany in some Christian circles). Judaism becomes in such discourse a negative foil: whatever Jesus stands for, Judaism isn't it; whatever Jesus is against, Judaism epitomizes the category. No wonder even today Jesus somehow looks "different" from "the Jews": in the movies and artistic renderings, he's blond and they are swarthy; he is cute and buff and they need rhinoplasty and Pilates. Jesus and his followers such as Peter and Mary Magdalene become identified as (proto-)Christian; only those who chose not to follow him remain "Jews."

This divorcing of Jesus from Judaism does a disservice to each textually, theologically, historically, and ethically. First, the separation severs the church's connections to the Scriptures of Israel—what it calls the Old Testament (see below, pp. 199–202). Because Jesus and his earliest followers were all Jews, they held the Torah and the Prophets sacred, prayed the Psalms, and celebrated the bravery of Esther and the fidelity of Ruth. To understand Jesus, one must have familiarity with the Scriptures that shaped him (or, as a few of my students will insist, that he wrote). Second, the insistence on Jesus's Jewish identity reinforces the belief that he was fully human, anchored in historical time and place. This connection is known as the "scandal of particularity": not only does the church proclaim that the divine took on human form, it also proclaims that it took on this form in a particular setting among a particular people. The church claims that divinity took on human flesh—was "incarnated"—in Jesus of Nazareth. The time and the place therefore matter. Christianity follows Jesus of *Nazareth,* not Jesus of Cleveland or Jesus of Mexico City; the incarnation dates to the first century, not the twenty-first. Further, the Jewish tradition into which Jesus was born and the Christian tradition that developed in his name were "historical religions," that is, their foundational events took place in history and on earth, rather than in some mythic time and mythic place; they have a starting point and a vision for the future. To disregard history, to disregard time and place, is to be unfaithful to both Judaism and Christianity.

Historically, Jesus should be seen as continuous with the line of *Jewish teachers and prophets,* for he shares with them a particular view of the world and a particular manner of expressing that view. Like Amos and Isaiah, Hosea and Jeremiah, he used arresting speech, risked political persecution, and turned traditional family values upside down in order to proclaim what he believed God wants, the Torah teaches, and Israel must do. This historical anchoring need not and should not, in Christian teaching, preclude or overshadow Jesus's role in the divine plan. He must, in the Christian tradition, be more than just a really fine Jewish teacher. But he must be that Jewish teacher as well.

Further, Jesus had to have made sense in his own context, and his context is that of Galilee and Judea. Jesus cannot be understood fully unless he is understood through first-century Jewish eyes and heard through first-century Jewish ears. The parables are products of first-century Jewish culture, not ours; the healings were assessed according to that worldview, not ours; the debates over how to follow Torah took place within that set of legal parameters and forms of discourse, not ours. To understand Jesus's impact in his own setting—why some chose to follow him, others to dismiss him, and still others to seek his death—requires an understanding of that setting. If we today have difficulty fathoming how our grandparents could function without the Internet and cell phones, let alone without television, how can we possibly presume to understand the worldview of Jesus and his contemporaries without asking a few historical questions?

When Jesus is located within the world of Judaism, the ethical implications of his teachings take on renewed and heightened meaning; their power is restored and their challenge sharpened. Jews as well as Christians should be able to agree on a number of these teachings today, just as in the first century Jesus's followers and even those Jews who chose not to follow him would have agreed with such basic assertions as that God is our father, that his name should be hallowed, and that the divine kingdom is something ardently to be desired. Conversely, the failure to understand the Jewish Jesus within his Jewish context has resulted in the creation and perpetuation of millennia of distrust, and worse, between church and synagogue.

Understanding Torah

Jesus's connections to the basic Jewish teachings were right on target. Mark 12:28–34 recounts that a scribe (a Jewish expert in the interpretation of Torah) heard Jesus teaching and, finding his answers solid, asked him, "Which commandment is the first of all?" Jesus responded, "The first is, 'Hear, O Israel: the Lord our God, the Lord is one; you shall love the Lord your God with all your heart, and with all your soul, and with all your mind, and with all your strength.' The second is this: 'You shall love your neighbor as yourself.' There is no other commandment greater than these." The scribe affirms Jesus's response: "You are right, Teacher; you have truly said that 'he is one and besides him there is no other' and 'to love him with all the heart, and with all the understanding, and with all the strength,' and 'to love one's neighbor as oneself'—this is much more important than all whole burnt offerings and sacrifices." The same story, with different details, appears in Matthew 22:34–40 and Luke 10:25–28.

This "Great Commandment," as Matthew terms it, is a combination of Deuteronomy 6:4–5 and Leviticus 19:18. The first reading, called the Shema (from its first word, "Hear!" or, better, "Listen!"), is a major part of the synagogue liturgy. The next verses in Deuteronomy enjoin the people: "Keep these words that I am commanding you today in your heart. Recite them to your children and talk about them when you are at home and when you are away, when you lie down and when you rise. Bind them as a sign upon your hand, fix them as a frontlet on your forehead, and write them on the doorposts of your house and on your gates" (6:6–9). The injunctions were taken literally: the caves of Qumran—and so the community associated with the Dead Sea Scrolls, a community contemporaneous with Jesus—yielded examples of those very "signs" bound on the hand and forehead. Called in Hebrew *tefillin* or, from the Greek, phylacteries, these are boxes that contain small scrolls on which are written Deuteronomy 6:4–9 as well as Exodus 13:1–10; 13:11–16 and Deuteronomy 11:13–21; the boxes are attached to leather straps and worn by Jewish men at worship. (The Babylonian Talmud *Eruvin* 96a suggests that *tefillin* were worn by women as well.) Today, some Jewish women as well as men wear them.

Deuteronomy's words are reinforced also by the literal understanding of "write them upon the doorposts of your house and on your gates." This is the origin of the *mezuzah* (Hebrew, "doorpost"), a parchment bearing the words of Deuteronomy 6:4–9 and 11:13–21 that is placed inside a small case and then attached to the door of the house. Josephus, a younger Jewish contemporary of Jesus whose works provide substantial information about Jewish life in the first century, mentions in his *Antiquities of the Jews:* "They [the Jews] are also to inscribe the principal blessings they have received from God upon their doors" (4.8.13). *Mezuzot* (plural) have also been found at Qumran, although with different scriptural passages.

Despite these connections, Mark's version of the citation from Deuteronomy is not a direct quote from the Hebrew. Deuteronomy speaks of loving God with all "your heart, and with all your soul, and with all your might"; the citation in the Gospel changes "might" to "mind" and adds as a fourth component, strength. The slight shift and addition may well have come from Jesus himself, or they may be Mark's adaptations to his Greek-speaking audience based on an alternative Greek version of the passage.

Jesus's second point, "You shall love your neighbor as yourself," is also a central verse in Jewish thought. The great Rabbi Akiva, who lived a century after Jesus, is said to have stated, "Love your neighbor as yourself—this is the major principle of the Torah" (Jerusalem Talmud *Nedarim* 9:4).

The combination of love of God and love of neighbor actually appears in other books from early Judaism, such as the *Testament of Dan* ("Love the Lord with all your life, and another with a sincere heart," 5:3) and the *Testament of Issachar* ("I loved the Lord with all my strength; likewise, I loved every man with all my heart," 5:2).

Jesus does not have to be unique in all cases in order to be profound.

His connection with basic Jewish teaching continues. According to the Babylonian Talmud, a sixth-century commentary on the Mishnah, a potential convert once asked Rabbi Hillel, one of Judaism's greatest teachers, "Teach me the Torah, that is, teach me all of your traditions, your values, your practices, and your theology, *al regel achat* [while standing on one foot]" (*Shabbat* 31a). Hillel wisely responded: "What is hateful to you, do not do to your fellow. All the rest is commentary; go and learn." A few decades later, Jesus also instructed his followers, "In everything, do to others as you would have them do to you." The connection to Hillel's summary of the teachings of Judaism is reinforced by Jesus's very next comment: "for this is the Law and the Prophets" (Matt. 7:12).

Christians and Jews on occasion debate which is the better formulation, the negative version offered by Hillel or the positive version offered by Jesus. The negative version could be charged with promoting a passive or at least nonproactive stance, whereas the positive enjoins action. The positive could be seen as promoting an egocentric form of action that does not consider the distinct needs and wants of the other. But the arguments are ultimately neither accurate nor helpful. Hillel hardly restricted his understanding of the Torah to this one line, and the Jewish tradition as a whole requires proactive engagement. Jesus is hardly talking about forcing one's views on another. Ultimately, although philosophers who can abstract these two statements from their contexts may want to debate the benefits and debits of each, the discussion on religious grounds tends to devolve into the rhetoric of "My teacher is better than your teacher." Such an approach hardly demonstrates love of God or neighbor. Perhaps if church and synagogue stopped debating who had the better formulation of the Golden Rule—which is by no means restricted to Jesus and Hillel—and started living by it, we'd all be better off.

Jesus's connection to Judaism can be seen not only in his general comments about Torah but also in his practice of its commandments. For example, Jesus dresses like a Jew. Specifically, he wears *tzitzit*, "fringes," which the book of Numbers enjoins upon all Israelite men (and a number of Orthodox Jewish men still wear) and which can be seen today most readily in the *tallit*, or "prayer shawl," worn in the synagogue during worship. Numbers 15:37–40 reads: "The Lord said to Moses, 'Speak to the Israelites, and tell them to make fringes on the corners of their garments throughout their generations and to put a blue cord on the fringe at each corner. You have the fringe so that, when you see it, you will remember all the commandments of the Lord and do them, and not follow the lust of your own heart and your own eyes. So you shall remember and do all my commandments, and you shall be holy to your God.'"

These *tzitzit* thus may be compared to WWJD bracelets. Just as the bracelets remind their Christian wearers to ask, "What would Jesus do?" so the fringes remind Jewish wearers of all 613 "commandments," or *mitzvot* (Hebrew; singular, *mitzvah*). The Gospels do not shy away from the fact that Jesus wore these fringes: it is these fringes that the woman with the twelve-year hemorrhage touches in hopes of a healing (Matt. 9:20). Similarly, Mark 6:56 records: "And wherever he went, into villages or cities or farms, they laid the sick in the marketplaces, and begged him that they might touch even the fringe of his cloak, and all who touched it were healed." That Jesus, according to Matthew 23:5, criticizes the Pharisees and scribes because "they make their phylacteries broad and their fringes long" suggests that his phylacteries were narrow and his fringes shorter. Jesus thus does not dismiss Torah; in the modern idiom, he "wears it on his sleeve."

The reminder of the fringes has a practical payoff for Christians. The Gospels' preservation of this detail indicates that the Old Testament must be acknowledged as more than just an anticipation of the coming of the messiah, after which it can be discarded or, more respectfully, put on the shelf next to the other antiques, to be admired but not used. By preserving the detail that Jesus wore fringes, the New Testament mandates that respect for Jewish custom be maintained and that Jesus's own Jewish practices be honored, even by the gentile church, which does not follow those customs.

Not only does Jesus dress like a Jew; he eats like a Jew as well. He keeps kosher; that is, he keeps the dietary requirements established in Torah. Leviticus 11:3 (and see Deut. 14:4–8) is explicit about what animals are permitted for human consumption: "any animal that has divided hoofs and is cleft-footed and chews the cud"; thus the pig, the camel, the rock badger, and the hare are not kosher. Jesus would never have consumed a ham sandwich. Nor, by the way, would the occasion often have presented itself—archaeological investigation finds few pig bones in Galilee.

The only contact Jesus has with pigs is described in its most complete form in Mark 5:1–20. Following their expulsion from a severely possessed man, a group of demons so numerous that their former host identifies himself as "Legion, for we are many," requests that Jesus send them into a herd of swine. Jesus agrees, "and the unclean spirits came out and entered the swine; and the herd, numbering about two thousand, rushed down the steep bank into the sea, and were drowned in the sea." Mark's narrative anticipates the mission to the Gentiles, for the city of Gerasa, where the story is set, is part of the Decapolis, a league of ten predominantly gentile cities, and the presence of the pigs is a less than subtle clue to the non-Jewish composition of the population. The story also allows a nice political dig against Rome, given that the "unclean spirits" identify themselves as "Legion," the Latin term for an army cohort. But as for Jesus's Jewish identity, neither he nor his Jewish associates would have mourned the loss of a herd of hogs, animals that are not kosher and that represent conspicuous consumption, in that they cost more to raise than they produce in meat.

There is one verse, Mark 7:19, that states Jesus declared all foods clean, but this is Mark's editorial comment and not something Jesus himself said. Many English versions of the Bible place that line in parentheses to signal its editorial nature (if parentheses had been invented in Mark's time, perhaps he would have used them as well). Not only did Jesus keep kosher; all of his immediate followers did as well. Had Jesus declared all foods clean, the story Luke recounts in Acts 10 would make no sense. Staying at the home of Simon, a tanner, Peter goes up to the roof about noon to pray. "He became hungry and wanted something to eat; and while it was being prepared, he fell into a trance. He saw the heaven opened, and something like a large sheet coming down, being lowered to the ground by its four corners. In it were all kinds of four-footed creatures and reptiles and birds of the air. Then he heard a voice saying, 'Get up, Peter, kill and eat.' But Peter said, 'By no means, Lord; for I have never eaten anything that is profane or unclean'" (Acts 10:9–14). The tanning process required boiled urine, so Peter's vision about less-than-desirable food products and his demurral about eating are understandable, given the aromas wafting up from Simon's shop; nevertheless, the point of the story is that Peter believed the dietary regulations to be still valid.

Acts 15, the description of the council of the leaders of the group gathered in Jesus's name to determine if Gentiles in the church had to be circumcised and "keep the Law of Moses" (15:5), similarly presumes that at least the Jewish members abided by the dietary regulations. There would have been no reason to debate whether Gentiles in the church needed to keep kosher if the Jewish members began lunch with a shrimp cocktail (shellfish are forbidden) or a bacon-wrapped appetizer. One of the major debates in the early church was not whether Jews who followed Jesus needed to keep kosher, but whether Gentiles who followed him needed to do so as well. The conclusion was that they didn't, for the commandments given to Moses at Sinai were for the Jewish people, not for the Gentiles.

Finally, had Jesus declared all food clean, the disagreement between Peter and Paul about table fellowship recorded in Galatians 2 would have made no sense. As Paul recalls the scene, Peter "used to eat with the Gentiles." But after some emissaries came from James, the leader of the Jerusalem branch of the movement, "he drew back ... and other Jews joined him in this hypocrisy" (2:12–13). Paul speaks of challenging Peter; who won the food fight is not recorded (Paul's silence on the result suggests that the outcome was not to his taste).

For Christians, the practical point to be drawn from these details about Jesus's dietary practices is that he, like his fellow Jews who also followed the dietary regulations, was committed to the idea of the sanctification of the body; he attended to what went into it and what came out of it. Although he did like to eat and drink (hence the charge that he was a glutton and a drunkard in Matt. 11:19), he did so with respect for the dietary traditions of his people.

Jesus followed the commandments (*mitzvot*) given to Moses on Mt. Sinai as he understood them. Consequently, he necessarily rejected the understanding of those commandments put forth by rival teachers. He would not, for example, have agreed with the people at Qumran that the best way to live out the teachings of the Torah was to withdraw from society and move to the desert.

The extent to which Jesus would have agreed with the "rabbis"—that is, with the teachings recorded in the Mishnah (codified ca. 200, but preserving much earlier material) as well as the Talmud (a commentary on the Mishnah that includes anecdotes, parables, long digressions, and additional legal materials and that also preserves much older material; the Babylonian Talmud, on which Jewish tradition eventually became based, was completed ca. 600)—is a much more complex topic. Although numerous commentaries on the New Testament (including this one) compare Jesus's words to some text from the rabbinic tradition, the comparison always creates problems with regard to accuracy and dating. We do not know how much of the material in the Gospels was actually spoken by Jesus himself, as opposed to being a product of the church's oral tradition or coming from the hands of the Evangelists themselves. Similarly, we cannot be certain that rabbinic material ascribed to a particular teacher was actually spoken by that teacher.

Nor can we be sure of the dates of the rabbinic materials—the Talmud happily puts into conversation teachers who lived centuries and hundreds of miles apart. Consequently, to compare a word of Jesus to a statement from the Talmud may be comparing a first-century statement made in the villages of Galilee to a fifth-century statement made in the capital of Babylon. To presume that the rabbinic rulings all go back to the first century and, more, that they antedate the destruction of the Temple in 70 is an act of faith, not history. The better comparison to the rabbinic documents is not the Gospel material but rather the writings of the church fathers, from Ignatius to Irenaeus to Cyprian to Augustine to Jerome and everyone else in between. Nor again are all the rabbinic statements consistent, for the legal texts record both majority and minority opinions. Finally, the rabbinic legal literature establishes the rabbis' ideal world; it is their vision of what should be, not of what is.

The rabbinic legal material is sometimes called the "oral Law" because of the teaching that it was delivered to Moses on Mt. Sinai as a commentary on the written Torah. *Pirke Avot*, a Mishnaic tractate that offers a compendium of great rabbinic teachings, begins with a description of how the oral Law was conveyed: "Moses received the [oral] Law from Sinai, and handed it on to Joshua, and Joshua to the elders, and the elders to the prophets, and the prophets to the men of the Great Synagogue,..." and so on to Hillel and his rival, Rabbi Shammai, and on to Judah the Prince. Inevitably, the "oral Law" was written down, but the name stuck. For the rabbinic tradition, the oral and written Torahs function together. For example, the rabbinic texts explain how the commandments of the written Torah are to be practiced. The teachings are not only helpful; they are necessary, because Leviticus and Deuteronomy do not come with instruction manuals for implementing their laws and statutes. The Torah says that one must put the words of Torah on one's doorposts and gates; the oral Law explains which words and how they are to be affixed.

To return to Jesus, it has been claimed that Jesus rejected the "oral Law," or the "oral Torah," the interpretations of the Torah that eventually found their way into Mishnah and Talmud. Therefore, he diverged from what most Jews in the early first century would have found to be the appropriate, faithful following of the tradition. David Klinghoffer best articulates this argument. He finds it "unsurprising that some Jews of the time might have chosen to confront and debate with" Jesus, since he "knowingly rejects the oral tradition, not from ignorance but from willfulness."[2] The problem with this view is that the oral Law itself is variable; not all rabbis agreed with one another either. The story of Rabbi Hillel and the potential convert is actually the second part of an anecdote that begins with the visit of that same potential convert to Shammai. Asked to summarize Torah while standing on one foot, Shammai instead beat the man with a stick. The story, told by those rabbis who saw themselves as Hillel's heirs, at least acknowledged the rival view. As the Talmudic interpretation, also written by those who identified with Hillel, puts it: "A heavenly voice declared, 'The words of both schools [of Hillel and Shammai] are words of the living God, but the Law follows the rulings of the school of Hillel'" (*Eruvin* 13b).

Even if one were to accept the highly disputed claim that the oral Law, eventually written down in the Mishnah close to two centuries after Jesus's death, was fully in place at the time of Jesus, that still does not mean that Jesus was out of step with his fellow Jews, including those with whom the rabbinic tradition would agree, on most practices. In fact, there is no indication that Jesus had a *systematic* interpretation of the Torah. He did not, as did the rabbis, discuss the various distinctions of tort law with other rabbinic scholars. Rather, the Gospels suggest that he responded to questions as they were posed to him, either by circumstances ("Can one heal on the Sabbath?") or by those seeking either to learn from him or to test him ("What is the greatest commandment?"). Jesus is thus neither part of the rabbinic tradition nor clearly antithetical to it. In some cases he would have agreed with the majority views; in other cases he'd have sided with the minority; and in a few cases, such as his forbidding of divorce, he would have been well outside of it (here on the conservative, not the liberal, wing).

Jesus would have expected to be challenged, and he would have issued his own challenges. That he was willing to engage in discussion of how to follow the commandments shows that he cared about them, deeply. In his teaching, he shows enormous respect for the *mitzvot*, the commandments, so much so that he debates how they are best to be understood and enacted.

For example, he "honors the Sabbath and keeps it holy," as one of the Ten Commandments requires. The Sabbath is something Jews and Christians share, although churches (with a few exceptions, such as the Seventh-Day Adventists) and synagogues celebrate it on different days and for different reasons. Judaism celebrates *Shabbat* (Hebrew) or *Shabbos* (Yiddish, the language of Ashkenazi, or eastern European, Judaism), first because it is the day blessed by God at the conclusion of creation: "Thus the heavens and the earth were finished, and all their multitude. And on the seventh day God finished the work that he had done, and he rested on the seventh day from all the work that he had done. So God blessed the seventh day and hallowed it, because on it God rested from all the work that he had done in creation" (Gen. 2:1–3; see also Exod. 20:8–11, which includes as part of its presentation of the Ten Commandments: "Remember the Sabbath day, and keep it holy. Six days you shall labor and do all your work. But the seventh day is a Sabbath to the Lord your God; you shall not do any work—you, your son or your daughter, your male or female slave, your livestock, or the resident alien in your towns. For in six days the Lord made heaven and earth, the sea, and all that is in them, but rested the seventh day; therefore the Lord blessed the Sabbath day and consecrated it").

The book of Deuteronomy gives a second reason for honoring the Sabbath: *Shabbos* guarantees that Israel will never be enslaved again. In another formulation of the Ten Commandments, Moses speaks to the people: "Remember that you were a slave in the land of Egypt, and the Lord your God brought you out from there with a mighty hand and an outstretched arm; therefore the Lord your God commanded you to keep the Sabbath day" (5:15). Although the separate explanations may raise a problem for those committed to chiseling the Ten Commandments on granite stones to be placed in courthouses, the general point of honoring the Sabbath is one upon which at least Jews and Christians might agree.

Jesus and his initial followers, like their fellow Jews, lived within a tradition replete with Sabbath joy. Jews, whether followers of Jesus or not, would have known Isaiah's summary of righteous worship: "If you refrain from trampling the Sabbath, from pursuing your own interests on my holy day; if you call the Sabbath a delight and the holy day of the Lord honorable … then you shall take delight in the Lord, and I will make you ride upon the heights of the earth; I will feed you with the heritage of your ancestor Jacob, for the mouth of the Lord has spoken" (58:13–14). Among the antecedents of these lines is Isaiah 58:6: "Is not this the fast that I choose: to loose the bonds of injustice, to undo the thongs of the yoke, to let the oppressed go free, and to break every yoke?" Jesus's initial Sabbath teaching in the synagogue of Nazareth, a scene developed in Luke 4, quotes these lines.

Jews told the gospel story originally, and they insisted on retaining the Sabbath. Eventually, the followers of Jesus shifted from celebrating the last day of the week to celebrating the first day of the week, Sunday, the day the church proclaims that Jesus rose from the dead. The meaning of the Sabbath thus shifted from a focus on the creation of the world and the liberation from slavery to a focus on what Christians would see as a new creation and a new liberation: Jesus's resurrection, his creating a new people, and his conquering death.

The distinction also served, for better or worse, to distinguish Jews from Christians. Such distinctions continue because of unfortunate conclusions drawn from limited understandings of the Gospels. On several occasions, Jesus challenges what appear to be prevailing views on how the Sabbath should be kept. The following story, from Luke 6:6–11 (recounted also in Mark 3:1–6; Matt. 12:9–14), is typical:

> On another Sabbath he entered the synagogue and taught, and there was a man there whose right hand was withered. The scribes and the Pharisees watched him to see whether he would cure on the Sabbath, so that they might find an accusation against him. Even though he

knew what they were thinking, he said to the man with the withered hand, "Come and stand here." He got up and stood there. Then Jesus said to them, "I ask you, is it lawful to do good or to do harm on the Sabbath, to save a life or destroy it?" After looking around at all of them, he said to him, "Stretch out your hand." He did so, and his hand was restored. But they were filled with fury and discussed with one another what they might do to Jesus.

From this and other narratives of Jesus healing on the Sabbath, a number of Christians have received the impression that Jesus completely revised the way the day was observed. In this "Christian" view, "the Jews" had turned the Sabbath from a day of rest and celebration to a day of constraint: don't do this, don't do that. The impression is symptomatic of a larger view of Judaism as a straitjacket with thousands of picky injunctions, and of Jews as fearful that if they were to violate one commandment, they would face the wrath of an angry God. Thus, all Jews at the time of Jesus had to have been hopelessly sanctimonious, obsessive, and paranoid. Only Jesus, defined over and against Judaism, escaped this early need for psychoanalysis, since his outlook was so healthy, so liberal, and so profound that he was able to declare: "The Sabbath was made for humankind, not humankind for the Sabbath" (Mark 2:27).

Sabbath observance, in the first century and for the past two millennia, has been a hotly debated issue. No Jew, then or now, would have upheld any Sabbath ruling preventing work were a life in danger. But there are issues that were, and can, be discussed. Should one practice medicine and so "work" in order to heal a nonpainful, chronic condition such as the one in Luke's story? More, what constitutes "work"? In the case of the healing of the man's hand, Jesus actually does no "work" per se; he does not even touch the man. The Greek cleverly notes that the man's hand "was restored"—passive voice. No one, including Jesus, could be accused of violating the mandate for Sabbath rest. Thus, one common interpretation goes, the church celebrates Jesus's breaking open a legalized, ossified tradition; that he both shamed and frustrated "the Jews" who opposed him is an added benefit to this particular interpretation. The problems are numerous, from a negative and false stereotype of Jewish Sabbath observance to a promotion of Christianity not through what it positively promotes (such as healing) but through a negative comparison to Judaism.

The stereotype is unfortunate; it is also disproved by the details of the Gospels themselves. A number of Jews would have agreed with Jesus that healing takes precedence over the Sabbath; others might have thought that a chronic, nonpainful condition could wait until sundown, lest the healing in this case give the impression that the healer did not honor the day or the commandment. For example, Luke 13:10–17 recounts how Jesus "was teaching in one of the synagogues on the Sabbath. Just then there appeared a woman with a spirit that had crippled her for eighteen years. She was bent over and was quite unable to stand up straight." Jesus sees her, calls her to him, and states, "Woman, you are set free from your ailment." "When he laid his hands on her, immediately she stood up straight and began praising God. But the leader of the synagogue [a lay position comparable to "president of the congregation"; the Pharisees are not in charge of synagogues], indignant because Jesus had cured on the Sabbath, kept saying to the crowd, 'There are six days on which work ought to be done; come on those days and be cured, and not on the Sabbath day.'"

At this point, Luke shifts to confessional language by replacing Jesus's name with a title: "But *the Lord* [Greek *Kyrios*] answered him and said, "You hypocrites! Does not each of you on the Sabbath untie his ox or his donkey from the manger, and lead it away to give it water? And ought not this woman, a daughter of Abraham whom Satan bound for eighteen long years, be set free from this bondage on the Sabbath day?" Luke concludes with the notice: "When he said this, all his opponents were put to shame, and the entire crowd was rejoicing at all the wonderful things that he was doing."

The story highlights Jesus's action as in contradistinction from what the synagogue leader would have preferred. But the crowd—that is, the Jewish majority—has no problem with Jesus's healing the woman, and they would have recognized his argument to be a standard form for discussion of legal matters. He argues on the basis of what is called in Hebrew a *qal v'homer*, or "from the lighter to the greater," model. The form is also known as an *a fortiori* (Latin, "by the stronger"), and it follows the logic: "If you already do X, then you should surely do Y, which is even more important." Jesus's healing itself is a matter of touch, which is not forbidden on the Sabbath: he makes no potions; he unties no cords. Further, the story is not arguing that anyone with any medical skill should be spending the Sabbath checking for chronic conditions that might be cured. The forbidding of work on the Sabbath remains in place—physicians such as Luke, then and now, got a day off—while miracle working remained permitted. Christians today (and Jews as well) may rejoice that Jesus was able to heal the woman and so allow her fully to celebrate the Sabbath, *without having to change their own Sabbath practices.* The synagogue leader thus represents not "the" Jewish view but rather *a* Jewish view, and one against that of the majority of the people in his congregation.

Rather than depicting "Judaism" as promoting a joyless Sabbath during which neighbors watch each other for the slightest violation of a prohibition, rabbinic texts, although later than the first century, make the same point Jesus made. Commenting on Exodus 31:14, "For the Sabbath is holy to you," the Babylonian Talmud (*Yoma* 85b) interprets, "The Sabbath is given to you; you are not to be delivered to the Sabbath," and then adds, "Profane one Sabbath for a person's sake, so that he may keep many Sabbaths." That the rabbis called the Sabbath the "pearl of creation" (*Midrash Tehillim* 92.1) does offer an interesting gloss on Jesus's parable of the pearl of great price (Matt. 13:45–46).

Jewish tradition further suggests that one greets the arrival of the Sabbath as one would greet a queen or a bride. The Babylonian Talmud (*Shabbat* 119a) states that on Friday evening, at sunset, Rabbi Chanina would dress in fine clothes and call out, "Come, let us go forth to welcome the Sabbath queen." Similarly, Rabbi Yannai would dress in fine garments and exclaim, "Come, O bride! Come, O bride." These two rabbis are of the Amoraic period, the time after the codification of the Mishnah; therefore it is problematic to suggest that people would have held their views in the first century. However, the notice of their practice does undercut the stereotype that "the rabbis" were a group of dour, sour scholars. Although later than the time of Jesus as well, the song sung in the synagogues to greet the Sabbath is *L'cha dodi likrat kalah* … , "Come, my beloved, to greet the bride, the presence of the Sabbath let us welcome." As with any royal arrival or any wedding, the people celebrate the Sabbath by dressing in their finest clothes, preparing their finest food, and ensuring that no one goes hungry. With these images, the tendency to depict "Judaism" as in need of correction by Jesus yields to a picture of Jesus firmly within his tradition. At the same time, his critique of any who would deny the joyful time of rest that Sabbath promotes can be more easily addressed to anyone, Christian or Jew, who would seek to do so.

Parables

In addition to his direct teachings, Jesus also evokes the prophets before him and the rabbis after in his parables, a style of teaching well known to his fellow Jews. The term "parable" literally means, in its Greek original, "to place or cast things side by side"; thus the parable compares two items. The Hebrew term for the genre is *mashal,* a similitude or metaphor.

Following David's adultery with Bathsheba and then murder of her husband, Uriah, the court prophet Nathan tells the king the parable of the ewe lamb:

> There were two men in a certain city, the one rich and the other poor. The rich man had very many flocks and herds, but the poor man had nothing but one little ewe lamb, which had had bought. He brought it up, and it grew with him and with his children; it used to eat of his meager fare, and drink from his cup, and lie in his bosom, and it was like a daughter to him. Now there came a traveler to the rich man, and he was loath to take one of his own flock or herd to prepare for the wayfarer who had come to him, but he took the poor man's lamb, and prepared that for the guest who had come to him. (2 Sam. 12:1b–4)

The story appalls David. He tells Nathan, "As the Lord lives, the man who has done this deserves to die." Nathan responds, "You are the man!" (12:5–7). David is not a little discomfited.

Less well known is the parable of the trees, told by Jotham in Judges 9:7–15. This satire on the monarchy suggests that those who aspire to political power are not productive like the olive or the fig or the vine but are, like the bramble, worthless.

The rabbinic tradition is replete with parables. As *Song of Songs Rabbah* (1:1), a rabbinic commentary on the Song of Songs (also called Song of Solomon or Canticles), puts it: "Do not let the parable be of little worth to you. Through a parable, a person can fathom words of Torah."

Parables seek to arrest the listeners, to show another perspective on the world, to call into question the status quo. They often convey news that audiences do not want to hear, and yet they do so in ways that may bring a smile, through wild exaggeration, ridiculous scenarios, and startling juxtapositions. David Stern offers a translation of a parable from *Lamentations* (*Eikhah*) *Rabbah* (3:21) about a king who wrote his wife a generous *ketubah*, or marriage contract: "So many bridal chambers I am building for you; so much jewelry I make for you; so much gold and silver I give you." When her husband then went on a tour of the provinces, the woman's neighbors would taunt her: "Hasn't your husband abandoned you? Go! Marry another man." The wife "would weep and sigh, and afterward she would enter her bridal chamber and read her marriage settlement and sigh [with relief]." When, after many years, the king finally returned, he expressed his amazement that his wife had remained faithful. She responded: "My master, O king! If not for the large wedding settlement you wrote me, my neighbors would long ago have led me astray."[3] The interpretation of the parable compares the wife to Israel, who is faithful to her God despite the impression that she has been abandoned. The parable concludes: "And the people of Israel enter their synagogues and houses of study, and there they read in the Torah, 'I will look with favor upon you and make you fertile.... I will establish my abode in your midst, and I will not spurn you' (Lev. 26:9–11), and they console themselves."[4] The rabbinic interpretation of the parable goes on to cite Psalm 119:92, "Were not your teaching my delight, I would have perished in my affliction," and it concludes with Lamentations 3:21, "This I call to my mind; therefore I have hope."

Stern not only points out the numerous connections the parable has to other rabbinic statements, the intricate word associations it draws from the Torah, and the several puns that carry the interpretation (which, alas, are all lost in English translation) but also brings up the parable's daring aspects. It is not afraid to depict God as an absent spouse; it raises the question of whether the Torah is really a consolation for the absence of redemption; and in the process of seeming to console Israel for its humiliation among the nations, it winds up kvetching to God. The parable even depicts Israel as a literate woman who may well have found the nations' invitation to marry one of them appealing. The parable thus leaves readers with a sense of both discomfort and closure: difficult ideas are not repressed but channeled into story. The surprise of the husband/king/ God at Israel's faithfulness is both humorous in the narrative and profound in the real world, as is the faithfulness of Israel, the wife.

Rabbinic parables are often attached to biblical verses; Jesus's parables are closer to those of Nathan and Jothan in that they relate, not to the words of Scripture, but to the "kingdom of God" or "kingdom of heaven." They too raise difficult questions and should prompt reactions ranging from surprise to outrage, but too often they are domesticated. Centuries of Christian reading have taken the punch out of the parables, so that they become nice, if banal, stories about good Samaritans who help people on the highway, prodigal sons who are welcomed home, sowers who sow, women who bake. The occasional king who burns down a city or bridegroom who shuts the door in the face of five virgins who have run out of oil—that is, the parables in which the difficult readings cannot be swept away—tend not to get much sermon time, especially in liberal Christian settings.

To recover the punch of Jesus's parables, one must hear them with first-century Jewish ears. Although such an exercise cannot be fully accomplished without detailed historical study, even a cursory knowledge of the cultural influences on all Jews in the first century, such as the narratives in Scripture, already begins the process. Any Jew who heard a story beginning, "There was a man who had two sons"—the opening of the famous parable of the prodigal son (Luke 15:11–32)—would know immediately that the brothers would not get along very well and that the father would be generally ineffectual in bringing harmony to the household. The stories of Cain and Abel, Ishmael and Isaac, and Esau and Jacob, for example, do not set up an auspicious model for the prodigal and his dutiful older brother.

Jesus's teaching that the kingdom of heaven may be compared to "leaven," or yeast (Matt. 13:33), would have gotten a rise out of his Jewish audience, for "leaven" often had negative associations, such as in Paul's comment that "your boasting is not a good thing. Do you not know that a little yeast leavens the whole batch of dough?" (1 Cor. 5:6). Paul uses the same language in Galatians 5:8–9, where he is arguing against those who want the men in the local church to become circumcised: "Such persuasion does not come from the one who calls you. A little yeast leavens the whole batch of dough." Allusions to removing the leaven from the house at the time of Passover (Exod. 12:15; 1 Cor. 5:7–8) and to the evil "leaven" of the "Pharisees and the Sadducees" (e.g., Matt. 16:6, 12) confirm the point. Today, when congregations hear about "leaven," the image that comes to mind is not the work of a fungus that feeds off the dough in a dark, damp place, but rather a red packet that sits in the refrigerator door.

Jesus's parable of the Pharisee and the tax collector, found in Luke 18:9–14, shows both the wallop of the story and the weakness of the standard interpretations that fail to consider the Jewish context of the events described. The parable goes as follows:

> Two men went up to the Temple to pray, one a Pharisee and the other a tax collector. The Pharisee, standing by himself, was praying, "God, I thank you that I am not like other people: thieves, rogues, adulterers, or even like this tax collector. I fast twice a week; I give a tenth of all my income." But the tax collector, standing far off, would not even look up to heaven, but was beating his breast and saying, "God, be merciful to me, a sinner."

The next line, an editorial comment (whether from Jesus, Luke's source, or Luke's own imagination), reads in most translations, "I tell you, this man went down to his home justified rather than the other."[5] Luke then may have added the final line, "For all who exalt themselves will be humbled, but all who humble themselves will be exalted." The same final line appears in Luke 14:11, at the end of Jesus's teaching on humility and hospitality, and it may well have been a floating saying, tacked on wherever the Evangelist found it most appropriate. Or Jesus may well have repeated the point; the source of the saying does not matter for the interpretation of the parable.

The problem with the parable is that today it has lost its challenge. Most readers do not find this parable discomforting, for Luke the Evangelist has filled his narrative with stories of righteous tax collectors, including Levi (known in Matthew's Gospel as "Matthew"), who joins the twelve apostles, and Zacchaeus, whom we meet in the next chapter (19:1–10). Short of stature (but not of income), Zacchaeus climbs a sycamore tree to get a closer look at Jesus as he is passing through Jericho. When Jesus sees him, he calls out, "Zacchaeus, hurry and come down; for I must stay at your house today." The tax collector hurries down, but when the townspeople grumble that Jesus is going to the home of a sinner, Zacchaeus announces, "Look, half of my possessions, Lord, I give to the poor; and if I defraud anyone of anything, I pay back four times as much." Jesus responds, "Today salvation has come to this house." If taken out of its narrative context and placed into a historical one, we would hear the townspeople still grumbling: in Jesus's time, the tax collector was the agent of the Roman government occupying Judea. Thus "faithful tax collector" would have been an oxymoron. Congregations today, although no great fans of the Internal Revenue Service, don't see the shock value; rather, they see righteous tax collectors who respond positively to Jesus.

Luke's readers too have little difficulty expecting to see "good tax collectors," and so they find them. The audience has changed from Jews in the early first century to gentile Christians toward its end. Luke is not writing in Judea, under Roman occupation; Luke is writing somewhere in the Greek-speaking gentile world, where Roman patrons such as Theophilus, to whom the Gospel is dedicated, can help the Christian mission to grow. Luke and the members of his congregation can easily view the tax collector in the parable as "justified," that is, in a right relationship with God. Moreover, they can also identify with the tax collector. He becomes the ideal Christian: he recognizes his sin, he humbly begs forgiveness, and grace is accorded him. How nice. Of course he, not the Pharisee, receives divine approbation.

When the parable is heard with first-century Jewish ears, however, the response is by no means so simple. The very idea that a tax collector would receive approval over a Pharisee should, instead, shock. To see the tax collector as justified is tantamount to a member of the local population claiming that an agent of a foreign, invading government, an agent whose job is to take money from the local population and funnel it to the capital of the invading empire, is the one to be admired and to serve as a moral exemplar. Although a bit generous as an analogy, the Pharisee would be the equivalent of Mother Teresa or Billy Graham. The idea that either would not be in a right relationship with God is preposterous.

Nevertheless, Christian readers usually presume Pharisaic evil, and the Gospel is complicit in setting up this conclusion. The first words of the Pharisees in Luke's Gospel come as Jesus both heals a paralytic and speaks of forgiving his sins: "Who is this who is speaking blasphemies? Who is able to forgive sins but God alone?" (5:21). Next, Pharisees "grumble" at Jesus's association with tax collectors and sinners (5:30). Following a relatively neutral question about why Jesus's disciples eat and drink while John the Baptist's do not (5:33) and the possibly neutral query by some of the Pharisees about why the disciples are "doing what is not lawful on the Sabbath," namely, rubbing grain in their hands and thus winnowing (6:2), a second Sabbath controversy returns to the "evil Pharisee" depiction. This is the story of the man with the withered hand, and it concludes that Pharisees, "filled with fury," discuss among themselves what "they might do to Jesus" (6:11).

After the Pharisees reject John's baptism (7:29–30), the Gospel then depicts three banquet scenes, found only in Luke's account, where Pharisees host Jesus (7:36–50; 11:37–54; 14:1–24). No scene works to enhance the reputation of the group or its members. At these symposia, Jesus criticizes his Pharisaic host's behavior as elitist, exclusivist, and hypocritical. The dinner-table conversation is summed up by such comments as:

> Now you Pharisees clean the outside of the cup and of the dish, but inside you are full of greed and wickedness. You fools! Did not the one who made the outside make the inside also? So give for alms those things that are within; and see, everything will be clean for you. But woe to you Pharisees! For you tithe mint and rue and herbs of all kinds, and neglect justice and the love of God.... Woe to you Pharisees! For you love to have the seat of honor in the synagogues and to be greeted with respect in the marketplaces. Woe to you! For you are like unmarked graves, and people walk over them without realizing it. (11:39–44)

The icing on this anti-Pharisaic cake appears in brief remarks Jesus later makes to the disciples concerning how they must "beware of the yeast of the Pharisees, that is, their hypocrisy" (12:1) and that the Pharisees are "lovers of money" who ridicule Jesus for insisting that "you cannot serve God and mammon" (16:13). The few remaining references follow suit.

Just as Luke has set up the tax collector to represent the "good Christian," so readers are neatly led to see the Pharisee as the "bad Jew" (in both cases the adjectives are redundant). The poor Pharisee of the parable never had a chance.

But it is Luke, not Jesus, who provides the context for the parable. By Luke's time, the Pharisees had come to represent for the church the Jews who refused to follow Jesus; their portrait is primarily composed of polemic, not objectivity. Yet even in Luke's Gospel, hints of a more benevolent Pharisaic view do seem to peek through. Not only do Pharisees continue to host Jesus at dinner parties and so keep the doors of communication open in the intimate setting of a shared meal; they also advise Jesus, "Get away from here, for Herod wants to kill you" (Luke 13:31). There is no necessary reason to conclude that their warning is disingenuous.

If we hear the parable through first-century Jewish ears—the ears that would have been listening to Jesus himself—a much different picture develops than the negative one Luke conveys. First, the Pharisee need not be seen as hypocritical or arrogant. The Pharisee's prayer begins with "I thank" (the Greek term is *eucharisto,* whence the English term "Eucharist"), and the idea of thanking God is a major component of Jewish prayers. The Pharisee's prayer, *"on its own terms,* shows no more arrogance on his part than anyone who has prayed or thought, 'There but for the grace of God, go I.'"[6] The negative view of the Pharisee comes from Luke's narrative, not from Jesus's original context.

And because of that context, the parable works. It traps listeners brilliantly. As soon as one makes the determination that the tax collector is justified, the thought results: "Thank heaven I am not like that Pharisee over there." How absurd to think: "Thank heaven I am not like Mother Teresa; thank heaven I am not like Billy Graham." Even *if* one finds the Pharisee sanctimonious, the parable still works, because the identification with the tax collector results in the reaction, "Thank heaven I am not sanctimonious, like that Pharisee." The irony is delicious.

And the good news of the parable continues. By forcing readers to see something positive about the tax collector, it insists that even those who work for the enemy may still be part of the congregation, that even those who exploit members of their own community deserve consideration; perhaps they, like Zacchaeus, are doing the best they can while trapped in an impossible situation. In other words, the parable forces hearers to walk in the shoes of the criminal or the ostracized. At the same time, it requires listeners to assess acts of piety and the value placed on them in any religious setting. This Pharisee, who tithes, who fasts, who prays without asking anything for himself, is exactly the sort of congregant clergy adore. The parable then raises the question of who has honor in the congregation, who is the better role model, who is without sin, and who is without sanctity.

The ending of the parable may provide two additional shocks. First, most translations read Luke 18:14a as saying, "This man [the tax collector] went down to his home justified rather than the other." But neither the Greek nor the context of the line demands this exclusivist conclusion. It is possible that the Pharisee also is justified. As Robert Doran states, "As far as I can see, the only factor in the context that has led interpreters to choose such an exclusive meaning is that one does not want to say that a Pharisee is upright/justified (*dedikaiomenov*)."[7] The line need not be read "went down to his home justified rather than the other," but "went down to his home more justified than the other." In this case, the ancient audience is shocked that the tax collector has the greater recognition; today's audience is shocked that the Pharisee has any recognition at all.

Finally, perhaps the ending is even more surprising, for the tax collector's very justification may be dependent on the Pharisee. This Pharisee tithes more than he is required to do, he fasts more than he is expected to do, and this righteousness is not in dispute. Such actions can have vicarious effects—perhaps the Pharisee's righteousness actions are precisely what allow the tax collector to be put in a right relationship with God. As Timothy Friedrichsen suggests, the reaction from Jesus's Jewish audience would have been "shock, dismay, even anger" at the very idea that the Pharisee's righteous behavior and attitude "may benefit, of all people, their nemesis, a tax collector."[8] By modern analogy, the righteousness shown by the greatest saint in the church works for the redemption of the greatest sinner.

The parable thus continues to provoke, to challenge, to disturb. It is very Jesus, and very Jewish.

Prayer

The content of the Pharisee's prayer provides a negative contrast to the prayer most closely associated with Jesus, the so-called Lord's Prayer. The more familiar version is found in the Sermon on the Mount (Matt. 6:9–13):

> Our Father in heaven,
> Hallowed be your name.
> Your kingdom come.
> Your will be done, on earth as it is in heaven.
> Give us this day our daily bread.

And forgive us our debts, as we also have forgiven our debtors.
And do not bring us into temptation, but rescue us from evil.

Some churches add to this prayer a doxology (literally, a "word of praise") that is found not in the New Testament but in an early Christian text called the *Didache*, or the *Teaching of the Twelve Apostles:* "For the kingdom and the power and the glory are yours forever. Amen." Luke's Gospel presents a version of the prayer that lacks a number of the familiar Matthean lines: "Father, hallowed be your name. Your kingdom come. Give us each day our bread for tomorrow. And forgive us our sins, for we ourselves forgive everyone indebted to us. And do not bring us into temptation" (11:2–4).

Although scholars have argued and will continue to argue over which lines are original to Jesus, which translation is closer to the hypothesized construction of the Aramaic tradition, which verses were adapted to church needs, and so on, all versions of the prayer fit within a Jewish context. Nor is there any compelling reason to think that Jesus taught only one version of the prayer.

The problem with the Lord's Prayer is neither its content nor its historicity, but its familiarity. Many congregants don't actually think of the meaning of the words or, if they do, find only comfort rather than a challenge. Little children still happily conclude that the deity's name is "Harold," fear that the major sin they might commit is trespassing on someone else's lawn, and earnestly hope that they are never led "into Penn Station." When placed in a first-century Jewish context, the prayer recovers numerous connotations that make it both more profound and more political. It fosters belief, promotes justice, consoles with future hope, and recognizes that the world is not always how we would want it.

The famous opening line from Matthew's version, "Our Father [who is] in heaven," has, like the parable of the Pharisee and the tax collector, been interpreted as distinguishing the good Jesus, and so the good Christian, from those nasty Jews. Still popular is the view that only Jesus would have dared to call God "Father" and that only Jesus would have done so with the daring use of the Aramaic term *Abba*, meaning "Daddy." The claims are hopelessly flawed. In Jewish thought, the designation of the deity as "Father" develops substantially during the Second Temple period, that is, after the return from the Babylonian exile in 538 BCE. For example,

Malachi 2:10 states, "Have we not all one father?" The Mishnah (*Berakhot* 5:1) states that the ancient holy ones (called Hasidim) spent an hour in preparation prior to prayer "in order to direct their hearts toward their Father who is in heaven." This understanding of God as Father continues in synagogues today, where Jews speak of and to *Av ha-rachamim* ("merciful Father") as well as *Avinu malkenu* ("our Father, our King") and proclaim, *Hu avinu* ("He is our Father").

Passages in the Gospels also attest an image of God as the "father" in Jesus's new family. For example, Matthew 23:9 instructs, "Call no one your father on earth, for you have one Father—the one in heaven." The notion of the single Father, in heaven, is consistent with Jewish beliefs.

Although it is better to think of *Abba* as a first-century Aramaic term than a Swedish rock band, the translation "Daddy" is incorrect.[9] The term means "father," and it is not an expression associated primarily with little children. The New Testament writers themselves do not understand it to mean "Daddy" either, for in each of the three uses the Aramaic *Abba* is immediately glossed with the Greek vocative *o pater*, "Father." The only place in the Gospels Jesus himself is said to use the address *Abba* is Mark 14:36; in Gethsemane, he prays, "*Abba*, Father, for you all things are possible; remove this cup from me; yet, not what I want, but what you want." Paul twice cites the prayerful address to *Abba*. Romans 8:15 speaks of "when we cry 'Abba! Father!'" and Galatians 4:6 similarly notes, "God has sent the Spirit of his Son into our hearts, crying 'Abba! Father!'" Even Joachim Jeremias, the scholar who first proposed the translation "Daddy" along with its unique attribution to Jesus, retracted his thesis and called it "a piece of inadmissible naiveté."[10]

Nor was Jesus the only Jew to address God as *Abba*, although this may have been a hallmark of his teaching. That Paul preserves the Aramaic when writing to Greek-speaking gentile converts—the earliest use of *Abba* for the "Father in heaven" appears in Galatians 4—suggests that the invocation may well go back to Jesus. Perhaps Jesus emphasized the address more than did other Jews; he may have felt a personal connection, whereas his fellow Jews took a more communal approach. For example, Jewish addresses to the "Father" tend to be communal; when Jesus calls to *Abba* in Gethsemane, his address is entirely personal. He is not speaking on behalf of anyone except himself. But the Lord's Prayer is not an example of a unique address: the prayer begins "Our Father," not "My Father."

Although distinctive, the address to God as *Abba* is not anomalous in Judaism. The Talmud does record a few examples. Whether the material antedates Jesus cannot be determined, nor should the date become an issue. Jesus and other Jews used the term *Abba* for the deity; there need not be a spitting contest about who came up with a prayer using the term first. (The first person may well have been Jesus's mother or any one of the millions of Jews in the late Second Temple period, for all we know.) Geza Vermes records the following passage, from the Babylonian Talmud (*Taanit* 23b). The first figure mentioned, Honi the Circle-maker, was a Galilean rabbi from the first century BCE who was known both for claiming a particularly intimate relationship with God and for being able to control the weather (one might compare Jesus's ability to still storms and walk on water). Apparently, this meteorological ability was passed along to his grandson:

> Honi the Circle-maker's daughter had a son called Hanan ha-Nehba. When the world was in need of rain, the sages would send school-children to him; they would take hold of the hem of his garment and say to him, "Abba, Abba, give us rain." Then he would plead with the holy one: "Master of the universe, render a service to those who do not know the difference between the Abba who gives rain and the Abba who does not."[11]

The address to God as Father, whether offered by Jesus or anyone else, signals more than piety. It also has a political edge. Whereas these various notices about dress and food, parables and prayer distinguish Jesus and his fellow Jews from their gentile neighbors, neither Jesus nor his fellow Jews should be seen as living in some sort of Hebrew bubble. Judaism since the fourth century BCE, the time of Alexander the Great, had existed in a Hellenistic environment, and since 63 BCE Roman appointees had ruled both Judea and Galilee. Not in the first century, likely never, was there a "pure" Judaism uninfluenced by its neighbors. That is not how culture works, and it is not how religion works. Consequently, Jesus cannot be located only within a constrained definition of "Judaism"; he is also a resident of the Roman Empire.

The Caesars on the throne in Rome were called "father"—as Washington was called "father of our country" or as the Russian czars were called by their populations (with relative degrees of warmth) "little father." For example, the Roman historian Cassius Dio (ca. 165–229) writes, "The appellation of 'father' perhaps gives them, with regard to us all, a certain authority which fathers once had over their children, not, indeed originally for this, but as an honor and as an admonition that they should love those being ruled as children and that they in turn should revere them also as fathers."[12] By speaking of the "Father in heaven," Jesus thus insists that Rome is not the "true" father.

More, by encouraging his followers not to call anyone "father," he evokes the prophetic insistence that individuals not rest assured on their lineage. The same point appears in the proclamations of "a good man" who, according to Josephus, "exhorted the Jews to lead righteous lives, to practice justice toward their fellows and piety towards God, and so doing" to engage in an act of ritual immersion, not to "gain pardon for whatever sins they had committed, but as a consecration of the body that implied that the soul was already thoroughly cleansed by right behavior" (*Antiquities* 18.5.2). According to this popular leader, individuals should not rely on ancestral privilege; he is quoted as saying, "Do not presume to say to yourselves, 'We have Abraham as our father,' for I tell you, God is able from these stones to raise up children to Abraham." In Hebrew, the invective is a play on words: "children" is *banim*, and "stones" is *evanim*; Aramaic offers a similar pun. This quotation attributed to the leader is not from Josephus; it is from the Gospels (Matt. 3:9; Luke 3:8, RSV), where the speaker is known as John the Baptist.

The next line in the Matthean version of the Lord's Prayer, "Hallowed be your name," is a component of most Jewish prayers. For example, the Kaddish—perhaps best known for being recited by mourners, and a prayer that is in Aramaic, the language Jesus spoke—begins, "Magnified and sanctified be [God's] great name." Jews early on concluded that the name of God is both sacred and ineffable. A number of the Dead Sea Scrolls, from Qumran, write the four letters of the divine name (Hebrew *yod, heh, vav, hey;* in English transliteration, YHWH) in paleo-Hebrew, an ancient style of writing, rather than in regular script. The hallowing of the divine name through the use of circumlocutions appears even in the New Testament. For example, Matthew's Gospel tends to speak of the "kingdom of heaven" rather than the "kingdom of God."

"Your kingdom come" correlates in Jewish tradition with the expression *olam ha-bah*, "the world to come." The "world to come" is the messianic age, a time distinguished from and infinitely better than "this world" (*olam ha-zeh*). Jesus's plea for the kingdom to come also has a conspicuous political edge. The prayer seeks the *divine* kingdom, not the one of Caesar or his lackeys, such as Herod Antipas, the ruler of Galilee who executed John the Baptist, or Pontius Pilate, the Roman governor who crucified Jesus.

Today a number of Christians (and Jews) think that Judaism lacks a notion of a messianic age or an afterlife. The view stems in part from centuries of Jews and Christians defining themselves in relation to each other. The more the church stressed what Jews call "the world to come" and so focused on salvation for which a certain orthodoxy of belief was requisite, the more the synagogue emphasized life in this world and the sanctification of life through actions. In part, branches of modern Judaism chose to deemphasize or even eliminate from the liturgy materials that suggested supernaturalism. Yet even for these congregations, the view that the world can be repaired (known as *tikkun olam*, "reparation of the world") and the stress on working toward this repair keep the idea of a better world, a "world to come," in place.

The Jewish concern for action or practice, already evident in the Torah, lies behind the next line in the prayer. Jesus is also fully involved with doing the divine will or, as the prayer puts it, "Your will be done." He shows this involvement by doing what Jews call "building a fence about the Law" (*Pirke Avot* 1:1). The point is to take an additional precaution so that a commandment is not violated. One humorous example from the rabbinic tradition (Babylonian Talmud *Shabbat* 13a) advises, "To a Nazirite [one who has vowed to remain in a state of ritual purity particularly marked by eschewing "wine and strong drink" (Num. 6:1–8) along with haircuts and contact with corpses] we say: 'Go round and round, but not near a vineyard.'" In other words, to avoid the temptation to drink wine, the Nazirite is to avoid places where wine can be obtained. The best-known explanation of such fence building in the Jewish tradition today is the dietary practice of not mixing milk with meat products (thus, a cheeseburger would not be kosher). The biblical basis for the practice is the threefold repetition of the injunction "You shall not boil a kid in its mother's milk" (Exod. 23:19b; 34:26b; Deut. 14:21).

Examples of fence building attributed to Jesus appear most clearly in the so-called Antitheses of the Sermon on the Mount (Matt. 5:21–47). To those who heard it said, "You shall not murder," Jesus says, "If you are angry with a brother or sister, you shall be liable to judgment." To those who heard it said, "You shall not commit adultery," Jesus says, "Everyone who looks at a woman with lust has already committed adultery with her in his heart." To those who heard it said, "You shall not swear falsely," Jesus says, "Do not swear at all" (a point ignored by those who insist on "swearing on a stack of Bibles" or being "sworn in" by placing one's hand on a Bible). In each case, Jesus is taking the Law, the Torah, so seriously that he extends prohibitions regarding action to prohibition regarding thought. The term "Antitheses" itself is an unfortunate label that gives the impression of separating Jesus from Jewish tradition, for it suggests that Jesus is antithetical to the Torah. Jesus does not "oppose" the Law; he extends it. Moreover, his attitude toward it is not liberal, but highly conservative.

The only actual "antithesis" of this section of the Sermon on the Mount is Matthew 5:43–44: "You have heard that it was said, 'You shall love your neighbor and hate your enemy.' But I say to you, Love your enemies and pray for those who persecute you." No law commands hatred of enemies. On the contrary, Proverbs 25:21 advises, "If your enemies are hungry, give them bread to eat, and if they are thirsty, give them water to drink." Granted, there is a compensatory aspect to this bit of wisdom, for the proverb does indicate that those who do behave in such a beneficent manner toward enemies "will heap coals of fire on their heads, and the Lord will reward you" (25:22). Jesus therefore goes a step beyond the biblical tradition. Nevertheless, at least the enemy gets fed, and it might be a good reminder to those who hear his words in the Sermon on the Mount that "loving the enemy" also involves physical care, including "daily bread."

The next line in the Lord's Prayer, "Give us this day our daily bread," is redundant. "Give us this day our bread" or "Give us our daily bread" would be direct, but asking for "daily bread" for "this day" overstates. The problem with the verse is the Greek word usually translated "daily," *epiousion*. The term does not show up elsewhere in the contemporaneous literature, and according to the church father Origen (185–254), it was actually coined by the Evangelists.[13] Definitions range from "necessary for existence" to "for the current day" to "for the following day" to "be coming." Perhaps the best translation, then, would be, "Give us tomorrow's bread today," for that makes the most sense in a first-century Jewish setting. Jewish texts speak of the *olam ha-bah*, the world to come, as a glorious banquet. Isaiah 25:6 foresees that "on this mountain the Lord of hosts will make for all peoples a feast of rich food, a feast of well-aged wines, of rich food filled with marrow, of well-aged wines strained clear." From *2 Baruch*, an apocalypse written after the destruction of the Jerusalem Temple in 70, comes this beautiful vision:

> And Behemoth will reveal itself from its place, and Leviathan will come from the sea, the two great monsters which I created on the fifth day ... and they will be nourishment for all who are left. The earth will also yield fruits ten-thousand-fold. And on one vine will be a thousand branches, and one branch will produce a thousand clusters, and one cluster will produce a thousand grapes, and one grape will produce a *cor* of wine. And those who are hungry will enjoy themselves. (29:4–7)[14]

Pirke Avot, from the Mishnah, attributes to Rabbi Jacob the saying "This world is like a vestibule before the world to come: prepare yourself in the vestibule that you may enter into the banqueting hall" (4:16).

Even today, at the synagogue on a Friday night or Saturday morning Jews welcome the Sabbath by serving food, because the Sabbath is a foretaste—literally—of the world to come. The same idea appears on the lips of Jesus, when he speaks of the day that "many will come from east and west and eat with Abraham and Isaac and Jacob" (Matt. 8:11) and when he describes Lazarus as reclining (as if he were on a dining couch) in Abraham's bosom (Luke 16:23). In the church, taste of the messianic age is what should be encountered at the Eucharist (Communion), at "the Lord's *table*."

"Give us tomorrow's bread today" therefore means "Bring about your rule, when we can eat at the messianic banquet." This is the prophetic hope, the prophetic vision. And yet the other meanings of that problematic Greek term need not be excluded by this emphasis on the messianic table. The pun is not an unknown form of expression to the Jewish culture. The same line can also mean "Dear Father, please give us enough food to get us through the day, so that our children will not starve." Thus, the prayer leads to action, for God actually gives, not "bread," but grain. Bread comes from human effort. In like manner, the standard Jewish blessing said before eating, "Blessed are you, Lord Our God, King of the Universe, who brings forth bread from the earth," holds the same paradox, since "bread" does not come forth from the earth. Neither the Lord's Prayer nor the Jewish blessing is an abstract wish for food to drop down from heaven; each is a concrete petition that God will motivate our hearts to do the right thing. Both insist that humanity and divinity work together.

As for "Forgive us our trespasses," the original was most likely "Forgive us our debts" (as the Sermon on the Mount puts it in Matt. 6:12). The line does not promote some vague notion that God should forgive us for the occasional taking of the divine name in vain or for yelling at the cat. It goes directly to the pocketbook; it says, "Don't hold a debt. If someone needs, you give." The call is for economic justice. As Habakkuk laments, "Alas for you who heap up what is not your own! How long will you load yourselves with goods taken in pledge?" (2:6).

Yet "trespasses" or "sins" may well have been part of the prayer as well. I had been convinced that the version reading "debts" was the original, given Jesus's frequent excoriations of the rich and his comparable solace for the poor. I had relegated the idea of forgiving "trespasses" to the growing institutionalized church, which promoted the forgiveness of sins and did adapt away from the community described in the early chapters of Acts in which people held their goods in common. "Forgiving trespasses" is, further, often easier than forgiving debts.

However, in the fall of 2005, I taught my regularly scheduled divinity school course on the Gospel of Matthew, not on the Vanderbilt campus, but at Riverbend Maximum Security Institute, the prison in Tennessee where death row is located. In discussion of the Lord's Prayer, one of the Riverbend students who had undertaken a program of restorative justice spoke eloquently and passionately about receiving forgiveness from the family of his victims. As he put it: "Economics don't mean nothing compared to that word of forgiveness." It's hard to argue with his point. Given Jesus's association with "sinners," that is, with people who deliberately treat others as they themselves would not want to be treated (Hillel's version of the commandment; Zacchaeus the tax collector would be a good example), the notion of forgiving trespasses makes a great deal of sense as part of his ministry. Nothing prevents the conclusion that Jesus offered two versions of the prayer.

The Greek phrase usually translated "Lead us not into temptation" is better rendered "Do not bring us to the test." Judaism speaks about tests given to human beings—particularly worthy human beings. God decided to "test" Abraham, as the story known as the Akedah, or "binding" of Isaac, in Genesis 22 begins: "God tested Abraham. He said to him,... 'Take your son, your only son, the son whom you love, Isaac, and go to the land of Moriah, and offer him there as a burnt offering on one of the mountains that I shall show you.'" The testing of Job took from him his property, his family, and his health. "Do not bring us to the test" thus means "Do not put us in a situation where we might be temped to deny our faith or our morals." For Jews facing abuse by the Roman Empire or, alternatively, the offer of career advancement if they would only be willing to exploit their own people and renounce their own traditions, the words would have had an immediate import. Similarly, for followers of Jesus subject to rejection by their families and, later, persecution by the state, the prayer could not be more apt.

"Evil" in the line "but rescue us from evil" is more precisely "the evil one" (it is unlikely that the Aramaic underlying the Greek would have contained the abstract concept of evil, and the Greek itself is literally "the evil one") and is a reference to Satan, who "tested" Jesus in the wilderness following the baptism (Matt. 4:1–11; cf. Mark 1:12–13; Luke 4:1–13). In the Hebrew text of Job, a book written several centuries before the birth of Jesus, Satan is actually called "the Satan"—literally, "the Accuser"; his role was that of the heavenly prosecuting attorney. Although he operates in this early text as a functionary in God's court, he already shows in his dealings with Job that he is capable of inflicting horrific tests on humanity. By the first century, "the Satan" had become simply "Satan," a supernatural being who sought to lead people away from God. First-century Judaism also had a lively sense of fallen angels, called "watchers," who attempted to lure people away from Torah by teaching them such things as the making of war instruments, astrology, and the use of cosmetics.[15] "Rescue us from the evil one" thus also makes a great deal of sense in historical context.

To put this final pair of verses, "Do not bring us to the test, but rescue us from evil," on the colloquial level, the couplet may be seen as saying,

"Look, God, I don't need testing from you, and I certainly don't need being brought to the test by Satan." Provocative, directly related to human experience, intimate enough with God to be direct, it is an ideal prayer for a first-century Jew.

The issue of whether the prayer is ideal for a twenty-first-century Jew is more delicate. I am not advocating that Jews and Christians should be reciting the Lord's Prayer together, for the prayer is too associated with Jesus, and so with the past two thousand years of difficult relations between Christians and Jews. Further, Judaism has its own liturgy in which all of these concerns are addressed one way or the other. Nevertheless, perhaps this very Jewish prayer, recorded in the very Christian New Testament, is something that grandparents and grandchildren in intermarried families could say together. The prayer is not "*to* Jesus"; it says nothing uniquely Christian; and it fits neatly within Jewish piety. In this way, Jesus truly does provide a bridge, rather than a wedge, between Christians and Jews. In turn, a number of Jewish prayers—that is, prayers recited in antiquity as well as today by Jews—might have equal resonance with Christians.

Reclaiming the Jewish Jesus

Jesus of Nazareth dressed like a Jew, prayed like a Jew (and most likely in Aramaic), instructed other Jews on how best to live according to the commandments given by God to Moses, taught like a Jew, argued like a Jew with other Jews, and died like thousands of other Jews on a Roman cross. To see him in a first-century Jewish context and to listen to his words with first-century Jewish ears do not in any way undermine Christian theological claims. Jesus does not have to be fully unique in order to say something or do something meaningful.

To see and hear him in his historical context enriches the meaning of those all too familiar images and sayings. They become striking again, not just for their spiritual potential, but also for their social engagement. The kingdom of heaven is not, for the Jewish Jesus of Nazareth, a piece of real estate for the single saved soul; it is a communal vision of what could be and what should be. It is a vision of a time when all debts are forgiven, when we stop judging others, when we not only wear our traditions on our sleeve, but also hold them in our hearts and minds and enact them with all our strength. It is the good news that the Torah can be discussed and debated, when the Sabbath is truly honored and kept holy, when love of enemies replaces the tendency toward striking back. The vision is Jewish, and it is worth keeping as frontlets before our eyes and teaching to our children.

From Jewish Sect to Gentile Church

Jesus's earliest followers—Peter and Mary Magdalene, James and John, Joanna and Matthew—were, like Jesus himself, Jews. This designation signals not only their identification with the people of Israel but also their participation in a common set of practices and beliefs. Like Jesus, they honored the Torah and followed Mosaic law as they interpreted it. But when the man for whom they had given up their livelihoods, their homes, their families—the man whom they believed to be God's anointed one, the Messiah—was nailed to a Roman cross, their personal loyalty, social vision, and theological convictions were tested; with the proclamation of his resurrection, those loyalties, visions, and convictions were transformed.

As those followers began to proclaim the message that Jesus of Nazareth, the Messiah, had been resurrected, they met with a spectrum of responses from their fellow Jews. Some believed the message of a crucified and resurrected Lord and so were convinced as well that the "world to come," the messianic age, the resurrection of all the dead, and the final judgment would soon arrive. Others, perhaps doubtful of the claims concerning Jesus, found compelling the righteousness practiced by the members of the community: daily prayer, sharing goods in common, care for widows, and faithful trust in divine providence. The various extraordinary signs manifested by his followers, such as their visionary experiences, charismatic healings, and speaking in tongues, convinced others.

Although historians have challenged the details recorded in the book of Acts, the description of the Pentecost event is not incommensurate with cross-cultural manifestations of what is known as glossolalia, or "speaking in tongues." The same phenomenon apparently gripped the church in Corinth; in 1 Corinthians Paul insists that the practice be constrained, for it was disrupting the church's gatherings. Paul's version of glossolalia is that of speaking in an "unknown" language; Luke enhances the impression by describing people speaking in real languages:

> When the day of Pentecost [the Jewish pilgrimage holiday of Shavuot, also known as the Festival of Weeks] had come … all of them were filled with the Holy Spirit and began to speak in other languages, as the Spirit gave them ability. Now there were devout Jews from every nation under heaven living in Jerusalem. And … each one heard them speaking in the native language of each. Amazed and astonished they asked, "Are not all of these who are speaking Galileans? And how is it that we hear, each of us, in our own native language? Parthians, Medes, Elamites, and residents of Mesopotamia, Judea and Cappadocia, Pontus and Asia, Phrygia and Pamphylia, Egypt and parts of Libya belonging to Cyrene, and visitors from Rome, both Jews and proselytes, Cretans and Arabs." (Acts 2:1–11)

The message of "the Way," as these earliest followers called themselves, took root among members of the local population, along with pilgrims and traders. Luke puts the number of the initial converts at three thousand (Acts 2:41), although ancient demographics are notoriously difficult to confirm. However many affiliated, whether three or thirty thousand, not all the attention was positive.

Luke also notes that "others sneered and said, 'They are filled with new wine'" (Acts 2:13), which may hint at the usual practice of glossolalia, which can sound like babbling. The verse indicates that some thought the whole affair was nonsense, that the visionary experiences were signs, not of heavenly communication, but of either demon possession or insanity. Speaking in tongues was the babbling of drunks. Communal living was all well and good, especially if one believed the kingdom of God was arriving within a week or so, but providing for the direct needs of one's family was more important. The vast majority of those who came into contact with these Galilean messianists would continue to pray, care for the poor, and trust in divine providence as they had always done; they didn't need the Jesus community for that.

Whenever a new religious movement, political view, or social practice emerges, some resistance is to be expected, usually from the representatives of the status quo. As long as Peter and his colleagues lived in relative obscurity, with their common meals and their care for their own, they would not have come to the attention of Rome's local allies, the Jerusalem establishment. But as the movement began to spread, danger followed. To proclaim the resurrection of an individual is one thing; to proclaim that the Messiah was a man crucified by Rome was something else entirely. There was, according to Rome, only one king, and that was Caesar, not some Galilean criminal with royal pretensions. The Temple establishment may have feared a public revolt; scribes and teachers of the Law might have worried about this rival school of thought. The followers of Jesus may have contributed to the tension by preaching about the end of the age, the destruction of the Temple, the guilt of all the people for crucifying Jesus, or Jesus's place in the heavenly throne room. To proclaim oneself a follower of Jesus consequently meant to risk ridicule, ostracism, and even persecution.

Still others thought the movement was a danger to the way of life they cherished, a way of life that stressed concern for one's parents and children and sought to maintain the stability of the family. Jesus's group had a different focus. Anticipating the inbreaking of the kingdom of heaven, when they would be "neither married nor given in marriage,... like angels in heaven" (Mark 12:25), they promoted a system of family values that ran counter to the dominant Jewish view of the time. According to Matthew's Gospel, Jesus applied the following verses from the prophet Micah to his own program: "I have not come to bring peace, but a sword. For I have come to set a man against his father, and a daughter against her mother, and a daughter-in-law against her mother-in-law, and one's foes will be those of one's own household" (10:34–36; see Mic. 7:6). Whether Jesus made this statement or it was attributed to him by his followers, who had personally experienced such division, the point is correct, for Jesus did divide families. James, John, and their mother chose to follow him, while their father, Zebedee, stayed in Galilee with his boats and his hired men. Joanna followed him, while her husband, Chuza, Herod's steward, remained absent (see Luke 8:1–3). To the man who asked to bury his father before joining the movement, Jesus tersely responded, "Let the dead bury their own dead; but as for you, go and proclaim the kingdom of God"

(Luke 9:60). To another who stated, "I will follow you, Lord; but let me first say farewell to those at my home," Jesus responded, "No one who puts a hand to the plow and looks back is fit for the kingdom of God" (Luke 9:61–62). The family that Jesus offered was determined not by marriage or blood but by loyalty to him and his teachings. There was no great communal support for any movement that placed its own ethos and its own members ahead of one's parents, spouse, siblings, and children.

Nevertheless, the message would not be silenced. As it began to enter the wider gentile world, it would be played in new keys for new audiences. The ethical concerns remained strong, but accompanying this message of the kingdom of heaven was an increasing focus on Jesus himself: the meaning his death and resurrection had for the individual and for the cosmos as well. The Jewish messianic expectations of Jesus's first followers would coalesce around the cross and the proclamation of the resurrection.

Messianic Expectations

Not all Jews in the first century—or ever—have believed that a messiah was coming. Neither was there general agreement upon messianic attributes; there was no checklist that included

Being born to a virgin mother
Receiving a direct commission from God
Defeating Satan's temptations
Walking on water

Despite Paul's insistence that Jesus "was buried, and that he was raised on the third day in accordance with the Scriptures" (1 Cor. 15:4), no Jewish source, outside those associated with the followers of Jesus, shows any expectation that the messiah would be killed and after three days rise. The closest possible reference is Hosea 6:1–2: "Come, let us return to the Lord; for it is he who has torn, and he will heal us; he has struck down, and he will bind us up. After two days he will revive us; on the third day he will raise us up, that we may live before him." The reference is not to a single individual, but to the people Israel. The Scriptures to which Paul refers are the Law and the Prophets, not the Gospels (which had not yet been written).

But there was one general point of agreement shared by those Jews who had messianic expectations, namely, that the messiah would inaugurate the messianic age. The coming of the messiah meant that there would be a manifest difference in the world. The prophet Micah envisions the "days to come" when

> Many nations shall come and say:
> "Come, let us go up to the mountain of the Lord,
> to the house of the God of Jacob;
> that he may teach us his ways
> and that we may walk in his paths."
> For out of Zion shall go forth instruction,
> and the word of the Lord from Jerusalem.
> He shall judge between many peoples,
> and shall arbitrate between strong nations far away;
> they shall beat their swords into plowshares,
> and their spears into pruning hooks;
> nation shall not lift up sword against nation,
> neither shall they learn war any more;
> but they shall all sit under their own vines and under their own fig
>   trees,
> and no one shall make them afraid. (4:2–4)

The messianic age, or the "world to come," was the time of proclaiming "release to the captives, and recovery of sight to the blind" (Luke 4:18, in which Jesus cites Isa. 61:1–2)—not just some captives, but all; not just some who are blind, but all. Even more marvelous, the messianic age would witness a general resurrection of the dead, as parents and children, patriarchs and matriarchs together with their descendants would feast at the final banquet, and there would be no more reason to pray, "Give us this day our daily bread."[1]

All Jews did not share in this belief in a final resurrection. The Sadducees, who were associated with the upper echelons of the priesthood and elite Jewish society, did not accept the view. They apparently saw the idea of the reintegration of the body and soul after death as an unnecessary innovation, for the concept is not present in the Torah. It only begins to appear in the relatively late sections of Isaiah and then the book of

Daniel. Luke 20:27 recounts how "some Sadducees, those who say there is no resurrection [of the dead]," tested Jesus with a question about the afterlife (see also Mark 12:18; Matt. 22:23). Acts 23:8 observes: "The Sadducees say that there is no resurrection, or angel, or spirit; but the Pharisees acknowledge them all." Josephus baldly states: "The doctrine of the Sadducees is that souls die with the bodies" (*Antiquities* 18.2.4).

That the New Testament and Josephus both mention the Sadducees' lack of belief in resurrection suggests that their view was distinctive; the majority belief was that the dead would rise, although some thought that all people would rise to face a final judgment and some believed that only the righteous would rise while the wicked would just stay dead. The belief in a general resurrection can even be heard from the lips of Martha, the sister of Mary and Lazarus and the friend of Jesus. At Lazarus's tomb, Jesus informs Martha, "Your brother will rise again." Martha responds with the view held among traditional Jews to this day: "I know that he will rise again in the resurrection on the last day" (John 11:23–24). Jesus responds with the well-known lines "I am the resurrection and the life. Those who believe in me, even though they die, will live, and everyone who lives and believes in me will never die" (11:25–26). John's Gospel shifts away from an end-time view of the resurrection; eternal life, according to the Fourth Gospel, means living fully, today, in the abiding presence of God.

This view that the coming of the messiah presages the time the dead will rise appears also in the Gospel of Matthew: "At that moment the curtain of the Temple was torn in two, from top to bottom. The earth shook, and the rocks were split. The tombs also were opened, and many bodies of the saints who had fallen asleep were raised. After his resurrection they came out of the tombs and entered the holy city and appeared to many" (27:51–53). This is Matthew's notice that the resurrection of Jesus was accompanied by a general, although by no means universal, resurrection. For the Pharisees as well as for Martha and the tradition motivating Matthew's unique observation, when the messiah comes, the dead are raised. There is no thought of a second coming or of a two-stage messianic event.

Because Jesus's followers believed him to be the Messiah, they saw in his mission and message the inauguration of the messianic age. They reasoned, quite logically given their Jewish presuppositions, that if Jesus were the Messiah, then death could not hold him; if Jesus were the Messiah, the dead would rise.

Paul, the Pharisee from Tarsus who became the church's first great evangelist, confirms this messianic view, albeit filtered through his understanding of Jesus as the Christ, the "anointed one." He resists detaching the resurrection of Jesus from the general resurrection of the dead. Asserting that "in fact Christ has been raised from the dead, the first fruits of those who have fallen asleep" (1 Cor. 15:20), he insists as well on this connection between Jesus's resurrection and the general resurrection of the dead: the agricultural metaphor suggests that the final harvest is coming, and that would occur during the same season. As Paul puts it: "Each in his own order: Christ the first fruits, then at his coming those who belong to Christ. Then comes the end, when he hands over the kingdom to God the Father, after he has destroyed every ruler and every authority and power" (1 Cor. 15:23–24).

In his earliest Letter, 1 Thessalonians, written about the year 49—less than two decades after the death of Jesus—Paul writes to restore the fledgling congregation's trust in his teaching. He had told them that the resurrection of the dead was soon to enter human history, but meanwhile members of the Thessalonian church had died. Church members were concerned about the salvation of their dead brothers and sisters. The apostle writes:

> We do not want you to be uninformed, brothers and sisters, about those who have fallen asleep, so that you may not grieve as others do who have no hope. For since we believe that Jesus died and rose again, even so, through Jesus, God will bring with him those who have fallen asleep. For this we declare to you by the word of the Lord, that we who are alive, who are left until the coming of the Lord, will by no means precede those who have fallen asleep. For the Lord himself, with a cry of command, with the archangel's call and with the sound of God's trumpet, will descend from heaven, and the dead in Christ will rise first. Then we who are alive, who are left, will be caught up in the clouds together with them to meet the Lord in the air; and so we will be with the Lord forever. (4:13–17)

The Thessalonians understood "we who are alive" to refer to themselves and Paul. But the years passed, the trumpets remained silent, and the archangel's call was not heard. Consequently, Paul's description of what has come to be called the "rapture" (from the Greek term meaning "to be taken up" or "to be assumed") has been reinterpreted. Today, 1 Thessalonians 4 provides the impetus for the best-selling Left Behind series, in which faithful Christians are literally lifted up to heaven—leaving their clothes behind!—while the rest of the world suffers through the reign of the Antichrist. These books are the latest in a series of depictions of the rapture throughout the centuries, the means by which Paul's statement, directed to a small, first-century Greek congregation, has been interpreted through the generations. When the end didn't come, Paul's followers did what all groups convinced that they are living in the last times do: they reflect, they research the Scriptures, they reinterpret, and they either recalculate, retract their views, or disband.

The early eschatological enthusiasm sparked by the announcement that Jesus, the Messiah, had been resurrected is confirmed in the Acts of the Apostles, the continuation of the story started in the Gospel of Luke. In the first chapter of Acts, the apostles ask the resurrected Jesus, "Lord, is this the time when you will restore the kingdom to Israel?" (1:6). They are still looking for the recognizable, universal change that will show the justice of God in operation in the world. Jesus deflects the question: "It is not for you to know the times or periods that the Father has set by his own authority" (1:7). Their task is rather to return to receive the Holy Spirit, after which they will witness to Jesus throughout the Roman Empire. Then, in a bit of narrative, chiding humor, Luke continues: "When he [Jesus] had said this, as they were watching, he was lifted up, and a cloud took him out of their sight. While he was going and they were gazing upward toward heaven, suddenly two men in white robes stood by them. They said, 'Men of Galilee, why do you stand looking up toward heaven? This Jesus, who has been taken up from you into heaven, will come in the same way as you saw him go into heaven'" (1:9–11). Luke, who in both the Gospel and Acts defers the end time to the distant future, thus hints at Paul's view of the "rapture" even as he gently nudges those who are continuing to look up toward heaven in anticipation of the return of Jesus to look forward to the evangelizing of the world instead.

The Galilean followers of Jesus proclaimed their Lord had been resurrected, and they anticipated the general resurrection of all the dead to follow. Paul assured the Thessalonians that the "dead in Christ" would rise first; Matthew offered a version of this general resurrection with the opening of the tombs; Luke insisted that the end was coming, but his emphasis was on certainty rather than immediacy; John reframed the question. In each case, Jesus's followers either anticipated a "second coming" in which the resurrected Lord would bring about the messianic age of universal health, justice, and peace, or they offered a counter and a comfort to take the place of an imminent end.

For the majority of Jews, these various revisions failed to convince. Whatever their views about the messiah, the "world to come," or the "kingdom of God," they did not find persuasive the detaching of the messiah from the messianic age. The problem was not the claim that Jesus had been raised; the problem was the claim that he *alone* had been raised. Although many expected the messiah would bring about a resurrection, a single resurrection did not prove messianic identity.

It is plausible that some Jews could have accepted the idea that Jesus was raised from the dead but still not believed that he was the Messiah. For example, Jesus could have been regarded as a martyr vindicated by God. In the mid-second century BCE, the Syrian ruler Antiochus IV Epiphanes, together with certain members of the Jewish upper classes, resolved to transform Jerusalem into a Hellenistic city, eliminate distinctive practices such as circumcision and the abstention from pork, and otherwise assimilate the Jews into the empire.[2] Second Maccabees, a book found in the Deuterocanonical Writings (also known as the Old Testament Apocrypha), describes in painful detail how one of seven brothers, faced with the choice of transgressing the laws of his ancestors or being tortured to death, in the midst of his suffering taunts Antiochus: "You accursed wretch, you dismiss us from this present life, but the King of the universe will raise us up to an everlasting renewal of life, because we have died for his laws" (7:9). Another brother, suffering the same fate, echoes the point about vindication: "One cannot but choose to die at the hands of mortals and to cherish the hope God gives of being raised again by him. But for you there will be no resurrection to life" (7:14).

Some Jews heavily influenced by pagan views may have equated the news of Jesus's resurrection with the presumed return to life of pagan heroes, such as Asclepius. Other Jews rejected the idea that Jesus was resurrected. They saw no reappearance of Jesus; the world had not changed; they were unlikely and unwilling to accept the word of a group of Galileans. These doubters claimed, according to Matthew's Gospel (28:11–15), that the whole resurrection proclamation was a hoax: the disciples had stolen the body. A few might have thought that Jesus's followers had seen a ghost, such as the shade of Samuel called up at King Saul's request by a medium at Endor (1 Sam. 28:3–19).

As the delay of justice, the finality of death, and the rapacity of Rome continued, some of Jesus's early followers may well have returned to their homes and families. The social experiment of living by forgiving debts and trespasses, treating all in the group as members of one's own family, and recognizing that they were part of the inbreaking of the kingdom of heaven remained only a beautiful memory and an unfulfilled hope. They would need to wait for someone else.

The small band that remained faithful, inspired by Jesus's teachings and convinced by his resurrection that he was God's anointed, had to contend with the inevitable questions raised by their belief in Jesus as the Messiah:

1. How could the world—so manifestly different in the hearts of Jesus's followers but so evidently the same to empirical observation—be experiencing the messianic age?

2. If the messianic age was a time when Gentiles would also worship the God of Israel, did they bear the responsibility of facilitating that conversion?

3. How were they to continue to live as they waited for the end to come and as more people joined their group?

4. If Jesus is to be proclaimed not just a vindicated martyr but the Messiah, how should his death be explained?

Among others, it would be Peter, Paul, and James who provided answers to these questions, and as they did, they transformed the Jewish sect into a gentile phenomenon. They created a movement in continuity with the Jewish message Jesus proclaimed, but they also adapted that message— along with the announcement of Jesus's crucifixion and proclamation of his resurrection—to new times, settings, and congregations.

Peter, the Rock

Peter, the fisherman from Galilee, emerged as the spokesman for the disciples and became the first leader of the early Jerusalem community. Peter's actual name was Simon bar Jonah (*bar* is Aramaic for "son of"), but Jesus designated him Kepha, Aramaic for "rock." The Greek translation of "rock" is Petros, as in the term "petrified." Matthew's Gospel sets the occasion for this designation at Caesarea Philippi, where Simon announces his belief that Jesus is "the Messiah, the Son of the living God." Jesus responds: "Blessed are you, Simon son of Jonah. For flesh and blood has not revealed this to you, but my Father in heaven. And I tell you, you are Peter (*Petros*) and on this rock (*petra*) I will build my church" (16:16–18a).

That Peter emerged as a leader at all is astonishing, for the Gospels report his continual misunderstanding, vacillation, and even denial of Jesus. Mark's Gospel states that at Jesus's arrest, the male disciples "deserted" their leader and "fled" (14:50). What Peter experienced after the crucifixion remains a matter of some debate, and conflicting details in the Gospels prevent any firm historical conclusion. According to Matthew 28:16–20, Peter encountered the risen Jesus on a mountaintop in Galilee. Luke cryptically has several disciples tell the two travelers who had met Jesus on the road to Emmaus that "the Lord has risen indeed, and he has appeared to Simon" (24:34). However, the circumstances of this appearance go unnoted. John offers two appearances to the male disciples in Jerusalem (20:19–25, 26–29) and then another meeting by the Sea of Tiberias (chap. 21). In this final scene, Peter and a few of his fellow apostles breakfast with Jesus on the shore, and there Jesus commissions him to "feed my lambs" (21:15).

However, wherever, and whenever Peter experienced his encounter with the risen Jesus, he eventually settled in Jerusalem, where according to the book of Acts he and the apostle John directed the inchoate church. Peter and the few dozen men and women with him lived as Jesus had taught them, as if the messianic age were already breaking in. Eschewing the desires of private property and self-preservation, they established a utopian community in which they were all one family of mothers and brothers and sisters. Luke describes their lifestyle:

Now the whole group of those who believed were of one heart and soul, and no one claimed private ownership of any possessions, but everything they owned was held in common. With great power the apostles gave their testimony to the resurrection of the Lord Jesus, and great grace was upon them all. There was not a needy person among them, for as many as owned lands or houses sold them and brought the proceeds of what was sold. They laid it at the apostles' feet, and it was distributed to each as any had need. (Acts 4:32–35)

Their beliefs and practices were bolstered, according to Luke's account in Acts 2, by the descent of the Holy Spirit at Pentecost. Just as Jesus's healings had attracted crowds in Galilee, so the public—and unusual—activities of the followers of Jesus served to draw in the people of Jerusalem. To this audience, Peter, John, and their companions began to proclaim the news that a crucified man—Jesus of Nazareth—had risen from the dead. They proclaimed the cross not an ending but a beginning, not a tragic death of a charismatic prophet but the inauguration of the messianic age. To prepare for this inbreaking of the kingdom of God, Peter and his colleagues demanded, the people must repent. Soon the movement grew, as did opposition to it.

Eventually and inexorably came persecution, and some of the followers fled Jerusalem. In Damascus and Antioch, Greece and Egypt and Rome, their message began to be heard in the local synagogues and small shops, on street corners and at banquets. The mission was growing, and it was changing.

The Gentile Mission

Along with Jerusalem's residents, pilgrims and the merchants visiting the city also witnessed the charismatic performances of the followers of the Way and heard, whether firsthand or indirectly, the news about Jesus. From these individuals, who would return to their homes in Damascus and Antioch, Ephesus and Rome, the proclamation of the Jewish Messiah spread. But with the spread of the gospel to the Diaspora, to those Jews outside the homeland, the same ridicule, ostracism, and persecution that almost inevitably attend new religions followed as well.

It is in the context of such persecution that the New Testament introduces Saul, the Pharisee from Tarsus, later to be called "St. Paul." According to Acts 9:1–2, Saul, "breathing threats and murder against the disciples of the Lord, went to the high priest and asked him for letters to the synagogues at Damascus, so that if he found any who belonged to the Way, men or women, he might bring them bound to Jerusalem." In his Letter to the Philippian church, he recounts his own background: "as to zeal, a persecutor of the church" (3:6). He notes in Galatians 1:13 that the Gentiles of the church had heard of his "earlier life in Judaism," how he was "violently persecuting the church of God and was trying to destroy it."

Why Paul persecuted the church is a matter of some speculation. Was he concerned that members of the Way were seeking to replace the Torah with Jesus? If so, his action resembles that of Protestants of all types— frontier Evangelicals (Methodists and Baptists), urban mainline Christians (Presbyterians), and other restorationists (Campbellites)—who attacked members of the Church of Jesus Christ of Latter-day Saints; the charge was that this group was teaching something contrary to the basics tenets of their theology and moral vision. Had he heard that followers of the Way were teaching that the Law was unimportant or marginal or somehow replaced by Jesus? If so, such teaching would have gone against what he described as the center of Jewish life, and his life. Writing to the Philippian church, Paul emphasizes his Jewish identity: "If anyone else has reason to be confident in the flesh, I have more: circumcised on the eighth day, a member of the people of Israel, of the tribe of Benjamin, a Hebrew born of Hebrews; *as to the Law, a Pharisee; … as to righteousness under the Law, blameless*" (3:4b–6).

Could Paul have been worried about the safety of his fellow diaspora Jews? Local majorities, then and now, tend not to look favorably on people who cry out ecstatically, make assertions based on mystical visions, forsake traditional family roles, and proclaim as Lord someone executed by the state. Or again, was he fearful that these messianists would put the synagogues and so his fellow Jews in danger? According to the *Lives of the Caesars*, a gossipy book by the early-second-century Roman historian Suetonius, the emperor Claudius (49–54 CE) had expelled all Jews from Rome because of controversy over a fellow called "Chrestus"—perhaps a mishearing of "Christ." If this "Chrestus" is a reference to the Christ, then Paul had good reason to worry. Internal religious tension can spill over into public fights, and public fights under Rome's rule were stamped out, harshly.

Or had Paul heard that Jesus and his followers uttered threats against the Temple? Mark records that, in the trial before the Sanhedrin, "some stood up and gave false testimony against him": "We heard him say, 'I will destroy this Temple that is made with hands, and in three days I will build another, not made with hands'" (14:57–58). According to the Acts of the Apostles, false witnesses also accused Stephen, a member of the early Jerusalem gathering, of the same charge: "This man never stops saying things against this holy place [the Temple] and the Law; for we have heard him say that this Jesus the Nasorean will destroy this place and will change the customs that Moses handed on to us" (6:13–14). Luke then records that Stephen, after an impassioned speech ending with a condemnation of the people for consistent evil culminating in their corporate betrayal and murder of Jesus, is dragged outside the city and stoned. As Stephen was being martyred, "the witnesses laid their coats at the feet of a young man name Saul.... And Saul had approved of their killing him" (Acts 7:58–8:1). Or, perhaps Paul had heard that these messianists were praying *to* Jesus or *through* Jesus, for that practice may have suggested a second God, something anathema to his Pharisaic sensibilities.

Whatever Paul's reasons for persecuting the followers of the Way, they became utterly irrelevant one day on the road to Damascus. There Paul had an experience both he and Acts describe as an encounter with the risen Christ. And at that moment, Paul turned from persecutor into proclaimer.

Paul states in Galatians 1:16–17 what he did after his encounter: "I did not confer with any human being, nor did I go up to Jerusalem to those who were already apostles before me, but I went away at once into Arabia, and afterwards I returned to Damascus." During those years he would have met with other followers of Jesus, and together they started the process of articulating a theology that would translate the Jewish Jesus into a gentile Savior.

For Paul, the cross and the resurrection were more than an assurance that the messianic age was breaking in, and Jesus was more than a true prophet or righteous martyr. The payoff had to be greater, and it had to encompass not just Jerusalem, but Athens, Antioch, and Alexandria as well. Since the sign of the messianic age inaugurated by Jesus was not, at least yet, the resurrection of the dead or the final judgment, Paul provided it a different, and in his view even better, effect. He concluded that the cross could be understood as a sacrifice: it proved that Jesus had paid the penalty for all human sin, that he had "died for the ungodly" (Rom. 5:6). Reconciling humanity and divinity from the chasm created by the fall of Adam, Jesus had "justified by his blood" fallen humanity. Thus, he asserts, "will we be saved through him from the wrath of God" (5:9). The Christ, in other words, died as a sacrifice, and in so doing he defeated the powers of sin and death and provided humanity with both reconciliation with God and access to eternal life.

For Paul, that eternal life was to come in the near future. In contrast to the proclamation heard so often today that "I am saved," Paul tends to put the idea of salvation in the future. Jesus justifies and sanctifies (in the present), but one is saved in the future. A generation later, the church would rephrase Paul's statements, so that salvation became coeval with baptism.

Most Jews would not have accepted Paul's claims any more than they would have accepted a messiah without a messianic age. They already had the belief in the resurrection of the dead, and they believed in a just God who forgave sin. Thus, this new Galilean savior would be for them a redundancy—there was nothing broken or missing in their system that his death and resurrection could fix or fill. Further, most would have found the entire notion of a crucified messiah who brings about by his death salvation from death and sin ridiculous. As Paul puts it in 1 Corinthians 1:23, "We proclaim Christ crucified, a stumbling block [*skandalon*] to Jews and foolishness [*morian*, i.e., moronic] to Gentiles."

Some may have perceived Paul's views to be more akin to those of mystery cults than to the Scriptures and practices of Israel. This business about dying to sin and rising to Christ and immersion in water as an initiation rite representing rebirth smacked of something the followers of Isis, Dionysus, or Attis or those folks who participated in the Eleusinian mysteries would do. Off-putting as well was the idea of a human sacrifice who establishes a "new covenant in his blood" (1 Cor. 11:25). Paul's message was not likely to get a good hearing with the synagogue membership. This did not stop him from trying.

During his years in Arabia and Damascus, Paul and other Jewish followers of the Way would have spread their gospel in the synagogues as well as in the markets, streets, apartments, and villas. In these settings, along with Jews would have been found Gentiles. Synagogue gatherings— "synagogue" is from a Greek term that literally means "gathering together"—were attended not only by Jews but also by Gentiles. Called "God-fearers," these Gentiles admired Judaism's ethos and antiquity, its rituals and its ethics, but they did not make full conversion.

There was no need for them to convert. Although some Jews in antiquity did think that the reign of God was confined to Jews alone and to their particular group of Jews (just as some Christians believe that only Christians of a certain sort will enter heaven), most synagogue congregations did not. They welcomed converts, but they did not seek them. It was only in the second century CE, when pagan Rome and then its Christian heirs made conversion to Judaism illegal, that the synagogue developed the practice of dissuading would-be proselytes.

As for what would happen to the Gentiles when the messiah came, different Jews had different opinions. The Dead Sea Scrolls typically regard the Gentiles as well as most of the Jews who did not join the Qumran community as damned. But there was another option, this one already hinted at in the Prophets. According to Zechariah 8:22–23: "Many peoples and strong nations shall come to seek the Lord of hosts in Jerusalem, and to entreat the favor of the Lord. Thus says the Lord of hosts: In those days, ten men from nations of every language shall take hold of a Jew, grasping his garment and saying, 'Let us go with you, for we have heard that God is with you.'" They do not say, however, "circumcise us when we get there." They would worship the God of Israel *as Gentiles.*

For Zechariah, Gentiles would be brought into the world to come by divine fiat. Jews need not engage in a mission to them. To put this in Christian parlance, one did not have to be Jewish in order to be saved. There was, and there remains, in Jewish thought no reason for Gentiles to convert to Judaism, although in the Hellenistic and early Roman periods a number did. In the early days of the covenant community, one could not convert to become a Hebrew or an Israelite any more than an Italian could "convert" to become a Navaho or a Kenyan could "convert" to become Japanese; affiliation did not create a recognition that one had actually changed ethnic groups. To describe a non-Israelite in its midst, Israel used the term *ger toshav,* meaning "sojourning stranger" or, colloquially, "resident alien." Yet sometime after the Babylonian exile in the sixth century

BCE, the nation of Israel took on more formally the attributes of what we today would call a "religion." One could not convert to become a "Judean" or a "Galilean," but one could become a "Jew" and so affiliate with both the God of Israel and the people of Israel.

By the first century, Jewish thought offered Gentiles three major options regarding affiliation: Gentiles could formally join the people Israel, as did one Nicolaus, the proselyte from Antioch whom Luke mentions in Acts 6:5. This fellow was a Gentile who converted to Judaism, moved from Syria to Judea, and then became a recognized leader of the Way. Or Gentiles could become God-fearers and affiliate with the Jewish community to greater or lesser degrees without undergoing conversion. Given that conversion required circumcision and maintaining the dietary laws (and so likely prohibited dining at the local temple, where families bonded and networking got accomplished), and a host of other problems that accrue when one changes citizenship, the God-fearer option had a number of takers. Or Gentiles could simply be Gentiles who behaved in a righteous way. Righteous Gentiles populate the Scriptures of Israel— from Abraham's servant in Genesis who finds Rebekah as a bride for Isaac to Pharaoh's daughter in Exodus, who, ignoring her father's commands to kill the Hebrew babies, adopts Moses, to the helpful eunuchs in the books of Esther and Daniel. (The term "righteous Gentile" is used today to refer to Gentiles who, at risk to their own lives, sheltered Jews from the Nazis and their collaborators.)

Paul, good Jew that he was, knew about righteous Gentiles. He also knew that the God of Israel was also the God of the Gentiles and that the Gentiles, *qua* Gentiles, would accept this theological truth in the last days. In other words, for Paul, the Gentiles would come into the messianic realm *as Gentiles;* they did not have to be Jews in order to be in a right relationship with God. The Babylonian Talmud, that compendium of Jewish Law, agrees with him: "Righteous people of all nations have a share in the world to come" (*Sanhedrin* 105a). And so Paul proclaimed to the Gentiles that the Jewish God was their God; the Jewish messiah was their messiah, but they did not have to convert to Judaism to receive his love or his beneficence.

Convinced that the only correct path was the one he promoted, Paul thus offered Gentiles full rather than subsidiary membership in the people Israel, minus the requirements of circumcision and Jewish dietary laws.

Moreover, Paul's gospel offered Gentiles the most precious commodity in the ideological market: eternal life. Even better, unlike the mystery cults the Pauline communities did not require membership fees; on the contrary, they included rich and poor, slaves as well as free, women as well as men, and Jews as well as Gentiles (see Gal. 3:28). The erasure of sin, the connection to Israel's respected ancient past, and the morality of the church all added to the new movement's appeal. The enhanced status church patrons might acquire made the message especially desirable to those seeking honor, or clients. Thus, Paul's communities of Jews and Gentiles, convinced the Messiah had come and the end times were around the corner, began to stake out their own identity.

Working with Barnabas, a fellow member of the Way from Cyprus, Paul began a major program of attempting to proclaim the gospel of Jesus to Gentiles in Antioch, about three hundred miles north of Jerusalem by geography and about 180 degrees different from Jerusalem in ethnic makeup (a gentile rather than Jewish majority). There and elsewhere, the two missionaries founded communities of Jews and Gentiles, united in the belief that the Messiah had come. These groups would receive the name "Christian"—a likely pejorative term meaning a "partisan of Christ" or member of the "Christ party."

At this point, matters get dicey. To preach to Jews the idea of a crucified messiah is dangerous enough or, as Paul puts it, a "scandal." To speak of the "son of God" or "god from god" or "savior" and to mean Jesus rather than Caesar (for these were titles given to the Roman emperor) was to suggest disloyalty to the state. To tell Gentiles that there were certain religious or social practices that they would have to give up was not only "folly"; it was seditious. Paul enjoined his gentile converts from sacrificing to their family gods or worshiping at their families' altars. They were to stop eating meat sacrificed to idols, which in the urban cities of antiquity meant social suicide for the upper classes; to refuse to participate in the temple-based cultic meals was to refuse table fellowship with friends, family, and patrons. Paul explicitly addressed the matter in 1 Corinthians 8. The chapter begins, "Now concerning food sacrificed to idols" and warns, "if others see you, who possess knowledge, eating in the temple of an idol, might they not, since their conscience is weak, be encouraged to the point of eating food sacrificed to idols?" (vv. 1, 10).

From the gentile perspective, the claim that followers of Jesus must cease being followers of the gods was horrifically unpatriotic, for the gods of the city were its protectors. Forsake the gods, and the gods will forsake you. No wonder Jews in local synagogues were upset, for the message about a Jewish messiah, proclaimed by Jews, would impact them. Having the Gentiles forsake their gods and their pagan practices in the messianic age is desirable; having them do it before the end has come is suicidal.

For Paul and Barnabas, the political fallout along with occasional persecution by the local synagogue was a small price to pay in order to save the world. Nor was it a huge problem, since Jesus was returning soon.

Jews and Gentiles

Meanwhile, back in Judea, Peter was engaging in his own missionary activity and, like Paul, he was also experiencing resistance. Acts 12:1–3a reports that King Herod Agrippa, Herod the Great's grandson who ruled from 37 until his death in 44, "laid violent hands upon some who belonged to the church. He had James, the brother of John, killed with the sword. After he saw that it pleased the Jews, he proceeded to arrest Peter also." Given Peter's political vulnerability, after getting out of prison (Luke recounts a miraculous escape with striking parallels to other "jailbreak" legends in antiquity), he wisely leaves Jerusalem. Acts reports his travels to Joppa and Caesarea as well as to Samaria. Although Acts 10 credits Peter with the conversion of the centurion Cornelius, a God-fearing Gentile, his mission field remained the Jews. Paul confirms this division of evangelistic labor in Galatians. Speaking of his meeting with the leaders of the Jerusalem church, he states in his typically prolix way:

> When they saw that I had been entrusted with the gospel for the uncircumcised, just as Peter had been entrusted with the gospel for the circumcised (for he who worked through Peter making him an apostle to the circumcised also worked through me in sending me to the Gentiles), and when James and Cephas [i.e., Peter; "Cephas" is the Greek rendering of the Aramaic "Kepha"] and John, who were acknowledged pillars, recognized the grace that had been given to

me, they gave Barnabas and me the right hand of fellowship, agree-
ing that we should go to the Gentiles and they to the circumcised.
(2:7–9)

The agreement also meant that Gentiles in the church need not be circumcised; as Paul states in the same Letter, he went up to Jerusalem with
Barnabas and met there with the church's leaders, and "even Titus, who
was with me, was not compelled to be circumcised, though he was a
Greek" (2:3).

Paul was to evangelize the Gentiles apart from the Law; Peter was to
proclaim the good news of Jesus to the Jews under the Law. Everything
should have been fine. Even a bit of poaching was permitted, since both
were working for the common cause of bringing the world the good news
of the Christ. In the first few years of the church, everything was fine,
more or less. Much can be accommodated in daily practice if one believes
the end is coming soon. But time dragged on, and decisions had to be
made. If Jews who believed Jesus was the Messiah and Gentiles who
believed the same were to worship together—if they were to celebrate
together the meal that had become the hallmark of the new community—policies needed to be established.

Anyone involved with multicultural initiatives should have a sense of
the difficulties the church faced in determining where it could adapt and
what had to remain sacrosanct. Do Jews and Gentiles in the church remain
distinct, or should there be, as Ephesians 4:4–6 puts it, just "one body
and one Spirit ... one Lord, one faith, one baptism, one God and Father"?
Among the essential questions the emerging churches faced were matters
of diet and circumcision. Circumcision and following the dietary regulations mandated in Torah would mark the church as a Jewish movement;
lack of circumcision and the proclamation that all foods are clean would
distinguish the church from its Jewish origins.

A Brief Feminist Excursus

By insisting that his gentile congregants did not have to be circumcised
and by teaching baptism as the rite of initiation into the church, Paul was
not, contrary to one common stereotype, adopting a feminist view. He
was not replacing the "male" symbol of circumcision with the "egalitar-

ian" symbol of baptism. The church father known as Justin Martyr (so called because Rome executed him in 165) did question whether Jewish women could be saved, since they are not circumcised (*Dialogue with Trypho* 46.3). Jewish women would have been happy to tell him that his question was misguided, if not simply stupid. Although sources on women's personal experience are scant, there is no evidence that Jewish women felt the need to be circumcised (who could blame them?). Their community considered them full members, and the Jewish literature never refers to them as "uncircumcised." The Jewish philosopher Philo of Alexandria states that Jewish women do not need to be circumcised. Circumcision is required to check male pride as well as male sexual impulses; women, according to this writer, have no such problems (*On the Special Laws* 1.1.1–3). His psychology may be distasteful to twenty-first-century sensibilities, but the point about women as fully belonging to the Jewish community is nevertheless clear.

Women are, moreover, hailed for participating in circumcising activity. According to 1 Maccabees, another book in the Deuterocanonical Writings (or Old Testament Apocrypha), when the Syrian-Greek king Antiochus IV Epiphanes and his upper-class Jewish allies in Jerusalem decided to hellenize the Jewish population, the process entailed not only sacrificing a pig, forbidden to Jews, on the Temple altar but also the proscription of circumcision. "According to the decree, they put to death the women who had their children circumcised and their families and those who circumcised them; and they hung the infants from their mothers' necks" (1:60–61).

Looking at initiation rites from the other side, Christian baptism emerges as a no less patriarchal practice. Baptism is a form of "rebirth" or being "born again"—the language is from John 3—that substitutes the mother's biological role with that of the church. Further, the entry rite to salvation for a woman, according to 1 Timothy 2:15, is just as biologically particular as circumcision: "She will be saved through childbearing."[3] Both church and synagogue are patriarchal institutions; neither was egalitarian in the first century. Therefore, neither should be judged solely according to twenty-first-century standards. Paul rejected circumcision for his gentile converts because circumcision indicated conversion to Judaism, not because he was concerned that women did not bear the mark of circumcision on their own bodies. Paul promoted the idea of baptism not because of some feminist impulse, but because it was a popular form of ritual practice known in both Jewish and gentile contexts.

The Failed Two-Track System

To circumcise or not to circumcise; to keep kosher or to eat pork and shrimp; to have one church for both Jews and Gentiles or to have separate tables, beliefs, and practices ... The church was fighting for its life. For the movement to live to see the return of Jesus, something needed to be done. James, the brother of Jesus, also called "James the Just," was the one to make the determination.

There is no good evidence that James followed Jesus prior to the cross. In the synoptic Gospels (Matthew, Mark, and Luke, so named because they "see together" in telling basically the same story with the same words and in the same order), Jesus dismisses his natal family, his "mother and brothers and sisters" in favor of "whoever does the will of God" (Matt. 12:46–50; Mark 3:32–34; Luke 8:19–21).[4] John's Gospel states with no equivocation, "Not even his brothers believed in him" (7:5)! The noncanonical *Gospel of the Hebrews* (as described by the church fathers Origen [185–254] and Jerome [ca. 340–420]) claims, however, that James was at the Last Supper: "James had sworn that he would not eat bread from the hour in which he had drunk the cup of the Lord until he should see him risen from among them that sleep. And shortly thereafter the Lord said: 'Bring a table and bread!' And immediately it is added: He took bread, blessed it and broke it and gave it to James the Just and said to him: 'My brother, eat thy bread, for the Son of Man is risen from among those who sleep.'" This appears to be a bit of Christian spin control designed to explain how James emerged as such a principal architect of the early movement.

Paul reports the tradition, which early became creedal, that the resurrected Jesus appeared to James: "For I handed on to you [the Corinthian church] as of first importance what I in turn had received: that Christ died for our sins in accordance with the Scriptures,... and that he appeared to Cephas, then to the twelve. Then he appeared to more than five hundred brothers and sisters at one time, most of whom are still alive, though some have fallen asleep. Then he appeared to James, then to all the apostles." Paul concludes by noting that "last of all, as to one untimely born, he appeared also to me" (1 Cor. 15:3–8). The appearance to James legitimates his role in the church's leadership, just as the experience Paul had on the road to Damascus sanctions the validity of his gospel.

Along with his familial connections and the report of a resurrection appearance, several other factors facilitated James's ascendancy in the Jerusalem church. Peter's imprisonment coupled with his frequent absences from Jerusalem may have created a leadership vacuum. His volatility may also have prompted some to seek a steadier leadership. James not only had the connections but also had the consistency and the piety. His well-known fidelity to the Laws of Moses and his strong affiliation with the Temple enhanced his reputation among both Jews who followed Jesus and those who did not.

Practical and pious, James sought a solution to the gentile question. His first attempt, and first failure, was to sanction a two-track mission: Peter would evangelize the Jews, and Paul the Gentiles. According to Galatians 2:9, "James and Cephas and John, who were the acknowledged pillars [of the church]," recognized that Paul and his colleague Barnabas should go to the Gentiles, while they would be in charge of evangelizing the "circumcised." Occasionally, there were crossovers, such as Peter's conversion of Roman centurion Cornelius and his family (Acts 10) and Paul's occasional success with a few diaspora Jews. As Paul notes in 1 Corinthians: "To the Jews I became as a Jew, in order to win Jews. To those under the Law I became as one under the Law (though I myself am not under the Law) so that I might win those under the Law" (9:20). But once the communities mixed, the default was no longer clear. Gentile Christians, at least in Paul's system, did not need circumcision, Jewish dietary regulations, specific Sabbath observance, and so forth. Jewish Christians, however, sought to follow the Way as Jews, complete with the practices that had always distinguished their community from those of their gentile neighbors. The center could not hold.

In his Letter to the Galatians, Paul mentions that "people from James," whom he calls the "circumcision faction," had convinced Peter to stop eating with Gentiles. Peter complied, and Paul complains that "the other Jews joined him in this hypocrisy, so that even Barnabas was led astray by their hypocrisy" (2:12–13). However, once Paul's polemical language is eliminated, his own righteous indignation becomes suspect. Writing to the Galatians, a gentile church that was seeking at least to practice circumcision if not to follow the rest of the commandments enjoined upon Jews, Paul needed whatever leverage he could find to convince the congregation that they need not practice Judaism. By calling Peter's action hypocritical and blaming "people from James" for the hypocrisy, he could promote his own (nonhypocritical, directly authorized by the Christ) gospel.

Paul had hoped that the Jewish representatives of the church would prioritize the good of the church as a whole over their particular practices. For Peter to eat with Gentiles and so submerge his Jewish identity for the good of the group was for Paul the correct practice. Yet Paul himself had earlier spoken, approvingly, of a two-part mission: Peter to the Jews and Paul to the Gentiles. A two-part mission suggests that Gentiles would enter the church apart from Mosaic Law, and Jews would continue their ancestral and well-loved practices. The commitment of those Maccabean mothers who died and whose sons died as well, for the sake of practicing circumcision, could not simply be ignored. The fact that not only Peter but also all the other Jews at that Antioch setting save for Paul were determined to follow Jewish dietary practice might be seen as their recognition of the importance of their own cultural and religious identity. Multiculturalism, then or now, cannot function if there is a homogeneous default that causes one group to give up what is of enormous value to them, especially if what is to be forsaken is divinely mandated Torah.

For Peter and James, there was a two-track system. Gentiles and Jews, although marked by separate practices, were both full members of the church. For Paul, there was only one track, and it was his. But it would take several years for his gospel to receive general acceptance. Although Paul insists that "when Cephas came to Antioch, I opposed him to his face" (Gal. 2:11), he probably did not win the battle. For all his protestations, he does not actually tell the Galatians that he emerged triumphant in the debate. Nevertheless, Paul's Law-free gospel would win the war over the fate of Christianity.

Luke presents his own version of how the controversy over Jewish versus gentile practice was settled. Acts 15 begins with the notice that "certain individuals came down from Judea and were teaching the brothers, 'Unless you are circumcised according to the custom of Moses, you cannot be saved.'" In a bit of understatement, Luke describes how "Paul and Barnabas had no small dissension and debate with them." That Luke's own stamp marks the account is seen by what is not said: in this description, James is not associated with the "people from Judea" and there is no mention of the "defection" of Peter, Barnabas, and other leading men of the church. Instead, Luke, who tends to depict the early church as growing smoothly, in unity, and under the ongoing guidance of the Spirit, notes that the church does what any sensible institution would do when facing a controversy: it holds a meeting at its headquarters and awaits the decision from the chair of its board, in this case James.

Paul and Barnabas journey to Jerusalem, where they are welcomed by the "apostles and elders" but challenged by "some believers who belonged to the sect of the Pharisees," who insist that Gentiles in the church be circumcised and follow Mosaic Law. Again, Luke's agenda is apparent, given that both the Gospel and the Acts of the Apostles depict the Pharisees as the ones whose views are to be rejected. At the meeting itself, "after there had been much debate" (which Luke does not record), Peter gets up and describes how he converted the gentile centurion Cornelius apart from circumcision and the rest of Mosaic Law. Yet Peter's own description makes little sense historically. This same Peter, who according to Paul had refused table fellowship with Gentiles and who, according to an earlier account in Acts, had insisted, "I have never eaten anything that is profane or unclean" (10:14), now asks, "Why are you putting God to the test by placing upon the neck of the disciples a yoke that neither our ancestors nor we have been able to bear?" (15:10). Peter had faithfully followed the Law, as had his ancestors and his fellow Jewish disciples. At best the comment is overstatement. It also hints of Lukan apologetic: a non-Jew may find the Torah an unbearable yoke; an insider would not.

Then James offers his compromise. He "reached the decision that we should not trouble those Gentiles who are turning to God, but we should write to them to abstain only from things polluted by idols [i.e., meat offered in pagan temples], and from fornication [sexual indecency; the Greek term is *porneia*, whence "pornography"], and from whatever has been strangled, and from blood" (15:19–20). The injunctions show some connection to Leviticus 17–18 and the rules for the *ger toshav*, or "resident alien." They also bear some conformity with the Noachian commandments, seven rules that according to the rabbis were part of the covenant that God established with Noah and, so, requisite for all humanity: injunctions against murder (*shefichat damim*; literally, "spilling blood"), stealing (or kidnapping; *gezel*), idolatry (*avodah zarah*), sexual immorality (*giliu arayot*), eating the flesh from a live animal (*ever min ha-chai*), and blasphemy against the God of Israel ("Blessing the Name," *birhat ha-Shem*) and the insistence on honest courts (*dinim*).[5] In this configuration, the Gentiles have only seven commandments; the Jews have not just the Ten Commandments, but the 613 given to Moses. Acts brings the number for the Gentiles down to four.

The one place where all four concerns James adduces come together is in the pagan temples: that setting would find meat offered to idols, blood, what is strangled, and the presumption, if not necessarily the practice, of illicit sexual behavior. Thus, the letter may have been designed to keep Christians away from the formal setting of pagan worship. It does not, however, address practices by Jews in the churches. The model is "separate but equal." It too will not hold.

The Pauline Gospel

James's compromise allowed Jews in the churches to maintain their distinct practices and Gentiles to avoid pagan worship, but the compromise would ultimately fail. The common ground the church accepted was the common ground of its gentile members. The gospel it proclaimed was that of Paul, not that of James or Peter. Paul's Letters never mention the Jerusalem council, and no reference is made to James's Letter by any other New Testament document. Nor does history always, or even often, show that executive decisions are accepted by the masses. For Paul, whose gospel would carry the day and the next two millennia, Gentiles in the church could not live like Jews. To see how his argument worked, at least for the church, we return to Galatians.

Paul had told the Galatian congregation, which he had founded, that the Gentiles in the church were "children of Abraham." Jews, who considered themselves "children of Abraham" physically as well as spiritually, might have disagreed. He also told the Galatians that the Scriptures of Israel were their Scriptures as well. Again, Jews may well have disagreed. Paul's problems came about, however, when those Galatian Gentiles started to ask about the implications of Paul's good news: what does it mean to be a child of Abraham, and what do the Scriptures of Israel say? Someone in the Galatian church then read, or at least heard about, what the Torah, here in its Greek translation, records concerning these questions. According to Genesis 17:14, God tells Abraham, "Any uncircumcised male who is not circumcised in the flesh of his foreskin shall be cut off from his people" ("cut off" may be a pun, albeit a quite serious one). Taking the comment seriously, the men in Paul's Galatian church lined up for the operation.

Hearing of this practice, Paul reacts as any good first-century rhetorician would: he viciously caricatures the views of his opponents, attacks the heart of their teaching, and piles on the arguments in favor of his position. In his frantic attempt to convince the church he founded that "a person is justified (or reckoned righteous) not by the works of the Law but through faith in Jesus Christ" (Gal. 2:16), Paul lists a number of reasons why the Law, a set of practices that separate Jews from Gentiles, need not be followed. To each reason he offers, a scripturally based counterargument as well as a loyalist Jewish response is easily constructed.

For example, Paul argues that the promises of God were given not to Abraham's biological descendants, the physical children of Israel, but to his spiritual descendants. The argument here relies on a grammatical point: "The promises were made to Abraham and to his seed [Greek *sperma*]; it does not say, 'And to seeds,' as of many; but it says, 'And to your seed,' that is, to one person, who is Christ" (Gal. 3:16). Paul, following the Septuagint, the Greek translation of the Torah, highlights the singular form of the collective noun, "seed," which can also be translated "offspring." Thus Abraham's "offspring" is the Christ, and so those who follow the Christ. The interpretation is clever, but it does fly against the plain sense of the verse. Genesis 12:7, for example, states, "Then the Lord appeared to Abraham and said, 'To your offspring [seed] I will give this land.'" Paul does not speak of Jesus as inheriting the land of Israel nor of the gentile Galatians as about to possess Jerusalem real estate. Following the near sacrifice of Isaac, an angel, speaking for God, tells Abraham: "I will indeed bless you, and I will make your offspring [seed] as numerous as the stars of heaven and as the sand that is on the seashore. And your offspring shall possess the gates of their enemies, and by your offspring shall all the nations of the earth gain blessing for themselves" (Gen. 22:17–18). Paul would need better ammunition.

Likely recognizing the weakness of the "offspring" argument, Paul appeals to history. He notes, for example, that Abraham is justified apart from the Law, since at the time of Abraham the Law had not been given, and "the Law, which came four hundred and thirty years later [i.e., after Abraham], does not annul a covenant previously ratified by God, so as to nullify the promise" (Gal. 3:17; on the number of years, see Exod. 12:40). Therefore, the Sinaitic covenant cannot replace the covenant with Abraham, and the covenant with Abraham does not require following Mosaic Law. Thus Gentiles in the church, who are the heirs of Abraham, are also justified apart from the Law. Then again, as Paul—and likely his Galatian audience—also knew, although the Mosaic covenant does not annul the Abrahamic one, neither is it mutually exclusive to it. The synagogue saw the two covenants as complementary. Further, the legal argument does not resolve the question of circumcision, since Abraham and the men of his household certainly did submit to this operation. Finally, according to Jewish legend, the patriarchs Abraham, Isaac, and Jacob did keep the Torah. One legend, which may be much later than Paul (the dates of such legends are notoriously difficult to determine), reads: "R. Simeon ben Yohai [second century CE] said, 'Our father Abraham—his own Father did not teach him, nor did he have a master to teach him. From whom, then, did Abraham learn Torah? It was the Holy One, who had provided him with reins that were like two pitchers overflowing and filled him with Torah and wisdom all through the night. R. Levi, however, said, 'Abraham learned Torah all by himself'" (*Genesis Rabbah* 61:16; 95:3).[6]

Along with this ancient form of proof-texting, that is, citing individual verses often taken out of context to prove a point, Paul also offers utilitarian arguments. He insists, for example, that if the Gentiles in Galatia agree to circumcision, then it follows they should practice the entire Law. The gentile audience of the Letter may not have agreed; it is just as likely that they stopped with circumcision: ham, yes; foreskin, no. They had been taught that they were children of Abraham, heirs to the promises. Abraham was circumcised, but the biblical text does not state that he followed Mosaic Law (as Paul also notes in his appeal to the 430 years between Abraham and Moses).

Continuing to pile up arguments—with quantity increasingly replacing quality—Paul then explains that the Law was added because of human transgressions "until the seed would come to whom the promises had been made" (Gal. 3:19). Thus the Law is a temporary, stopgap measure designed not to make people good but only to keep them from sinking further into sin. Paul even states that the Law is a "disciplinarian" (Greek *paedagogus*, the slave who taught children the alphabet), "but now that faith has come, we are no longer subject to a disciplinarian" (3:25). On the contrary, the synagogue and perhaps even those Christians in Galatia would respond, the Torah is the eternal word of God, a "tree of life" to those who hold it. Nothing in the Scriptures of Israel suggests that the Law would pass away. Nor would most Jews have agreed with the idea that the Torah was given because of human transgressions. Rather, they would have regarded it as a sign of divine love.

Sounding a bit desperate, Paul states that the Torah was not given to Israel directly by God but "was ordained through angels by an intermediary" (Gal. 3:19). The reference to angels comes from the Greek translation of Deuteronomy 33:2; the Hebrew text states that God and Moses conversed directly. A response is easily found. Mediation should not make a difference in theological value; the words of God spoken by the prophets are mediated, but they are of no less value than a voice that comes directly from heaven. The word that came to Abraham to promise blessing to his "offspring" came from an angel: "The angel of the Lord called to Abraham a second time from heaven and said, 'By myself I have sworn, says the Lord.... I will indeed bless you, and I will make your offspring as numerous as the stars of heaven and as the sand that is on the seashore'" (Gen. 22:15–18). The legitimacy and importance of this promise are not in doubt.

Paul seeks to seal his argument in Galatians with an allegorical reading of Abraham's two wives, Sarah, the mother of Isaac, and Hagar, the mother of Ishmael. According to Paul, Hagar represents the old, outdated covenant established between God and Israel at Mt. Sinai: "She corresponds to the present Jerusalem, for she is in slavery with her children" (4:25). Sarah, on the other hand, represents "Jerusalem above" and the gospel of freedom. Her son, Isaac, a child "of the promise," is born like the Galatians, "according to the Spirit"; Ishmael is born "according to the flesh" (4:28–29). Thus those who claim physical descent from Abraham and follow Torah are children of Hagar; those who claim spiritual descent and do not follow Torah are children of Sarah. Who knew? Jews, of course, would disagree, as would have those Galatian Gentiles who, seeking to be like Abraham as well as both Isaac and Ishmael, desired circumcision.

The New Testament does not record how the Galatian situation was resolved. That the Letter found its way into the canon, however, indicates that Paul's view ultimately prevailed.

The Olive Tree and Its Branches

By the late 50s, or more likely early 60s, when Paul wrote his Letter to the Romans, a letter to a church he did not found, circumstances had changed. Quite likely the church had had a Jewish majority until 49, when Claudius expelled all Jews from Rome because of "Chrestus." The expulsion would have included those Jews who proclaimed Jesus to be the Christ, such as the "Jew named Aquila, a native of Pontus, who had recently come from Italy [to Corinth] with his wife Priscilla, because Claudius had ordered all Jews to leave Rome" (Acts 18:2). Upon their return to Rome at Claudius's death in 54, these Jews would have found their church in gentile hands. The congregation at Rome to which Paul wrote comprised both Jews and Gentiles, and each group appears to have maintained particular practices.

In a more pastoral tone compared to that of Galatians, Paul insists that the Roman church should not be split over dietary practices but should "pursue what makes for peace and for mutual upbuilding" (14:19). Both Jews and Gentiles, according to Paul, are on the same footing, and each needs the other in order for the divine plan of salvation to be implemented.

Paul begins by noting that both Jews and Gentiles are in need of the same mechanism for salvation. The Jews have the Law and the Prophets, but they do not follow what they have received; the Gentiles have the witness of creation as well as their own conscience, but they choose to ignore what they know to be true. There can be no two-track model, because the trains on both tracks derailed. Only the train conducted by Paul, the one in which distinction between Jews and Gentiles is erased, will pull into the heavenly station.

However, to prevent gentile congregants from boasting in the comparably greater success of the gentile mission, and because the fate of Israel was of deep concern to him, Paul insists that the promises given to Israel have not failed. His own anguish regarding Israel's "no" to the Christ can be heard across the centuries: "For I could wish that I myself were accursed and cut off from Christ for the sake of my own brothers, my kindred according to the flesh. They are Israelites, and to them belong the adoption, the glory, the covenants, the giving of the Law, the worship, and the promises. To them belong the patriarchs, and from them, according to the flesh, comes the Christ" (9:3–5). Although they have not agreed to believe in Jesus, God remains faithful to them: "I ask, then, has God rejected his people? By no means!" (11:1).

Paul, rather, proposes, first, that because some of Israel have already accepted the gospel, this righteous remnant proves the promises to Israel are still in place. But he goes on in a more expansive manner. Proposing that a "hardening has come upon part of Israel, until the full number of the Gentiles has come in" (11:25), Paul sees the failure of the Jewish mission as part of the divine plan. It is "through their transgression" that "salvation has come to the Gentiles" (11:11). Had the message remained only among the Jews, the gentile mission never would have had a chance. Thus the stumbling of Israel is for the benefit of the Gentiles. "As regards the gospel they are enemies of God" for the sake of the Gentiles, but concerning election "they are beloved, for the sake of their ancestors" (11:28).

Then, Paul suggests, the salvation of Gentiles would directly impact the salvation of Jews, for the success of the gentile church would "make Israel jealous" (11:11). The Jews had not succeeded in bringing the gentile nations to the worship of the God of Israel or even to a repenting of sin. Israel was to have been "a light to the nations," as Isaiah (49:6) had announced, so that God's "salvation may reach to the end of the earth," but they had failed in that mission. Now Israel would see, through the acceptance of Paul's gospel among the nations, that the church had fulfilled the role of being a light. But the Gentiles, despite their success, cannot boast in their own justification. On the contrary, Paul calls them wild olive shoots grafted onto the cultivated olive tree, which is Israel. They can be as easily broken off as are the natural shoots. As Paul states, "For if God did not spare the natural branches, neither will he spare you" (Rom. 11:21).

Paul's program of salvation continues once the "full number of the Gentiles" (Rom. 11:25) comes in. At that point, not only will Israel recognize the success of the gentile mission and become "jealous," but also "all Israel"—that is, ethnic Israel, the Jews—"will be saved" (11:26). The salvation of Gentiles is thus dependent on the Jewish rejection of the gospel, and the salvation of the Jews is thus dependent on the gentile acceptance.

It's a lovely picture of Jews and Gentiles responsible for each other's salvation: "God has imprisoned all in disobedience, so that he may be merciful upon all" (11:32).

Given its pastoral solution to the rivalries and tensions in the Roman church, Paul's Letter may have at least temporarily resolved the local congregation's difficulties. The Gentiles would not boast in their takeover of the church or condemn the Jews for the general failure of the Jewish mission. The Jews would retain the honor of their ancestors and perhaps still keep their distinct practices, as long as the church was able to remain unified.

By the end of the first century and certainly before the New Testament canon was fixed, the church had become predominantly gentile. Paul's Law-free gospel triumphed over Matthew's insistence that "not one iota, not one stroke of a letter, will pass from the Law" (5:18). Mark's insistence that Jesus "declared all foods clean" (7:19b) triumphed over James's insistence on minimum requirements for Christian Gentiles (Acts 15). Such shifts marginalized Jewish members of the church, for whom the Torah was an essential part of their identity. Two thousand years later, it is scant comfort for Jews to be told that they are "enemies of God" for the sake of the church (Rom. 11:28) or that they are lopped off the trunk of true Israel. Paul's vision that "there is no longer Jew or Greek ... in Christ Jesus" (Gal. 3:28) is not good news for Jews, whose identity is then erased. In the church, the vision came true.

The very practices that preserved the Jewish identity of Jesus's earliest followers, those practices that Peter and James had cherished, would become eccentricities; eventually they would become heresies. In his *Epistle* 79, written to Augustine, Jerome (d. 420) mentions a group called the Nazarenes, "who accept the Messiah in such a way that they not cease to observe the old Law." They practice circumcision, celebrate the Sabbath, and follow Jewish dietary regulations. Of them he states, "Desiring to be both Jews and Christians, they are neither the one nor the other" (*Epistle* 112).

Had the church remained a Jewish sect, it would not have achieved its universal mission. Had Judaism given up its particularistic practices, it would have vanished from history. That the two movements eventually separated made possible the preservation of each. But neither Peter, James, nor Paul would live to see that formal separation. Peter and Paul are reputed to have been killed during the persecution of Christians in Rome by the emperor Nero in 64; James was executed two years earlier, in Jerusalem, by an interim high priest for, as Josephus puts it, "having transgressed the Law" (*Antiquities* 20.197–203), although it is by no means clear that the charge had to do with Christian proclamation. Josephus even remarks that the "leading men among us" (certainly Jews, probably Pharisees) protested this execution.

The legends of Peter and Paul and James would grow. Books would be written in their names, miracles attributed to them, paintings made of them. But for all the accounts of the miracles they reputedly performed, one is beyond dispute. Through struggle and compromise, imagination and practicality, these three Jews preserved the message of Jesus.

Jesus did not engage in a mission to the Gentiles. His followers had to adapt his message, just as any successful missionary learns to speak the language of and use the images from the group being evangelized. The message had to adapt, given the proclamation of Jesus's resurrection. This first generation of Jesus's followers ensured continuity between the message spoken by Jesus of Nazareth and the messages spoken about him. The New Testament canon, by placing the stories of Jesus, Peter, and James prior to the Pauline Letters, affirms this continuity. Paul's Letters, although written before the Gospels of Matthew, Mark, Luke, and John, follow them in the canonical order; the writings of Paul must be read through the filter of the Gospels.

Although Paul and, to a lesser extent, James and Peter are sometimes today charged with transforming the message of the kingdom of God that Jesus proclaimed into a proclamation of Jesus himself, the charge is an overstatement. The claim presumes that Jesus himself had no messianic pretensions, whatever the particulars of their configuration. This is unlikely. Surely Jesus thought of himself as having a special commission from God to heal, to prepare the people for the breaking in of the kingdom of heaven, to speak on his own authority and not like the scribes, and to be an "anointed one," a "messiah." If Jesus did not think he was a or the messiah, however the term is defined, he may well have been the only one in his inner circle who did not. Moreover, the claim that Paul somehow invented Christianity by repackaging the message of Jesus for Gentiles ignores Zechariah's vision of the Gentiles streaming to Zion *as Gentiles*, and it ignores what Peter and Paul both witnessed, namely, the presence of charismatic activity such as speaking in tongues and visionary experiences among Gentiles. Whether Jesus *was* a or the messiah is another question, and that can be answered only by the voice of faith, not by the voice of the historian.

Inside the church, Jesus was proclaimed the Messiah, the redeemer from sin and death, the Son of God. Outside the church, Jews who did believe a messiah would come—and not all did—still awaited the messianic age, the time when wars would cease, the dead would rise, and righteousness would reign. But wars continued, the tombs stayed closed, and God's kingdom had not come. Although the borders between church and synagogue remained fluid even past the time of Constantine,[7] gentile church and Jewish synagogue had separated. Each claimed the name Israel; the existence of one questioned the claims of the other. Misunderstanding, polemic, and persecution would replace the branches on the olive tree.

THREE

The New Testament and Anti-Judaism

Jesus was a Jew speaking to Jews; Paul was a Jew who, in light of his visionary encounter with Jesus, concluded that the coming of the Messiah had erased the distinction between Jew and Gentile, male and female, slave and free. Yet he still identified as a Jew, "an Israelite, a descendant of Abraham, a member of the tribe of Benjamin" (Rom. 11:1), and he still cared passionately about his "own people," his "kindred according to the flesh" (Rom. 9:3). Despite his insistence that "there is no longer Jew or Greek ... in Christ Jesus" (Gal. 3:28), Paul cites certain privileges of the Jews: "They are Israelites, and to them belong the adoption, the glory, the covenants, the giving of the Law, the worship, and the promises; to them belong the patriarchs, and from them, according to the flesh, comes the Messiah" (Rom. 9:4–5). To call him anti-Semitic would be a mislabeling.

"Anti-Semitism" refers to hatred of Jews as an ethnic group, and it assumes an essential and unchanging Jewish identity. Anti-Semites believe that Jews are, in their very being, "different," and there is no way for them to remove that otherness. Anti-Semitism ascribes to Jews innate negative traits: Jews are rapacious; Jews are clannish; Jews are ugly. Given this definition, neither Jesus, Paul, nor the New Testament is anti-Semitic. The question of whether the New Testament is "anti-Jewish" causes different problems.

Anti-Judaism: Defining the Problem

Anti-Judaism is usually defined as a theological position rather than an essentialist or racialist one: it is the rejection of specific Jewish teachings and practices and/or of Judaism as a "way of life" or means of salvation. Problems abound with this vague definition. What is "rejection" of Judaism to one reader is the "fulfillment" of Judaism to another. Whereas Jews today who accept Jesus as the Messiah see themselves as "fulfilled" or "completed" Jews and so epitomizing the best of Judaism, other Jews regard this group as illegitimate at best or as misguided, ignorant apostates. "Secular Jews" who identify with the Jewish people culturally but not with regard to religious practice and who find outdated or even ridiculous Laws prohibiting the eating of pork or shellfish may be considered anti-Jewish by those Jews who maintain those practices. The current crisis in the Middle East brings the question of "anti-Jewish" views starkly into discussion. Is the promotion of a Palestinian state an anti-Jewish stance in that it denies the biblical promise of the land to Abraham? Is it anti-Jewish because it appears to support the agenda of homicide bombers who take Jewish lives? Or is it a pro-Jewish view because it seeks justice for an oppressed people and because it follows Hillel's injunction "What is hateful to you, do not do to your fellow"? If a Jew tells a joke that plays upon stereotypes about Jews, is that Jew "anti-Jewish"? If a non-Jew tells the same joke, is that non-Jew appropriately labeled "anti-Jewish"?

Defining "anti-Judaism" is as intractable as defining "pornography," and not simply because both are obscene. Neither term has secure criteria, so in assessing pornography or anti-Judaism interpreters must rely on subjective impressions. Potter Stewart's classic comment about pornography from *Jacobellis v. Ohio,* "I know it when I see it," applies as well to anti-Judaism in the New Testament. Because what is anti-Jewish to one reader is pro-Jewish to another and to a third a misinterpretation by later Christians, the discussion reaches stalemate. Thus, "Is the New Testament anti-Jewish?" is not a helpful question. However, that it has been read in a manner that condemns anything associated with Jews and Judaism, from practices to beliefs, is not in question. The text has, by far too many and for far too long, been interpreted in an anti-Jewish manner.

Further, any discussion of whether the New Testament is "anti-Jewish" falters on the equally intractable problems of who makes the decision and on what criteria. If one person contends that there is no anti-Jewish teaching in the New Testament but another insists that there is, who's right? Who gets to speak? Unlike Nazi newspapers and KKK pamphlets, the New Testament prompts different reactions from people of goodwill. For the church, the New Testament is a book of compassion, of the perfect love called *agape*, of inclusivity. But many Jews who pick up a copy of the New Testament—in a hotel room, in a hospital, from a missionary on the street corner—find instead a teaching of exclusivity, intolerance, and hate. Still other Jews find in the Gospels a message of truth and so accept Jesus as Lord and Savior, while some Christian readers, especially those sensitized to the atrocities carried out in the name of Jesus, will find themselves rejecting some of the New Testament's claims. The same book, the same words, can take on profoundly different meanings and make profoundly different impressions.

That such alternative readings exist is the result of the way all people make sense of the world they encounter. Each reader and community of readers brings to a text different presuppositions and experiences, and each will emphasize different parts of the text. This phenomenon is by no means limited to Scripture. Some actors interpret Shylock's speech— "Hath not a Jew hands, organs, dimensions, senses, affections, passions? If you prick us, do we not bleed? If you tickle us, do we not laugh? If you poison us, do we not die?"—as creating sympathy for Jews. Others use it to show just how depraved and hypocritical the Jew is, in that he is willing then to take a pound of flesh from Antonio, the Christian merchant of Venice, who certainly if pricked will bleed. Public school systems debate whether to ban *Huckleberry Finn* as a racist tract or require students to read it because they see in it the recognition of the dignity of the slave and the hypocrisy of those who support slavery. Mel Gibson's *The Passion of the Christ* evoked similarly polarized reactions. For some viewers, it offered a magnificently compelling treatment of Jesus's sacrifice on behalf of sinful humanity; for others it was an anti-Semitic travesty; for others it was a snuff film; for others it was a snooze; for still others it was incomprehensible since the film never made clear why "the Jews" hated Jesus so much.

Doctrinal matters lead to similarly polarized views. For example, many Christians hold a position of soteriological exclusivity, that is, the belief that salvation is granted only to those who accept Jesus as Lord and Savior. The logical consequence of this belief is that Jews (and all others) who do not accept Jesus as Lord and Savior will face an eternity in hell. A number of Jews who have been told, with relative degrees of compassion, that if they do not believe in Jesus they will fry in hell understandably find such a view anti-Jewish. The message of soteriological exclusivity,

particularly when accompanied by the threat of damnation, offends especially when it is proclaimed to little children or pronounced at a funeral
for an agnostic. When the proclamation is then accompanied by the insistence that Christians believe in a God of mercy and compassion, the entire
dogmatic system becomes, to non-Christians, absurd. Any number of
Jews and others outside the Christian fold would have difficulty grasping
the concept of a "compassionate" deity who damns individuals for something they cannot control.

But the vast majority of Christians who hold that salvation is only
through the Christ should not be regarded as anti-Jewish, and they would
be appalled by the suggestion that they are. On the contrary, they see
themselves as loving their Jewish brothers and sisters. They are also being,
in their view, biblically faithful to their understanding especially of John
14:6. Doubting Thomas says to Jesus: "Lord, we do not know where you
are going. How can we know the way?" (14:5). Jesus responds: "I am the
way, and the truth, and the life. No one comes to the Father except
through me." The matter is not, or not necessarily, anti-Jewish prejudice.
It is an issue of biblical authority. Christians may not like the terms of
salvation the gospel proposes, but their respect for biblical authority
trumps the discomfort they may feel about restricting heaven's neighbor-
hoods.

The matter of biblical authority extends to other issues in the culture
wars. The most prominent example today concerns sexual practices. Christians who conclude from Leviticus 18:22 ("You shall not lie with a male as
with a woman; it is an abomination"), Romans 1:26–27 ("Their women
exchanged natural intercourse for unnatural, and in the same way also the
men, giving up natural intercourse with women, were consumed with passion for one another"), and a few other passages that the Bible condemns
homosexuality and therefore that churches should not sanction same-sex
sexual relationships may well be homophobic. However, they may also be
struggling with a biblical message that conflicts with their own sense of
social justice, human nature, psychology, or civil rights.

Ministers in churches that do not ordain women struggle when their
daughters ask to proclaim the gospel from the pulpit may be "sexist" or
"misogynistic"; alternatively, they may be wrestling with how they understand 1 Corinthians 14:34–35 ("Women should be silent in the churches.
For they are not permitted to speak, but should be subordinate, as the

Law also says.... For it is shameful for a woman to speak in church")
and 1 Timothy 2:12 ("I permit no woman to teach or to have authority
over a man; she is to keep silent"). Other Christians, equally concerned
with biblical authority, conclude that despite these passages full enfran-
chisement for gay men, lesbians, and all women is not inconsistent with
the biblical message, but in fact is the only correct interpretation of it.
The words used, the literary contexts in which they appear, the times in
which they were written—all impact how readers understand the passages.

Similarly, all readers set up a canon within a canon, or a touchstone of
truth. Jesus's great commandment concerns love of God and love of
neighbor; thus, these two criteria can become the guide for interpreting
specific passages. Christians completely faithful to the biblical text may
conclude that love of neighbor requires the ordination of women, gays,
and lesbians or the performing of "holy unions" for those couples forbidden by state law to marry. Personal experience (or revelation), the teachings of one's own church, and scientific information have all impacted
their biblical interpretation. Others find such conclusions an abomination,
completely contrary to biblical teaching.

Specifically concerning John's teaching that Jesus is the singular way
and truth, although some Christians find restriction or exclusivity, others
interpret "the way" not as Jesus himself but as his *teachings*. For this liberal
reading, entrance to heaven is determined not by belief, but by behavior.
The focus in this case is not "What do I believe about Jesus?" but "What
would Jesus do?" Still others look at the text in a historical context and
conclude that the Evangelist's major concern is not restricting the gates of
heaven, but rather combating rival sects, associated with the apostle
Thomas, that teach that anyone can achieve salvation through knowledge.
In this system, Jesus is more the guru who leads all to enlightenment than
he is the one who, singularly, teaches the correct interpretation of Torah
and dies on behalf of humanity.[1] When the Johannine Jesus states, "No
one comes to the Father except through me," he can even be seen as pre-
cluding any individual Christian or any church from determining the soteriological verdict. If Jesus is the Way, then *only* he determines entrance to
heaven.

The following scenario offers an alternative view to the restricted message:

After a long and happy life, I find myself at the pearly gates (a sight of great joy; the word for "pearl" in Greek is, by the way, *margarita*). Standing there is St. Peter. This truly is heaven, for finally my academic questions will receive answers. I immediately begin the questions that have been plaguing me for half a century: "Can you speak Greek? Where did you go when you wandered off in the middle of Acts? How was the incident between you and Paul in Antioch resolved? What happened to your wife?"

Peter looks at me with some bemusement and states, "Look, lady, I've got a whole line of saved people to process. Pick up your harp and slippers here, and get the wings and halo at the next table. We'll talk after dinner."

As I float off, I hear, behind me, a man trying to gain Peter's attention. He has located a "red letter Bible," which is a text in which the words of Jesus are printed in red letters. This is heaven, and all sorts of sacred art and Scriptures, from the Bhagavad Gita to the Qur'an, are easily available (missing, however, was the *Reader's Digest Condensed Version*). The fellow has his Bible open to John 14, and he is frenetically pointing at v. 6: "Jesus says here, in red letters, that he is the way. I've seen this woman on television (actually, she's thinner in person). She's not Christian; she's not baptized—she shouldn't be here!"

"Oy," says Peter, "another one—wait here."

He returns a few minutes later with a man about five foot three with dark hair and eyes. I notice immediately that he has holes in his wrists, for when the empire executes an individual, the circumstances of that death cannot be forgotten.

"What is it, my son?" he asks.

The man, obviously nonplussed, sputters, "I don't mean to be rude, but didn't you say that no one comes to the Father except through you?"

"Well," responds Jesus, "John does have me saying this." (Waiting in line, a few other biblical scholars who overhear this conversation sigh at Jesus's phrasing; a number of them remain convinced that Jesus said no such thing. They'll have to make the inquiry on their own time.) "But if you flip back to the Gospel of Matthew, which does come first in the canon, you'll notice in chapter 25, at the judgment of the sheep and the goats, that I am not interested in those who say 'Lord, Lord,' but in those who do their best to live a righteous life: feeding the hungry, visiting people in prison ..."

Becoming almost apoplectic, the man interrupts, "But, but, that's *works righteousness.* You're saying she's earned her way into heaven?"

"No," replies Jesus, "*I am* not saying that at all. *I am* saying that *I am* the way, not you, not your church, not your reading of John's Gospel, and not the claim of any individual Christian or any particular congregation. *I am* making the determination, and it is by my grace that anyone gets in, including you. Do you want to argue?"

The last thing I recall seeing, before picking up my heavenly accessories, is Jesus handing the poor man a Kleenex to help get the log out of his eye.

Enter the Historians

Although the problems of defining anti-Judaism, especially in the context of New Testament studies, cannot be resolved to everyone's satisfaction, scholars have not ceased to offer their views. A number remain convinced that one can determine objectively, through the application of various historical-critical approaches to the biblical text, whether the label "anti-Jewish" is warranted. Such readers believe they can, with some confidence, locate historically both the audience and the background of each ancient text as well as the agenda of the author. The point of historical criticism is to determine what the text meant in its original context. Some insist that a few New Testament texts can legitimately be labeled anti-Jewish. Others assert that the New Testament books bear no bigotry or guilt; the fault is not in the texts, but in ourselves.

Epitomizing this historical-critical perspective is the generally excellent study *The Jewish People and Their Sacred Scriptures in the Christian Bible,* published by the Pontifical Biblical Commission in December of 2001 (for more on this document, see below, pp. 157–58; 211–12). The effort by this Vatican-based group is a commendable one. It seeks to weed out anti-Jewish views in the church, and it begins with a sincere respect for the Bible as sacred Scripture. It is also an informed effort, for the authors are an international group of Roman Catholic biblical scholars (all men, of course) who have substantial knowledge of both the times in which the Bible was written and the ways in which it has been interpreted. The commission states:

> Real anti-Jewish feeling, that is, an attitude of contempt, hostility and persecution of the Jews as Jews, is not found in any New Testament text and is incompatible with its teaching. What is found are reproaches addressed to certain categories of Jews for religious reasons, as well as polemical texts to defend the Christian apostolate against Jews who oppose it. But it must be admitted that many of these passages are capable of providing a pretext for anti-Jewish sentiment and have in fact been used in this way. To avoid mistakes of this kind, it must be kept in mind that the New Testament polemical texts, even those expressed in general terms, have to do with concrete historical contexts and are never meant to be applied to Jews of all times and places merely because they are Jews. The tendency to speak in general terms, to accentuate the adversaries' negative side, and to pass over the positive in silence, failure to consider their motivations and their ultimate good faith, these are characteristics of all polemical language throughout antiquity, and are no less evident in Judaism and primitive Christianity against all kinds of dissidents.

The statement raises as many problems as it resolves. A reproach against "certain categories of Jews for [unspecified] religious reasons" may well be understood by Jews as an anti-Jewish statement. If Jews can be "reproached for *religious* reasons," it is difficult to understand how these reproaches do not constitute anti-Judaism. In like manner, a statement such as "The Roman Catholic ban on birth control and the ordination of women indicates a strongly misogynistic attitude" may be construed as a reproach addressed to certain members of the hierarchy who promulgate the bans, but it also threatens to convey a generally anti-Catholic attitude that encompasses all people within the church. Nor is it evident that all the New Testament documents are talking about "certain categories" of Jews rather than "all Jews" who do not affiliate with the church. Again, a statement condemning the "Roman Catholic Church" for allowing pedophile priests to continue to have contact with children technically must be a statement against certain members of the hierarchy and not at all against the vast majority of the laity and even other clergy. However, outsiders to the church may not see a distinction; instead, they may conclude that the entire church is condemned and corrupt. The claim that polemical language is designed to "*defend* the Christian apostolate against Jews" can easily be reversed, for that same language may be designed to *attack* those who choose to stay the course and not follow the new proclamation of Jesus the Christ. In the end, these well-meaning historical-critical studies are at best speculative. At worst, they erase rather than challenge the ambiguities of the ancient texts.

Whether addressing individual passages or books in their entirety, the attempts to find the materials innocent of anti-Jewish content remain speculative, and many are manifestly strained. Of the three passages most often cited as evidence of the New Testament's anti-Judaism, what is anti-Jewish to one interpreter is to another a mistranslation, a legitimate complaint, an atypical remark spoken in the heat of passion, or simply a metaphor.

"The Jews, Who Killed the Lord Jesus and Oppose Everyone"

In the earliest document in the New Testament, 1 Thessalonians, written about 49, Paul seeks to comfort his gentile audience facing not only the death of some of its members but also local persecution. He writes:

> For you, brothers and sisters, became imitators of the churches of God in Christ Jesus that are in Judea, for you suffered the same things from your own compatriots as they did from the Jews (*Ioudaioi*), who killed both the Lord Jesus and the prophets, and drove us out; they displease God and oppose everyone by hindering us from speaking to the Gentiles that they may be saved. Thus have they constantly been filling up the measure of their sins; but God's wrath has overtaken them at last. (2:14–16)

When I read this text to groups ranging from synagogue members to church members to students in the classroom, the general reaction is one of shame and often horror. Arguments insisting that the text should not be seen as anti-Jewish suggest a similar sense that, at least on the surface, the words are embarrassing to those interested in interfaith conversation.

Much discussion of 1 Thessalonians 2 begins with the claim that Paul is not talking about the "Jews" who killed Jesus, but "Judeans." The Greek of 1 Thessalonians can support this reading, for the term *Ioudaioi* can mean either "Jews" or, more narrowly, "Judeans." However, to speak of "Judeans" implies Jews, just as to speak of "residents of Vatican City" implies Roman Catholics or "students at Bob Jones University" implies "conservative Protestants." Maybe not all Judeans followed Jewish ritual or belief or even identified with "Judaism," however defined, but the majority did. Paul speaks of Judeans, not Hawaiians, Aleuts, or Maori. On this point, we might recall Luke's description of the Pentecost scene, where there were present "devout Jews (*Ioudaioi*) from every nation under heaven,... Parthians, Medes, Elamites, and residents of Mesopotamia, Judea and Cappadocia, Pontus and Asia,... both Jews and proselytes, Cretans and Arabs" (Acts 2:5, 9–11). The Thessalonian Christians hearing Paul's words would not have restricted their understanding of Paul's language to a geographically determined population, but would have heard a reference to all who identified with the Jewish way of life.

Another approach sees 1 Thessalonians 2:14b–16 as an interpolation, a passage not written by Paul, but inserted into the Letter after the apostle's death. In antiquity, this was not an uncommon phenomenon. The "woman caught in adultery" passage, famous for Jesus's comment "Let the one who is without sin cast the first stone," was inserted into the Gospel of John (7:53–8:11) after its initial publication. Also added later were the final verses of the Gospel of Mark (16:9–20), which describe Jesus's resurrection appearances. The earliest versions of Mark's Gospel ended with the three frightened women fleeing from the empty tomb. Scholars adopting the "interpolation theory" for 1 Thessalonians claim that the "wrath" of God refers to the destruction of the Temple in Jerusalem in the year 70. Some editor, viewing the devastation of Jerusalem as just punishment for the Jews, who not only rejected but also killed Jesus, opened up the Letter and inserted a few choice lines. The argument is not without merit, for 1 Thessalonians 2:14b–16 can be easily removed without breaking the narrative flow. Moreover, one could claim that the offensive words are inconsistent with Paul's own view, since elsewhere (e.g., Rom. 9–11) he does make positive comments about Jews.

Thus, the argument goes, Paul really didn't claim the Jews killed Jesus and so really didn't promote the view that God punished them for this injustice. The argument is remarkably utilitarian, for it allows the passage to be tidily dismissed or ignored. The same interpolation argument is used for 1 Corinthians 14:33b–36, Paul's statement that women should not teach in churches. It is easily removed without breaking narrative flow, and it is in contradiction to Paul's notices elsewhere of women prophesying (1 Cor. 7) and serving as deacons and apostles (Rom. 16) as well as to his assertion that "there is no longer male and female ... in Christ Jesus" (Gal. 3:28). The conclusion then to be drawn, for both problematic passages, is that a later editor must have added them. Since Paul didn't say them, Christians today don't need to follow them.

In both cases the interpolation theory may get Paul off the hook, but it fails to absolve the texts of, respectively, anti-Judaism and sexism. The fact that scholars seek to deny these texts Pauline authorship suggests that they find them offensive. Nor does denying Pauline authorship help anyone who cares about biblical authority, for the canon of the church is based on centuries of tradition, not current scholarly (split) opinion. Ultimately, the interpolation argument rests more on ideology than on textual evidence: it presumes both that Paul would not make statements we find offensive today and that any possible contradiction must be resolved. In effect, it removes from Paul the possibility that he may have changed his mind or, more pastorally, adapted his rhetoric to fit the needs of his congregations. The argument would be stronger if it had some actual manuscript support, as do the observations concerning the "adulterous woman" story and the ending of Mark, but no manuscript evidence suggests that the problematic words in 1 Thessalonians 2 are late editions; no copy of the Letter lacks the verses or displaces them to another setting.

Just as likely, Paul dictated 1 Thessalonians 2 (and 1 Cor. 14, but that is another book) exactly as it appears in Bibles today. It expresses his apocalyptic worldview in which humanity is divided into the people with the correct belief and those who are damned. Paul, believing himself to have had a direct commission from the Lord Jesus, was just as zealous for the gospel as he had early been against it. The apostle who, in his own words, "was violently persecuting the church of God and was trying to destroy it" (Gal. 1:13) is hardly one to shy away from strong language, especially when writing with a goal of keeping his flock safe from despair or heresy. As Ben Witherington observes:

Conversion radically changed Paul, as any fair reading of Galatians 1–2, 1 Corinthians 9, and Philippians 3.4–11 will show. To suggest that psychologically he would be incapable of a polemic of this sort against Jews who were involved in either the process that led to Jesus's execution or the more recent persecution of Christians in Judea is to ignore the evidence of the polemics of many converts to Christianity from Judaism over the course of the last two thousand years.[2]

The "wrath" to which Paul refers need not be limited to the destruction of Jerusalem by the Romans any more than a statement about divine wrath against the United States need be, or has been, limited to a particular disaster, whether it is the attacks on September 11, 2001, or any of a number of hurricanes, tornadoes, floods, or earthquakes that have devastated parts of the country. In speaking to the Thessalonians about Judea, Paul could be referring to any number of things, from an earthquake or storm or famine to the latest economic damage inflicted by Rome's policies. Perhaps his reference concerned the governorship of Cumanus, a particular brute among a series of brutish governors. According to Josephus (*War* 2.224–27; *Antiquities* 20.105–12), Cumanus arranged the slaughter of thousands of Jews in 49 or 50 during the Passover festival.

As for the presumed distinction in tone between 1 Thessalonians and Romans, Paul may have mellowed. Or, writing ad hoc letters directed to particular circumstances at particular times, Paul might have wanted to show his solidarity with the Thessalonian Gentiles and so rhetorically divorced himself from "the Jews." In Romans, Paul reconfigures his emphasis for the needs of that church and stresses his solidarity with the Jews.

Whether or not the words of 1 Thessalonians 2:14b–16 are "anti-Jewish" will remain a matter of debate. Historical-critical inquiry cannot resolve the question. Yet as long as scholars continue to argue that the passage is an interpolation, based on nothing other than the idea that the lines are "incompatible" with Paul's "nicer" views, the view that it *is* anti-Jewish gains credibility. Even if Paul did not "intend" by 1 Thessalonians 2:14b–16 to convey an anti-Jewish impression, however "anti-Judaism" is defined, the Thessalonian gentile audience, and today's scholars who are inclined to deny Pauline authorship to the passage, received an anti-Jewish impression nonetheless. What one intends and what another hears are not necessarily the same thing.

"His Blood Be on Us and on Our Children"

Matthew, following an earlier version of the story of Jesus before Pilate in Mark's Gospel, reports a Roman custom of releasing a prisoner to the crowds during the Passover festivities. Pontius Pilate, the Roman governor, places before the Jerusalem population two men, each named Jesus. The first, Jesus Barabbas (literally, "Jesus, son of the father") is an insurrectionary; the second is Jesus of Nazareth, the Son of the Father. The crowd clamors for Barabbas. Pilate, who finds no evidence that Jesus of Nazareth is guilty of any crime, questions the crowd, "Then what should I do with Jesus who is called the Christ?" They respond, "Let him be crucified!" Pilate asks, "Why, what evil has he done?" The crowd shouts again, "Let him be crucified!" (27:22–23).

As Matthew recounts the events: "When Pilate saw that he could do nothing, but rather that a riot was beginning, he took some water and washed his hands before the crowd, saying, 'I am innocent of this man's blood; see to it yourselves.'" Then comes the fateful verse, 27:25: "Then the people as a whole (*pas ho laos;* literally "all the people") answered, 'His blood be on us and on our children!'" From this verse, generations of Christians over hundreds of years concluded that all Jews for all times, and not just those present that fateful day, bore special responsibility for the death of Jesus. The guilt is inherited; it is a stain on Jewish identity; all Jews are "Christ killers."

From the perspective of history, the entire scene depicted in Matthew 27 is suspect. First, the tradition of this festival amnesty is not recorded anywhere except the Gospels. Although Rome was ruthless, it was not stupid. Releasing a political insurrectionary, especially during the Passover holiday celebrating the Jews' release from an oppressive, enslaving government of Egypt, would have been political folly. Second, Matthew presents Pilate more as a weak pawn, manipulated by the high priest and the crowd, than as the decisive ruler known from other ancient sources for deliberately provoking the sensibilities of his Jewish subjects. Although historically suspect, Matthew's account, however, is profound in that it encapsulates a central part of Christianity's theological vision: Jesus of

Nazareth, the innocent Son of the Father, goes to the cross, and thereby frees from death Jesus Barabbas, the manifestly guilty representative of humanity. The guilty are set free by the sacrifice of the Christ.

That "the people as a whole" in Jerusalem would have called out, "His blood be on us and on our children" is also historically unlikely. Like the Barabbas incident, however, it does fit Matthew's agenda. As early as chapter 2, Matthew had aligned Jerusalem with those who opposed Jesus. "Herod" and "all Jerusalem" (2:3) are discombobulated upon hearing that the Messiah has been born in Bethlehem, and Herod's plan is to kill the child. Matthew's Jesus identifies Jerusalem as the city that kills the prophets and stones those who are sent to it (23:37). The First Gospel even sets the scene of the "Great Commission," in which the resurrected Jesus commands his eleven remaining male followers to "make disciples of all nations, baptizing them in the name of the Father and of the Son and of the Holy Spirit," on a mountaintop in Galilee (28:16–20) rather than in the city of Jerusalem, where, according to Luke, John, and Paul, the early church had gathered. Thus, given Matthew's ongoing polemic against Jerusalem, "the people as a whole" who cry out for Jesus's blood can easily mean "all the people of Jerusalem." The reference to their children also fits this view, since the children of that Jerusalem crowd would have witnessed the destruction of the city in the year 70. Matthew blames that destruction on Jerusalem's failure to receive Jesus as Messiah.

In this argument, historical research can make a somewhat convincing case that Matthew 27:25 does not condemn all Jews as Christ killers. A few other explanations of the verse, although perhaps less convincing from a historical perspective, offer a theological rationale that some readers may find satisfying. One popular exculpatory move, this one with theological sensitivity but without evident support from Matthew's narrative, identifies "the people as a whole" not with the Jews, but with all humanity. When Christians hear the line, "His blood be on us and on our children," they are to see themselves as responsible for Jesus's crucifixion; he is killed not by "the Jews" but because of human sin and in conformity to the will of God. Churches that recite the line during Holy Week understand the point.

Finally, a third approach designed to remove the verse's anti-Jewish potential suggests that "the people as a whole" who call for Jesus's blood are ironically witnessing to if not actually accepting the cleansing blood of Jesus for themselves and their descendants. Thus the "blood cry" is a good thing. The thesis turns all Jews into "hidden Christians" wishing to participate in Jesus's sacrifice. This explication may resolve for some readers the labeling of Jews as Christ killers, but it produces the additional problem of turning the Jews into Christian wannabes and so erasing non-Christian Jewish identity.

However one interprets that fateful line today, the history of the church's interpretation cannot be ignored. Only in the twentieth century did the view of Jews as "Christ killers" begin to wane. Within the Roman Catholic tradition, this teaching of permanent, inherited guilt was rejected in 1965 with the promulgation of *Nostra Aetate*. The document declares:

> Even though the Jewish authorities and those who followed their lead pressed for the death of Christ (see John 19:6), *neither all Jews indiscriminately at that time, nor Jews today, can be charged with the crimes committed during his passion.* It is true that the church is the new people of God, yet the Jews should not be spoken of as rejected or accursed as if this followed from holy scripture. Consequently, all must take care, lest in catechizing or in preaching the word of God, they teach anything which is not in accord with the truth of the Gospel message or the spirit of Christ.

The shift in Roman Catholic attitudes is striking. Catholic children since Vatican II have not been raised to think of Jews as "Christ killers." Nevertheless, theology and history, teaching and practice do not always march hand in hand. The teaching of contempt still continues, which is in part why the Vatican continues to issue guidelines on how to present Jews and Judaism.[3] Most mainline Protestant churches agree with the Vatican's statement; most have also issued official statements indicating that they find anti-Semitism sinful and that "the Jews" are not to be blamed for Jesus's death. This teaching appears to be working. In the United States, polls suggest that the number of Americans holding this view of Jewish guilt at the beginning of the twenty-first century is between 2 and 8 percent.

Pockets of Islamic thought, although denying that Jesus died on the cross, nevertheless manage to blame the Jews for his crucifixion. The Qur'an states:

Therefore, for their [the Jews'] breaking their covenant and their dis-
belief in the communications of Allah and their killing the prophets
wrongfully and their saying "Our hearts are covered"; nay! Allah set
a seal upon them owing to their unbelief, so they shall not believe
except a few. And for their unbelief and for their having uttered
against Marium [Mary] a grievous calumny. And their saying:
"Surely we have killed the Messiah, Isa son of Marium, the apostle
of Allah"; and they did not kill him nor did they crucify him, but it
appeared to them so (like Isa) and most surely those who differ
therein are only in a doubt about it; they have no knowledge respecting it, but only follow a conjecture, and they killed him not for sure.
(4:155–57)

According to this teaching, the Jews boast in claiming to have killed Jesus,
but in reality they did not. They are condemned for something they did
not do, and the condemnation is, again, their own fault.

Regarding Matthew 27:25, whether one accepts these theological or
historical claims or not becomes a matter of interpretation. Again, the
question of whether the New Testament is anti-Jewish ends in personal
assessment of the arguments, and so it ends in stalemate.

"You Are from Your Father the Devil"

The Gospel of John, where the term *Ioudaios* ("Jew," "Judean") appears
approximately seventy times (the approximation is because of manuscript
variations), has received the most attention from scholars concerned about
the anti-Jewish potential of New Testament texts. Epitomizing the problem in the Fourth Gospel is chapter 8, where Jesus tells the Jews "who
believed in him," "You are from your father the devil, and you choose to
do your father's desires" (v. 44). Here is the origin of the view, popular
during the Middle Ages and still found even among well-meaning people
today, that Jews are literally "children of the devil," complete with cloven
hooves and horns. Michelangelo's statue of Moses, horned not because of
John 8 but because of the Latin translation of Exodus 34:29–35, which
describes "rays of light" that shone from Moses's face, serves to confirm
the forehead accessories. (I have twice been asked, each time by nice,
silver-haired Protestant women, where I had my horns removed. The

women, neither of whom had ever met a Jew before but both of whom had read John's Gospel and seen pictures of Michelangelo's horned Moses, asked in all innocence. They were both surprised and relieved to know that Jews don't have horns. I also mentioned that we don't have tails and cloven feet, just in case they thought that as well but were too embarrassed to ask.)

For some readers, calling Jews the "children of the devil" is sufficient evidence for the label "anti-Jewish." Others explicitly deny the charge of anti-Judaism. Again, the Pontifical Biblical Commission provides a good example. It explains that the Johannine polemic is "not made against Jews insofar as they are Jews, but on the contrary, insofar as they are not true Jews, since they entertain murderous intentions." The distinction between "Jews" and "true Jews" can be in some cases helpful. One might, for example, claim that the "Christians" who participated in Nazi action were not "true Christians." Then again, the Johannine Jesus is speaking to the "Jews who believed in him" (8:31). These are not the folks who, at least in chapter 8, were entertaining murderous intentions. If Jews who believe in Jesus are children of Satan, there is little hope for a positive view of those Jews who do not believe in him, especially given John's tendency to divide the world into those who follow Jesus and those who do not.

Others argue, as they did for 1 Thessalonians 2:14–16, that John is talking about Judeans and emphasizing a geopolitical or ethnic concern, not about Jewish beliefs and practices. It is true that whereas all Judeans are Jewish, not all Jews are Judean; some Jews are from Galilee, Tarsus, or Cyrene. However, as seen in the discussion concerning 1 Thessalonians 2, this is a distinction without a difference for the congregations. Any person in John's church who heard the term *Ioudaioi* in the Gospel would associate that term with those who affiliate with the Jewish synagogue, observe the Jewish Sabbath, and otherwise claim to be the heirs of Abraham.

In like manner, so falls the argument that John is really talking about the Jewish "leaders" rather than the Jewish people. This view frequently appears in today's liturgical readings, where, in order not to inculcate anti-Jewish views, pastors and priests speak of how the "Jewish leaders" rather than "the Jews" sought Jesus's life. The generous translation is well meaning, and it does help in preventing an anti-Jewish impression, as long as the congregation doesn't think too hard about the argument. However, since the vast majority of Jews chose to follow these leaders, and not Jesus, Peter, James, or Paul, the reading of "Jewish leaders" ultimately also offers a distinction without a difference.

More common in scholarly analysis is the assertion that John, writing toward the end of the first century, addressed a group that had been expelled from the synagogue. Ousted from his own community, he used entirely understandable reactionary language. John's Gospel could represent the thoughts of those who had been excommunicated. John three times, in chapters 9, 12, and 16, uses the expression *aposynagogos*—a word, unique to the New Testament, that literally means "out-synagogued"—to describe the fate of synagogue affiliates who choose to follow Jesus. For example, after Jesus heals a man who had been born blind, "the Jews" who "did not believe that he had been blind and had received his sight" called his parents to ask them about their son's condition. The parents advise the Jews to ask the man directly, "because they were afraid of the Jews, for the Jews had already agreed that anyone who confessed him [Jesus] to be the Christ would be put out of the synagogue" (9:18–22). However, the argument that therefore John's language cannot be considered "anti-Jewish" tends to be based more in Christian apologia than in historical evidence.

For example, the sanguine assignment of the Gospel to a Jewish author and the audience to a Jewish group of messianists is potentially belied by material in the Gospel itself. John both mentions a successful Samaritan mission (chap. 4) and notes that "Greeks" are interested in meeting Jesus (12:20–21). Thus, John might well have had Samaritans and Gentiles in his audience, and these congregants might well have concluded, upon hearing the Gospel read, that any "Jew," anyone affiliated with the synagogue down the street or across the empire, was a child of the devil.

Any argument based on the identity of the Gospel writer or on the composition of the original audience must remain speculative, since both who wrote the Gospels and where the Gospels were written remain unknown. We have no original manuscripts from the hands of the Evangelists, and the names "Matthew," "Mark," "Luke," and "John" were appended to the originally anonymous texts we do have. The Gospels themselves never identify their authors. Consequently, determination of author and audience must be made on the basis of the content of the text. The problem this determination poses for historians is obvious, although it often goes unacknowledged. In Gospel studies, scholarship proceeds according to an elegant circular argument: it determines the audience on the basis of the text, and then determines the meaning of the text on the basis of the audience. This process does not mean that the scholarship is sloppy or incorrect; it means that any conclusion based on the identity of the author and audience, including conclusions about anti-Judaism, must remain tentative.

Even if one grants that the author of the Fourth Gospel is a Jew writing primarily to Jews, which is in fact a viable thesis, the argument that therefore the Gospel cannot be anti-Jewish still falters. Scholars conclude that John's polemic, nasty as it is, should be regarded as an in-house fight. Therefore, the Gospel cannot be anti-Jewish, any more than, for example, the condemnation of one Episcopalian by another can be seen as "anti-Episcopalian." Further, because John's rhetoric results from an internal struggle, its effects were prompted by the Jews themselves, who started the whole mess in the first place by being intolerant and expelling followers of Jesus. That argument then neatly shifts the responsibility for the seemingly anti-Jewish rhetoric away from John and onto the Jews themselves. Christian readers thus need not worry about the rhetoric in John—it was never "anti-Jewish."

Alas, this approach is a tad too sanguine. Jews can adopt what other Jews, and non-Jews as well, may regard as an "anti-Jewish" stance. Today, for example, Jews who speak out on behalf of the Palestinian population and who have not a single positive thing to say about the state of Israel are often seen by other Jews, and non-Jews, as anti-Jewish or as "self-hating Jews." Some U.S. veterans who speak out against the war in Iraq have been labeled "un-American" by talk shows and editorials. Insider location does not preclude one's being seen as a hater of the internal group.

The argument that John's language is reactionary is a bit more complicated and requires several steps. First, the Fourth Gospel's language of *aposynagogos* is still often regarded as indicating a Mediterranean-wide program in which Jews were excommunicating Christians. Second, it is also understood as related to the so-called Council of Jamnia, a synod that supposedly took place around 90 CE in which Jews, still reeling from the destruction of the Temple, sought to reconstitute themselves as a pharisaically led movement, based in the synagogue and defined by Halakhah, that is, Jewish interpretation of biblical Law. Third, scholars further associate this council with the invention and promulgation of a prayer called the Birkhat ha-Minim, the "Benediction Against Heretics." The term *minim* refers to heretics or, better, members of parties in opposition to the rabbinic view. This passage, inserted into the longer liturgical prayer known variously as the Sh'mona Esreh ("Eighteen [Benedictions]"), the Amidah (the "Standing," since worshipers stand to recite it), or simply Tefilla ("[the] Prayer"), is then, fourth, seen as a curse against Christians. Two versions of the benediction, dating from approximately the tenth century and found in a geniza (a synagogue attic where worn sacred objects are preserved) in Cairo, distinguish among apostates, heretics, and Christians. The first states:

> For apostates (*meshummadin*) may there be no hope [unless they return to Your Law]; and the kingdom of arrogance may You quickly uproot in our days; and may *ha-Notserim* [Nazarenes, or Christians] and the *minim* [heretics] perish in an instant. [May they be erased from the Book of Life.] And along with the righteous may they not be written. Blessed are You, O Lord, who humbles arrogant ones.

The second similarly seeks the eradication of *Notserim* and *minim*.

Finally, the council and the prayer are both connected with evidence that in the second century and subsequently there may well have been cursing of Christians in the synagogues. Justin Martyr, writing in Rome about 160, speaks of Jews "cursing in [their] synagogues those who believe on the Christ."[4] Epiphanius (ca. 375) speaks of Jews saying, "Curse the Nazoraious, O God!" in the synagogues.[5] Jerome (ca. 410) similarly asserts that "three times each day in all the synagogues" the Jews "curse" the "Nazarenes."[6]

Of course, given this scenario—a synod proclaiming a prayer to curse Christians plus universal Jewish acceptance of the prayer—John would have had good reason for polemical language. The problem is that the entire argument is hopelessly flawed.

First, there is no evidence, for example, that Jews across the empire were expelling Christians from their synagogues in the first century. Paul indicates that Jews who confessed Jesus were not thrown out of synagogues; on the contrary, they were dragged in and beaten. Up to the fourth century, church fathers were still complaining that Jews welcomed members of their churches into the synagogues. Poor John Chrysostom (ca. 349–407) had to convince his congregants in Antioch, who were flocking to the worship services of the Jews, that the synagogue was a place of Satan. Moreover, even if John's account is an accurate depiction of a local practice, there is no reason to presume that Jews across the empire were expelling messianists. John's Gospel is not indicative of all first-century Christian practice and belief, as a quick comparison to the synoptic Gospels indicates; it is even less a summary of Jewish customs.

As for the so-called Council of Jamnia, this appears to be more historical fiction, already begun by the rabbis, and not historical fact. Nor can any "blessing against heretics" be firmly dated to that time. The Birkhat ha-Minim makes its first appearance not in the Mishnah (ca. 200) but in the Tosefta (*Berakhot* 3:25), a slightly later text, and as Daniel Boyarin observes, "the text itself indicates that the *birkat hamminim* is of recent origin."[7] Moreover, in this earliest version, the ones to be "cursed" include Pharisees along with *minim!* The account in the Babylonian Talmud (*Berakhot* 28b–29a) of the composition of this "benediction against heretics" dates, not to the first, but to the fourth or even the fifth century. Not only does it lack any reference to formal excommunication (and so cannot be directly applied to John's Gospel in any case), it bears the stamp not of history but of legend. The anecdote goes as follows: "Said Rabban Gamliel to the Sages: 'Can any one among you frame a benediction relating to the *minim*?' Samuel ha-Katan [Sam the Short, Sam the Lesser] arose and composed it. The next year he forgot it and he tried for two or three hours to recall it, and they did not remove him [as service leader]." Boyarin notes that a similar story is told in the Palestinian Talmud (*Berakhot* 9c) about this same rabbi's forgetting a prayer, but the text does not make clear that the prayer is the Benediction Against Heretics. As Boyarin concludes: "The very term *minim* is attested only from the Mishna at the end of the second century.... Neither Josephus nor Philo seem [*sic*] to have any idea of heresy."[8] Thus, the Benediction Against Heretics cannot be behind the language of *aposynagogos* in the Gospel of John.

Finally, lest readers today presume that Jews are cursing Christians in the synagogue, this is not the case. The Amidah, the longer prayer in which this benediction had been placed, is still recited in synagogue worship today, but it contains no references to Nazarenes or Christians. The reading of the benediction in question today is:

> Let there be no hope for slanderers, and let all wickedness perish in an instant. May all Your enemies quickly be cut down, and may You soon in our day uproot, crush, cast down and humble the dominion of arrogance. Blessed are You, O Lord, who smashes enemies and humbles the arrogant.

Despite this lack of evidence that there was an empirewide expulsion of Christians from synagogues or that Jews around 90 were cursing Christians by means of a standardized prayer, a number of biblical scholars remain convinced that the Birkhat underlies John's rhetoric. The Pontifical Biblical Commission goes so far as to suggest that Jews were not only expelling Christ-confessors but also murdering them: "One cannot seriously doubt that at certain times in different places, local synagogues no longer tolerated the presence of Christians, and subjected them to harassment that could even go as far as putting them to death" (the citation is to John 16:2, a future and probably eschatological prediction that reads: "They will put you out of the synagogues. Indeed, an hour is coming when those who kill you will think that by doing so they are offering service to God"). The picture this description presents is of nasty Jews who persecute innocent Christians for loving God, loving neighbor, and worshiping the Christ. Again, serious doubts abound.

Regarding the question of the expulsion recounted in John's Gospel, historical criticism frequently goes on holiday. Few bother to ask why such expulsion would occur. What was it about confessing Jesus that so disturbed the synagogue members? The possibilities are similar to those that might have prompted Paul's earlier persecution of the church.

Might Christ-confessors have sought to replace Torah with Jesus as the center of worship? That would get someone booted out of my synagogue. In the Christian apologetic literature, when the synagogue insists for its own integrity in determining the parameters of practice and theology, it is seen as recalcitrant and intolerant; when the church struggles for the same things, such as the elimination of distinct Jewish practice (and so cultural identity), it is seen as open and heroic.

Might they have been encouraging Gentiles in the synagogue to stop eating meat offered to idols or otherwise insisting on something that would create animosity within the wider gentile community? Jews might have seen such teachings as a threat to their own safety.

Might they have been encouraging God-fearers to join their movement and leave the synagogue? Not only would that have upset the congregation (poaching members is never appreciated); it may have threatened the protection friendly Gentiles granted Jews in the gentile world.

Might they have asserted that anyone who does not follow Jesus is a child of Satan? Again, that would not sit well in my *shul*.

Might they have been interrupting worship with ecstatic displays, such as speaking in tongues, dancing, or attempting to engage in miraculous healings? Churches today that have experienced outbreaks of charismatic worship will immediately recognize the problems such Spirit-filled enthusiasm can create.

Might they have proclaimed Jesus a "king," which in a diaspora context is for Jews a political liability?

Burton L. Visotzky suggests that perhaps Jews feared being associated with Christians and rounded up for the same persecutions Christians experienced on the local level. There are midrashim that describe the arrests of rabbis on suspicion of what looks like Christian sympathies.[9]

In other words, there are numerous very good reasons why Jews might have expelled messianists from their synagogues. Thus, John and his followers may have been expelled from the synagogue, and the Johannine language about the "Jews" may be reactionary rhetoric. To propose the possible reasons why the expulsions occurred is not to blame the Christian victims; rather, to ignore them is to presume Jewish guilt and continue the vilification of the Jews that John's rhetoric creates.

It is also possible that John has exaggerated the point of enmity between the synagogue and the followers of Jesus. Describing the death of Lazarus, the narrator announces that "the Jews" came to comfort Mary and Martha (11:31). Perhaps it is John, not the synagogue, who is seeking to separate the communities and force those who confess Jesus to dissociate with "the Jews."

Given these enormous historical problems in understanding the causes of John's rhetoric, the audience to which it was addressed, and the ways that audience understood the Gospel, the solution to the question of anti-Judaism in the Gospel of John specifically, and by extension in any passage in the New Testament generally, cannot be, or at least cannot solely be, a historical one. Historical investigation lacks the data needed to answer the question. The response to the matter of the text's anti-Jewish potential therefore must be a theological one: Christians must denounce anti-Jewish readings (however defined) because they are counter to the "good news" of Jesus. Only the theologian can firmly pronounce a New Testament text *not* anti-Jewish.

More Than a Prophet

When discussion moves from individual verses to the Gospels as a whole, additional explanations (if one agrees with them) or excuses (if one is looking for apologetic) for potentially anti-Jewish New Testament passages appear.[10] Some scholars conclude that the Jesus of the Gospels is to be compared to Israel's prophets, whose level of excoriation of the people was just as high as, if not higher than, Jesus's invectives against the scribes and Pharisees. Others insist that the New Testament is a Jewish book written by Jews, and therefore it cannot be anti-Jewish. Both arguments have merit, but neither ultimately convinces.

Jesus does sound like a prophet. Like Jeremiah, he predicts the destruction of the Temple (chapter 25); like Hosea, he "desires steadfast love and not sacrifice" (6:6). He condemns the leadership for not following in the ways of the Lord—that is what prophets have always done. Had Amos been alive in the first century, he might well have made several of the pronouncements beginning "Woe to you, scribes and Pharisees" (Matt. 23). However, although Jesus himself may be perceived as heir to the legacy of Amos and Jeremiah, the Gospels present him as more than a prophet. He is, according to the Evangelists, the Son of God, who adds something new to the prophetic concern for justice. He goes well beyond the role of Isaiah and Micah, who seek what is called in Hebrew *t'shuvah*, return and repentance. Jesus of the Gospels seeks something new, specifically, following him. He is important not only because of what he says, but also because of who he is.

Narrative context also disrupts the prophetic analogy. The prophets as well as the objects of their invectives all recognized themselves as members of the same community; the Jewish community preserved the words of the prophets and recognized itself as the recipients of the prophets' messages. The prophetic pronouncements are still read in the synagogues and understood as having meaning to present-day Jews. This is not the case with the narratives of Matthew or John. The Gospels were neither written for nor preserved by the Jewish community; they are not read in the synagogue. Thus, any assessment of Jesus's language as not anti-Jewish because he sounds like a prophet ignores the Gospels' narrative context.

Once the context of Jesus's words shifts, his words necessarily take on new connotations. The audiences to whom Jesus spoke are not in debate: Jesus was a Jew talking to other Jews, or as Matthew phrases it, "to the lost sheep of the house of Israel" (10:6; 15:24). Yet once Jesus's words became placed in the Gospel narratives and addressed to Christian churches, comments spoken *to* Jews became perceived, by the church as well as the synagogue, as comments spoken *against* Jews. When Christian readers identify with Jesus and his followers, then Jesus along with the apostles, the faithful women, Joseph of Arimathea, and other sympathetic figures become seen as (proto-)Christians. The "Jews" remain, as Matthew puts it, those who claim that the disciples stole Jesus's body or, as John has it, "children of the devil."

A Jewish Book?

Extending the view that Jesus should be seen as a prophet and therefore cannot be anti-Jewish is the argument that the New Testament is a "Jewish" book. According to numerous apologetic volumes, all the New Testament authors are Jews: Paul is Jewish; Mark and Luke are Jewish; Matthew, John, the author of Hebrews, the author of Revelation, all Jews. The argument also insists that these authors are writing mostly to Jews or at least to communities comprising Jews and Gentiles. Thus, the books of the New Testament cannot be anti-Jewish; on the contrary, they are as Jewish as can be. This sort of positivistic historiography falters on the circular argument. This argument, already seen prominently in discussion of the Gospel of John's (so-called) anti-Jewish polemic, stems from a well-meaning, but historically untenable, premise that equates "Judaism" with respect for the Scriptures of Israel.

Scholars argue that the Gospels of Matthew and John, along with the rest of the New Testament, are Jewish books because they are dependent on the Old Testament. They are thus rooted in Jewish soil, nurtured by

Jewish gardeners, and produce the fruit of a Jewish messiah. But, to continue the agricultural metaphor, the Gospels are at best hybrids rather than heirlooms. The gentile church too is grafted onto the root of Israel and nurtured by Jewish gardeners, like Paul and Barnabas. The Scriptures of Israel became the Scriptures of the gentile church. Yet dependence on them or citation of them is no more indicative of a home in Judaism than is a sermon today preached by a Christian minister on Genesis 1 indicative of a "Jewish" view.

The connection the church makes between the Scriptures of Israel and its own claims can be seen as "pro-Jewish," but it can also be seen as having nothing to do with "Judaism" and even as "anti-Jewish." For example, Christians have argued, and some still do, that they have the "right" interpretation of the shared materials, and that the synagogue never did understand its own Bible. The rhetoric thus does not show that the New Testament is a "Jewish" book; rather, it can easily be seen as indicating a co-optation of Jewish texts along with a rejection of anything distinctive about "Judaism." One of Paul's Letters written to a gentile church, 2 Corinthians, presents such a potentially anti-Jewish reading:

> Since, then, we have such a hope, we act with great boldness, not like Moses, who put a veil over his face to keep the people of Israel from gazing at the end of the glory that was being set aside. But their minds were hardened. Indeed, to this very day, when they hear the reading of the old covenant, that same veil is still there, since only in Christ is it set aside. Indeed, to this very day whenever Moses is read, a veil lies over their minds; but when one turns to the Lord, the veil is removed. (3:12–16)

The Pontifical Biblical Commission asserts that Paul is speaking not of the Jews' "total incapacity to read" but "only an inability to read it in the light of Christ." But Paul may well have been telling his gentile Christian readers that the Jews never did understand the meaning of their own Scriptures, "to this present day."

Old Testament usage and a positive view of Torah do not "Jewish" make, as those Gentiles in Galatia, lining up to be circumcised, sharply attest. Thus, when scholars make the claim that Matthew is the "most Jewish" of the Gospels, they might want to check their criteria. Matthew does cite Israel's Scriptures extensively, argues that not one stroke of the Law will pass away, restricts Jesus's mission to Jews, and uses the circumlocution "kingdom of heaven" rather than pronounce the name of the deity. All that looks pretty "Jewish." But "most Jewish" in the context of the four Gospels is not the same as "pro-Jewish" or even "not anti-Jewish." Matthew is not "more Jewish" compared to the Mishnah, since the Jewish community did not preserve or canonize the Gospel of Matthew.

Nor does the First Gospel claim the term "Jewish" for itself. Matthew, who throughout the Gospel uses such terms as "Pharisees" and "Sadducees," "scribes" and "elders" to describe the various Jewish groups, suddenly at the Gospel's end uses the telling term "the Jews." The context is not merely the rejection of the church's claims but an alternative, and from Matthew's perspective false, story:

> Some of the guard went into the city and told the chief priests everything that had happened [i.e., the resurrection]. After they had assembled with the elders, they devised a plan to give a large sum of money to the soldiers, telling them, "You must say, 'His disciples came by night and stole him away while we were asleep.' If this comes to the governor's ears, we will satisfy him and keep you out of trouble." So they took the money and did as they were directed, and this story is still told among the Jews [*Ioudaioi*] to this day. (28:11–15)

The story makes no sense from any historical perspective. The "chief priests and the Pharisees" who, according to Matthew (27:62), approach Pilate to request that a guard be placed at the tomb are a very odd combination. Matthew has lumped together two opposing groups in order to present a unified Jewish front against Jesus and his followers. Guards are not likely to say to their commanding officer, "Gosh, we fell asleep"; nor is the commanding officer likely to respond, "No need to worry, guys. I know you had a really long weekend here at this tomb, and we all get tired." Either the guards were among the stupidest military men ever to walk the earth, or Matthew has created a story that serves a number of needs. It functions as an etiology, a story of origins, to explain why "the Jews" claim that the body was stolen. It highlights the irony that, although the disciples did not recall Jesus's prediction of his resurrection, the "chief priests and Pharisees" did. It vilifies "the Jews" (summarized by the combination of lay and clerical leaders) by revealing that they knew the "truth" and deliberately attempted to suppress it. All this suggests the scene is Matthew's composition, not a record of what "really happened."

Hearing with New Aids

For the increasingly gentile church and for those Jewish members in it who had become alienated from the synagogue, "the Jews" are those who "killed the Lord Jesus"; they are his "betrayers and murderers," as Stephen, the first martyr for Jesus, calls them, "stiff-necked people ... forever opposing the Holy Spirit" (Acts 7:51–52). The followers of Jesus thus, although Jews themselves, become for the readers of the Gospels, then and now, identified with another group, whether it is called "the church" (*ekklesia*, the term Matthew uses) or "the Way." Context matters. The perspective of the reader matters.

It is therefore pastorally helpful to imagine how the words of some New Testament passages can sound to people who are not Christian. For example, Galatians 3:28 proclaims: "There is no longer Jew or Greek, there is no longer slave or free, there is no longer male and female ... in Christ Jesus." The verse may be very good news to the gentile men in Galatia, who now have the assurance that circumcision is neither warranted nor wanted. It might be good news to slaves (although slaves would likely prefer that all were free). Historically, it may be Paul's notice that the Christ returns humanity to its primary state, that of the unified, androgynous "Adam" before Eve was split off. But to state that in the ideal world, or even in the purview of the Christ, "there is no longer Jew or Greek" sounds like an erasure of Jewish (and Greek) identity. Christian universalism thus entails the erasure of anything distinctly Jewish. Those who seek to promote multiculturalism might wish to rephrase Paul's language to celebrate "both Jew and Greek, both male and female, and all, who should be free."

Anti-Jewish impressions can emerge even in texts that do not mention anything specifically concerning Jews. Several years ago, a rabbi in Nashville called to inquire about whether a particular New Testament reading, suggested by a member of the local clergy council, was appropriate for an interfaith Thanksgiving service. The passage was from the Sermon on the

Mount: "Therefore, I tell you, do not worry about your life, what you will eat or what you will drink, or about your body, what you will wear. Is not life more than food and the body more than clothing?" (Matt. 6:25). When (or if) Jesus said this to fellow Jews, he would not have been perceived as anti-Jewish at all. If a Christian homilist reads these lines to the church, no negative impression about Jews need be given. But when this same passage is recited in an interfaith gathering, a different message is delivered. For a Christian minister to state in a gathering where Jews are noticeable because of what they wear (the rabbi in Nashville, for example, would have worn a *kippa*, a yarmulke or skullcap) and what they eat (several Jewish participants would have had the vegetarian meal, because there is no local kosher butcher), the originally innocuous passage threatens to become anti-Jewish.

In like manner, parts of the synagogue's liturgy can sound "anti-Christian" to Christian ears. For example, the prayer recited before a Torah reading speaks of how God "chose us from among all the nations and gave to us his Torah." The language of chosenness signals the Jewish response to the offer of the Torah; rabbinic stories recount that it was offered to all the other nations, but only the Jews—whether through religious fidelity or because of divine coercion—accepted it. Jews may find the language comforting rather than exclusive, because Jewish theology states that everyone is called to a particular way of manifesting the divine in the world. But to outsiders, the language of "chosenness" sounds elitist at best, if not xenophobic, and unfortunately in parts of the ultra-Orthodox Jewish world these connotations do appear.

The Bible is capable of taking on innumerable interpretations. Historical-critical work can be very helpful in eliminating some of the negative interpretations, such as the ones that arise when today's readers encounter the Sermon on the Mount or Paul's formula of unification in Galatians. It can suggest that Jesus of Nazareth never called "the Jews" children of the devil; it can propose that the Jerusalem crowd never formally clamored for Jesus's blood, and it can argue that Paul never wrote that the Jews "killed the Lord Jesus and oppose everyone." But the historical arguments remain speculative.

Further, historical arguments risk being compromised, because they presume that the "original" audience or the "original intent" determines the meaning. To restrict the question of anti-Judaism to a text's author, let alone to claim to know the author's intent, and not to consider the audience is bad method, as any homilist knows. What the priest says from the pulpit is not always what the congregants hear in the pew. To suggest that the text cannot take on new meanings but must be interpreted only in the context of its original setting dooms both the church and the synagogue, because this argument precludes people from finding their own meaning in the text. Theologically speaking, a fully historical focus threatens to put the Holy Spirit out of business.

The only resolution to the question of New Testament anti-Judaism cannot come from historians. The elimination of anti-Jewish readings must come from the theologians, from those members of the church who conclude that anti-Judaism is wrong and who insist on Christian sensitivity to the issue.

The text remains, for both Jews and Christians, an ongoing means of communication among the community, the individual, and God; it is a conversation across time, across religious traditions, across cultures. Interpretation therefore can never be static. If we are to get past the forced politeness that often marks interreligious conversation and take the risk of engaging in honest communication, we must make every effort to see through each other's eyes, hear through each other's ears, and interpret with a consciousness of each other's sensitivities. Instead of immediately dismissing the claim that a text is anti-Jewish, we might rather understand how the readers making the claim reached this conclusion. Instead of immediately asserting that a text is anti-Jewish, we might rather ask those who do derive an anti-Jewish meaning what the text then means to them.

Helpful here is a classic story told by Rebbe Moshe Leib of Sassov (1745–1807). As the account goes, the rebbe had announced to his disciples, "I have learned how we must truly love our neighbor from a conversation between two villagers which I overheard":

The first said: "Tell me, friend Ivan, do you love me?"
The second: "I love you deeply."
The first: "Do you know, my friend, what gives me pain?"
The second: "How can I, pray, know what gives you pain?"
The first: "If you do not know what gives me pain, how can you say that you truly love me?"

"Understand, then, my sons," continued the rebbe, "to love, truly to love, means to know what brings pain to your comrade."[11]

To engage in interfaith conversation means to understand that what is dogma to one participant is danger to another, that what is profound may also be painful. Jews and Christians need to read the texts together. Christians need to recognize the impact that the problematic verses cited in this chapter and other texts as well have had on Jews. In turn, Jews should be aware that most Christians do not consciously read the texts anti-Jewishly and even resist any anti-Jewish implications. Although the New Testament can be seen as anti-Jewish, it need not be. Words—inevitably—mean different things to different readers. We need to imagine how our words sound to different ears.

My son, who was not quite four when we moved to Nashville, remarked upon first seeing the spire of Vanderbilt's Benton Chapel: "Look Mommy! Lowercase t!" The same symbol, the same text, may have quite different meanings, depending on whose eyes are seeing and whose ears are hearing.

FOUR

Stereotyping Judaism

Kinky Friedman—author, Texas politician, provocateur (a tautology with "Texas politician"), and leader of the band "Kinky Friedman and the Texas Jew Boys"—is well known, at least in certain circles, for the recording "They Ain't Making Jews Like Jesus Anymore." The title could serve as an anthem for the Jesus introduced in certain liberal Christian settings. Friedman is correct, first, in that New Testament scholarship is increasingly removing Jesus from Judaism. Through a chic apologetic that seeks to make Jesus politically relevant to the twenty-first century, Christians find in Jesus the answer to whatever ails the body politic, whether it is war, ethnocentrism, an institutional religion intertwined with the state, or misogyny. In order for Jesus to serve this liberationist role, he has to have something concrete to oppose. The bad "system" then becomes, in the scholarship and in the pulpit, first-century Judaism.[1]

Church homilies and sermons, daily and weekly Bible study, and even respected academic monographs depict, both explicitly and implicitly, a Judaism that is monolithic, mired in legal minutiae, without spiritual depth, and otherwise everything that (they hope) Christianity is not. Pastors, priests, and religious educators, Christians well aware that the New Testament has been interpreted in an anti-Jewish manner, wind up perpetuating anti-Jewish teaching nonetheless.

The Theological Problem

This caricature of Judaism meets several needs. On the most crass level, it allows Jesus to stand out from, if not be unique within, his social context. As long as Christians could believe that Jesus was fully divine, there was no need to distinguish him explicitly from Jews; he was already distinct.

No one else had a virgin mother or was raised from the dead. Once the church met the Enlightenment and the secular academy, however, Jesus no longer looked quite so original or quite so distinct. He appeared comparable to other figures of antiquity, from Bacchus to Apollonius of Tyana, whose biographies recounted divine births, healing powers, wise teachings, and survival after death. Moreover, the Enlightenment focus on "science" as opposed to "superstition" caused many to dismiss the biblical accounts of miracles entirely. Thus Jesus became seen, at best, as a provocative human being with several splendid ideas. Yet for the Christian claims to remain strong, Jesus had to be more than just a Galilean charismatic, cynic sage, clever teacher, or cultural critic. He had to regain his "unique" identity and his "distinctive" views.

If Jesus is simply a really good rabbi—that is, someone whose advice I can follow and still be in more or less good standing in my Orthodox synagogue, someone whose ethical message and storytelling ability can also be found in Jewish texts—then he is at best a fine teacher. But this portrait should be insufficient for those who want to call themselves "Christian." If Jesus is not the Messiah, "the way and the truth and the life," or the "Son of God," then there is no warrant to follow him as opposed to following Gandhi, the Buddha, Hillel, or any other great teacher. Once the supernatural and the transcendent are stripped away from Jesus, then there is no reason to recite the creeds, celebrate Christmas or Easter, or speak of the washing away of sin at baptism or the resurrection of the dead. As Paul tells his Corinthian congregation: "If Christ has not been raised, then our proclamation has been in vain and your faith has been in vain.... If Christ has not been raised, your faith is futile and you are still in your sins" (1 Cor. 15:14, 17).

Christian skeptics thus have an enormous problem. Why remain Christian if Jesus is one of several wise individuals with good ideas for social improvement? The easiest answer to the question is to argue that Jesus does what no one else ever did or could do; he is distinct, special, better. This process means depicting a Jesus who stands out as unique in his Jewish context; it also usually means enhancing the distinction, and this is done by painting that Jewish context in noxious colors. Hence, today a number of stereotypes of Judaism, based ever so tentatively on historical investigation, substitute for rigorous historical inquiry. Their value is utilitarian, for they allow Jesus to emerge as a unique ethical teacher who is able to cut through whatever hampers anyone from living life to the fullest. This religious need is what, to a great extent, prompts the current description of first-century Judaism as mired in legal minutiae that trampled on individual needs, promulgating a warlike theology that had no place for peace, and obsessed with a purity system that marginalized women and promoted hatred of foreigners. Within this context, Jesus then emerges as a member of the ACLU, Greenpeace, the National Organization for Women, and the United Nations (on a good day).

The social-justice Jesus who promotes a healthy interpretation of the Torah, peaceful response to oppression, the healing of women's bodies, and the recognition that the God of Israel is the God of the Gentiles as well is enormously appealing, and enormously useful. The image may also be substantially true. The problem emerges, however, when these observations are enhanced by the depiction of Judaism as rejecting such concerns. Jesus was not the only Jew to care about these issues; his social-justice interests make him a Jew rather than distinguishing him from Judaism. Today, alas, given the general ignorance about first-century Judaism, there are few means by which the pastor or the priest would ever know this.

The Educational Failure

Departments of religion, seminaries, and university-based divinity schools are substantially to blame, through sins of both commission and omission, for the perpetuation of anti-Jewish teachings. Christian clergy and professors of seminary subjects ranging from Old and New Testaments through church history, theology, ethics, and pastoral care are not typically trained in Judaica. What they know about "Judaism" thus becomes an often intuitive sense derived from select readings of the Old and New Testaments.

The situation is a particular problem for New Testament or early Christianity Ph.D. programs. Not all such programs require degree candidates to read such Jewish sources as the writings of Josephus and Philo, the Dead Sea Scrolls, the pseudepigraphical works (books dating to ca. 300 BCE–100 CE, usually written under the names of ancient worthies, such as 2 *Baruch* or 1 *Enoch*), or the rabbinic texts. Instead, popular today are required readings in methods. Rather than introducing students to the primary sources, faculty train their acolytes on "how" to read them. The result is a Ph.D. candidate who can apply any type of critical theory (from poststructural, postmodern, postcolonial, feminist, womanist, mujerista, Min-Jung, queer readings, and autobiographical critique to whatever is of greatest interest at this year's Modern Language Association meetings). There is much worth in these reading strategies and others, but there is no value to them if the student has no clue as to the content of the Letter to the Ephesians, let alone Philo's *Special Laws*, Josephus's *Antiquities of the Jews*, or tractate *Sanhedrin* in the Mishnah. The sad aspect of this methodological focus is that within ten years, the darling literary-critical theory will be outdated, and the academic whose focus is primarily on theory will be outdated as well. Even worse, a number of these strategies that seek to give voice to views that had previously been unheard in the academy preclude any critique. The voice from the margins claims the moral high ground, and all those who do not belong to the marginalized group can do is listen and, usually, feel guilty. Thus, scholarship devolves into solipsism, the social location of the interpreter is the only factor of determining the meaning of the text, and history becomes irrelevant.

Christian denominations that mandate formal training for their clergy require candidates for ministry to take courses in the Old Testament. From these introductory forays, students begin to fill in their knowledge of "Judaism" with what they learn about Abraham or David. Frequently, the narratives about the patriarchs and the monarchy then serve to provide a picture of what first-century Jews were doing. The comparable move would be for a Jew to read Paul's Letter to the Galatians or the Gospel of Mark and claim, on that basis, to know what members of the local Presbyterian church do on a daily basis.

Pentateuchal Law, save for the Ten Commandments, typically gets ignored in the Old Testament classes, for injunctions concerning how one plants crops or builds a temple are generally irrelevant to the modern church and boring to modern Christian students. However, this legal material does get cited, selectively, in *New Testament* classes and books about the New Testament as a principal source for understanding Jesus's Jewish context. Instead of looking at the writings of Josephus and Philo, the Dead Sea Scrolls, any of the noncanonical documents written by Jews in the first centuries BCE and CE, or even carefully mining the rabbinic texts for information about first-century practices, the default remains what the students actually have on hand, that is, their copy of the Old Testament.

Whether explicitly cited or implicitly assumed, ministerial candidates presume that first-century Jews followed biblical Law whole cloth. The normative view is that if one reads Leviticus, one understands what Peter and all his neighbors in Capernaum were doing.

Once this levitical view is in place, Christian readers come to the New Testament with the expectation that Jesus's Jewish context is marked by the practices of the legal code. The readers then, implicitly having dissociated Jesus and Paul from "the Jews," regard "the Jews" as either obsessive neurotics who "tithe mint, dill, and cummin" and neglect "the weightier matters of the Law: justice and mercy and faith" (Matt. 23:23) or complacent legalistic elitists who "boast in the Law" (Rom. 2:23).

In New Testament classes, many students get a single lecture, or half a lecture, on the four major parties of Jews mentioned by the Jewish historian Josephus: Pharisees, Sadducees, Essenes, and Zealots. With a paragraph or so for each of the different movements, they can continue on in the Gospels, confident that they know what there is to know about first-century Judaism. The modern analogy would be to think that if one knows a few details about the Knights of Columbus, the Kiwanis Club, the Masons, and the Boy Scouts, one understands American society. Making this situation even worse, the "backgrounds" chapter in the New Testament textbook rarely gets referenced when the study turns to the New Testament books themselves. Judaism thus is the "background" to the New Testament, rather than part of the common ground of Jesus and James.

The appropriate focus in New Testament studies on Jesus, Paul, James, and the other great figures makes another unfortunate contribution to anti-Jewish thinking. The professor and the textbook do not have the time or the inclination to emphasize, repeatedly, the diversity of Jewish beliefs in the first century. In churches, such historical details concerning diverse Jewish views, regardless of how accurate they are, have no place in the sermon already packed with comments about Jesus and justice. It is easier, especially from the pulpit, to speak of "the Jews," as in "The Jews were waiting for the messiah" or "The Jews sought the destruction of the Roman Empire." Pastors and priests are unlikely to stop at each use of the term, offer a brief historical synopsis, and then lecture the congregation on Jewish diversity; the New Testament does have other lessons to teach, and congregations do tire of hearing the same point week after week. It's easier, if not more rhetorically effective, to speak of how Jesus challenged "the Jews" rather than "a few Pharisees from Jerusalem." Moreover, even if the sermon does indicate that the opponents are a few members of one particular Jewish school of thought, the Christian congregation will still hear "the Jews." The same point holds in synagogue contexts. Jewish congregants often hear the reference to "Southern Baptist" initiatives to convert Jews as a "Christian" initiative, not a sectarian one.

This lack of direct attention to Jesus's Jewish setting and to the Jewish sources that aid in reconstructing this setting is especially ironic given the present state of academic emphases. The liberal wing of theological education requires students to take courses in "another religion"; Buddhism, Hinduism, and now Islam are the most popular. Yet, whereas Jews are mentioned directly in the writings of the New Testament, Jesus neither offers a "Woe to you, Buddhist" screed nor calls groups of Hindus a "brood of vipers." Some more conservative seminary curricula do require courses in Judaism, but these are geared to help Christian missionaries convert Jews, and they tend to be no more historically accurate than the average "Jewish Backgrounds to Jesus" lecture that begins most New Testament courses. Knowledge of religions is a splendid thing, as is the broadening of the clerical mind. But knowledge of Judaism on its own terms, and not (simply if at all) as a means to the evangelistic end, should have a special place in any serious study of Jesus and the New Testament, not only because Jesus and all his immediate followers were Jews, but also because the New Testament has been read and taught in a manner that perpetuates hatred of Jews.

Of the numerous overstatements concerning, misperceptions of, and slanders against first-century Judaism that appear with some consistency in classroom and church, seven (a good biblical number) are endemic in the Christian popular imagination:

1. The view that Jewish Law was impossible to follow, a burden no one could bear. In this construction, the injunctions are always identified as "Jewish Law" and very rarely "biblical Law" or "the instructions given by God to Moses" or "divine Law" despite the fact that the Laws are in the Bible the church considers holy.

2. The thesis that all Jews wanted a warrior messiah who would defeat Rome; therefore, "the Jews" rejected Jesus because he taught the way of peace.

3. The proclamation that Jesus was a feminist in a women-hating Jewish culture.

4. The conclusion that Jews were obsessed with keeping themselves pure from the contamination of outsiders, whereas Jesus, especially through his parable of the good Samaritan, broke through purity-based barriers.

5. The insistence that first-century Judaism was marked by a Temple domination system that oppressed the poor and women and that promoted social division between insiders and outcasts.

6. The assertion that Jews are narrow, clannish, particularistic, and xenophobic, whereas Jesus and the church are engaged in universal outreach.

7. The increasingly popular argument that the New Testament is not talking about Jews at all, but about "Judeans."

Each theory has instrumental value. By suggesting that Jesus redeems his followers from an abusive legal system, Christians have a greater rationale both for ignoring the first part of their canon and for deemphasizing the point the Letter of James makes unequivocally, "Faith *without works* is dead" (2:26). By speaking of Jews as warlike, Christians can ignore the warlike aspects of their own canonical tradition, including statements made by Jesus himself, and so claim for him the peaceful high ground. By making Jesus a feminist, Christians can address the misogyny that still permeates church and society. A focus on Jewish purity and xenophobia allows Christians to claim leadership in multicultural efforts, even if that effort decides that the one culture not worth celebrating is that of the Jews. The Temple domination system allows complaints about institutional religion to surface in a way that protects the church. The view of Judaism as particularistic deflects from the church the claim that, by insisting on salvation only through Jesus, it has the narrower, less universal vision. The "Judean" case provides a quick fix for those seeking to rid the text of anti-Jewish impressions.

In all these cases, Jesus is made relevant either by projecting a negative stereotype of Judaism or by erasing Judaism entirely. The proclamation of the church can, and should, stand on its own; it does not require an artificial foil, an anti-Jewish basis, or an overstated distinction.

The Law as an Unbearable Yoke

The view that Jews insist on following a "Law" that is not simply difficult to follow but is, as Peter puts it in Acts 15:10, "a yoke that neither our ancestors nor we have been able to bear" is a stereotype of much Christian (especially Protestant) teaching. Opposed to this Jewish system, Jesus invites: "Come to me, all you that are weary and are carrying heavy burdens, and I will give you rest. Take my yoke upon you, and learn from me; for I am gentle and humble in heart, and you will find rest for your souls. For my yoke is easy, and my burden is light" (Matt. 11:28–30).

Peter's statement about the Law makes sense if one is outside the system—there are a number of practices to learn, and people having no familiarity with Jewish tradition might have found the system daunting. However, average Jews did not find the "Law" any more burdensome than we citizens of the United States, who have many more laws on the books than are found in the entire Talmud, find our laws particularly burdensome. Americans manage to pass driver's license examinations by demonstrating an understanding of traffic laws; American foods are supervised by the FDA; Americans know they are not to steal or murder. Or, for another analogy, vegetarians do not consider their diet any more of a "burden" or an impossible yoke than Jews today who keep kosher find restrictions against cheeseburgers an impossible demand. First-century Jewish tithing practices are comparable to tithing practices in contemporary churches or, to update the analogy, to paying one's taxes. Were the Law such a burden, it is incomprehensible both that Jews chose to remain Jews and that numerous Gentiles chose to convert to Judaism.

As for Jesus's "easy yoke," Warren Carter makes a compelling case that Jesus is not talking about the "yoke of the Law" as interpreted by the Pharisees; rather, he is talking about the yoke of the Roman political system. As he notes in his *Matthew and Empire,* the connection of "yoke" imagery to the Law is exceptionally rare; most references in earlier biblical literature refer to some form of control (over slaves, over one's tongue, the yoke of wisdom). He further notes that a high percentage of language concerning yokes refers to "political control, particularly the imposition of harsh, imperial power."[2] The problem Jesus addresses, the problem the people face, is not the pharisaic understanding of Torah; it is the Roman understanding of power.

The idea that Jesus voided the Sabbath, declared all foods clean, and otherwise dismissed the Torah is an invention that met the needs of the growing gentile church, a church that did not define itself according to the practices that maintained the Jews' distinct identity. In the Sermon on the Mount, Jesus states: "Do not think that I have come to abolish the Law or the Prophets; I have come not to abolish but to fulfill." Whether these words came from Jesus himself or whether Matthew or some anterior source placed them on his lips, the point holds: Jesus upheld the Law, and he expected his followers to do the same. They would disagree with other Jews on the precise means by which the Law would be followed, and in doing so they would be expressing their Jewishness, not denying it.

The Warrior Messiah

Jewish messianic speculation was as diverse as Jewish theology and practice. Some Jews expected a messianic king, others a priest, others an archangel or heavenly figure such as Enoch, and others the coming of the world to come by divine fiat; still others were quite happy with the way things were. Nor was there consistency in the details of the messiah's roles. Some Jews yearned for the removal of the Roman presence from Judea and Galilee, if not from the earth; others were more concerned that fellow Jews who did not follow their particular beliefs and practices receive eschatological "correction" (usually in a quite malicious way); still others looked forward primarily to the end of poverty, disease, and death. There was no single view of a messiah other than the sense that his coming would manifestly change the world

Nor was it the case that all Jews, even those who opposed Roman rule, took the path of militarism. Although Judas the Galilean and a Pharisee named Zadok lead a revolt in Galilee in 6 CE to protest the census initiated by the Roman prefect Coponius[3]—a census was designed for the purpose of determining taxes—and a more widespread revolt against Rome took place in 66–70, most protests against the government were peaceful. For example, in 26 Pontius Pilate attempted to bring into Jerusalem standards depicting an image of the emperor. Regarding this provocative move as a direct violation of the biblical injunctions against "graven images," the population responded by sending a delegation to Pilate and by engaging in a five-day sit-down strike.[4] When Pilate raided the Temple treasury for funds to construct an aqueduct, numerous Jews surrounded his tribunal, but they did not attack. Pilate, less interested in peace than in pacification, responded by having the protestors executed.[5] In 41, when Caligula initiated plans to have his statue placed in the Jerusalem Temple, the Jews appealed to the Syrian legate Petronius rather than engaging in revolt.[6]

The "warrior messiah" idea derives from several factors. Undergirding the idea is the ancient canard that asserts a distinction between the "Old Testament God of war" and the "New Testament God of peace" and then associates that Old Testament God with the God of the Jews. The deity depicted by Deuteronomy and Joshua does have a bellicose streak. The following lines from Deuteronomy are not likely to be recited at a Quaker meeting:

I will take vengeance on my adversaries,
And will repay those who hate me.
I will make my arrows drunk with blood,
And my sword shall devour flesh. (32:41b–42a)

Joshua contains a description of a genocide: "When Israel had finished slaughtering all the inhabitants of Ai in the open wilderness where they pursued them, and when all of them to the very last had fallen by the edge of the sword, all Israel returned to Ai, and attacked it with the edge of the sword. The total of those who fell that day, both men and women, was twelve thousand—all the people of Ai" (8:24–25).

Nevertheless, it is not only incorrect but also heretical for Christians to distinguish between the God of the Old Testament and the God of the New. What must be noted first is that, according to Christian teaching, both Testaments depict the same God. There is no personality shift as the text moves from Malachi to Matthew, for the same bellicose deity appears in explicitly Christian texts. The book of Revelation, which is replete with military imagery, offers the unpleasant image of the angel who "swung his sickle on the earth and gathered the vintage of the earth, and threw it into the great wine press of the wrath of God. And the wine press was trodden outside the city, and the blood flowed from the wine press, as high as a horse's bridle, for one thousand six hundred stadia [two hundred miles]" (14:19–20). Jesus himself speaks of those who will be thrown either into the "furnace of fire, where there will be weeping and gnashing of teeth"

(Matt. 13:50), or "into the outer darkness" (Matt. 25:30). Regarding Jesus and militarism, according to Luke's Gospel, Jesus tells his followers: "The one who has a purse must take it, and likewise a bag. And the one who has no sword must sell his cloak and buy one.... They [the disciples] said, 'Lord, look, here are two swords.' He replied, 'It is enough'" (22:36–38). Their response indicates that they are already armed.

Along with "God of wrath" ideas in the New Testament, one can also find the "God of love" image in the Old Testament. The reputed Old Testament God of wrath is also the one about whom David sings, "The Lord is my shepherd" (Ps. 23:1). According to Isaiah, God says, "As a mother comforts her child, so will I comfort you" (66:13a). To argue that one Testament has a "better" or "nicer" or "more peaceful" God than the other is a gross misreading of the text.

The second major source for the idea that all Jews awaited a warrior messiah is the Bar Kokhba revolt of 132–35. The revolt may have been ignited by the emperor Hadrian's ban on castration, which was interpreted to include circumcision, by Hadrian's attempt to rebuild Jerusalem as the Roman city Aelia Capitolina, or by a combination of these and other events. Like Judah Maccabee centuries before him, Simon bar Kosiba refused to see his traditions profaned or proscribed, and so he began a campaign of armed resistance. Initially, his guerilla tactics proved effective, and more flocked to his call. Some, including the highly influential Rabbi Akiva, thought he was the messiah. Justin Martyr, writing after the revolt in the mid-second century, mentions that the general went by the name of "bar Kokhba," Aramaic for "son of the star."[7] The moniker suggests messianic pretensions. However, it is not clear that bar Kosiba thought himself to be the messiah or encouraged that belief in others. His letters do not make messianic claims; the inscriptions on his coins are at best difficult to interpret.[8]

Rabbinic tradition, developed after bar Kosiba's disastrous loss and the resulting Roman expulsion of all Jews from Jerusalem, fully dissociates him from any messianic role. According to the Palestinian Talmud (*Taanit* 68d): "Rabbi Akiva, when he saw bar Kosiba, said, 'This is the king Messiah!' Rabbi Jochanan ben Torta said to him, 'Akiva, grass will grow in your cheeks and still the son of David does not come.'"[9] The modern version of this idiom would be, "You'll be pushing up daisies before the messiah comes."

The third source for the "warrior messiah" image derives not from Jewish sources but from the Acts of the Apostles. According to Acts 1:6, the disciples question the risen Jesus: "Lord, is this the time when you will restore the kingdom to Israel?" "Restoration" likely means the return of independent sovereignty, and the question has scriptural warrant. Jeremiah states: "The days are surely coming, says the Lord, when I will raise up for David a righteous Branch, and he shall reign as king and deal wisely, and shall execute justice and righteousness in the land. In his days Judah will be saved and Israel will live in safety" (23:5–6). Ezekiel presents an oracle in which God promises the covenant community that "they shall be secure on their soil; and they shall know that I am the Lord, when I break the bars of their yoke, and save them from the hands of those who enslaved them. They shall no more be plunder for the nations, nor shall the animals of the land devour them; they shall live in safety, and no one shall make them afraid" (34:27–28). In each case the kingdom is "restored." However, in neither case is the restoration accomplished by a military operation.

Alternatively, the disciples' question may rather evoke the restoration of all things associated with the prophet Elijah. The last book of the prophetic canon Malachi predicts the coming of Elijah, who will "restore the heart of a father toward his son and the heart of a man toward his neighbor" (3:23, Greek translation [LXX]), a passage to which Luke 1:17 alludes.[10]

Finally, scholars sometimes quote or refer to a noncanonical Jewish text, dated about 63 BCE, called the *Psalms of Solomon* (especially chap. 17) as evidence of the general Jewish interest in a warrior messiah. When taken out of context, certain verses do suggest a "warrior messiah" ideal. *Psalms of Solomon* implores God: "Raise up for them [the people] their king, the son of David, to rule over your servant Israel in the time known to you, O God. Undergird him with strength to destroy the unrighteous rulers, to purge Jerusalem from Gentiles who trample her to destruction, in wisdom and in righteousness to drive out the sinners from the inheritance, to smash the arrogance of sinners like a potter's jar; to shatter all their substance with an iron rod" (17:21–24a). However, the next line pulls back from the blitzkrieg: "to destroy the unlawful nations with the word of his mouth; at his warning the nations will flee from his presence, and he will condemn sinners by the thoughts of their hearts."[11]

Thus, the "Jews" did not reject Jesus because Jesus was not a militaristic messiah, and the God Jesus proclaims is the same God who encountered Noah, Abraham, Moses, and David. As long as Christian teachers and preachers continue to suggest that Judaism is a militaristic, warmongering system missing a concern for shalom and that Christianity is the system of peace, devoid of any sense of militarism, violence, or revenge, anti-Jewish teachings will continue. As long as the God of the Old Testament is seen as distinct from the God of the New, anti-Jewish teachings will be reinforced. And as long as the churches refuse to acknowledge their own involvement in a text and a history marked by violence as well as peace, no religion is safe.

The Misogynistic Morass: Part I, The Samaritan Woman

More than twenty-five years ago, the second wave of feminist thought began to impact biblical studies. Seeking a Jesus who would provide "a lot more positive images for women than our upbringings in various churches or our academic doctoral training had led us to believe,"[12] Christian women began to look anew at the Gospels. The problem here was that direct evidence for Jesus's unique and progressive views on women was lacking. Instead, the counterevidence proved substantial. From the pages of the Gospels, Jesus emerges as a first-century man who for the most part subscribes to the normative gender roles present in Jewish as well as pagan settings. In his view, men and women had separate roles to play. He appoints no women among the inner group of twelve disciples; he locates men and women in the gender-determined roles of "brother and sister and mother" (Mark 3:34); he speaks of the night when "There will be two [men] upon one bed [or dining couch]; one will be taken and the other left. There will be two [women] grinding meal together; one will be taken and the other left" (Luke 17:35–36). As long as men do the eating and women do the cooking, liberation is not at hand.

Nevertheless, these early feminists had a ready-made mechanism for making Jesus one of their own: lower the bar on his Jewish context. The worse Judaism can be made to look, the better Jesus will look in comparison. If Judaism could be seen as a completely repressive system, then anytime Jesus is seen talking to a woman, healing her body, or receiving her support, he becomes a spokesman for women's liberation.

For example, commentators frequently insist that Jesus transgressed Jewish Law by talking with women, since "the rabbis" prohibited conversation between the sexes. Even more anomalous, he allowed Mary of Bethany to sit at his feet and receive instruction, while "the rabbis" prohibited women from learning Torah. "Jesus is the only rabbi who ..." became a litany in early feminist New Testament studies, and it remains a staple in pulpit and pew. The argument, no matter how helpful it proves to be in encouraging women to seek new roles in the church, is based on sloppy historical work.

Christian commentators interested in promoting a Jesus progressive on women's issues turn to select rabbinic materials to demonstrate how their Messiah rejects Jewish misogynism. Among the favorite citations is *Pirke Avot* 1:5, in which Rabbi Jose ben Jochanan of Jerusalem states, "Let your house be opened wide; and let the needy be your household; and do not prolong conversation with woman." The Mishnah then glosses the quotation: "His own wife, they meant, much less his neighbor's wife. Hence the sages say, 'Each time that the man prolongs conversation with the woman he causes evil to himself, and desists from words of Torah, and in the end he inherits Gehenna.'" It would be difficult to argue that the rabbinic texts are, uniformly, a major repository for promoting women's equality. Nevertheless, the selective juxtaposing of rabbinic quotations with material from the Gospels skews the discussion. "The rabbis" represent hundreds of people who wrote over several centuries, and the documents that record their writings postdate the time of Jesus. Some rabbis had misogynistic tendencies, as did some contemporaneous church fathers (for example, Tertullian [ca. 160–225], who tells all women, "You are the Devil's gateway!"[13]). Other rabbinic statements are progressive on women's concerns, as are other quotations from the church fathers. Comparing Jesus to "the rabbis" is like comparing the great Jewish teacher Hillel to "the church fathers."

Nor is Jesus a "rabbi" in the sense that the authors of the Mishnah and Talmud were rabbis. Jesus did not spend his time engaged in a (somewhat) systematic understanding of Torah or developing a plan for the sanctification of daily life through practice and prayer. Rather, he addressed issues when they presented themselves or when he was questioned about them. He is better seen as a charismatic teacher, healer, and speaker of traditional wisdom than as a rabbi who, in a study house, focused on understanding the words of Torah and determining how best to implement them.

The comparison only gets worse, for, as noted, New Testament experts tend to lack training in rabbinic sources; specialized training is needed, for these documents are often opaque to the uninitiated. Like legal documents today, they presuppose knowledge of the history of interpretation and they adopt an in-house jargon frequently incomprehensible to outsiders. Worse for the one unfamiliar with the texts, they jump from subject to subject, insert long digressions, and refuse to provide dates for their claims. One passage will put into conversation the views of rabbis who lived hundreds of miles and hundreds of years apart. And even worse, there are two major collections of rabbinic material, the Palestinian Talmud and the Babylonian Talmud, and they do not always agree. What's the poor scholar or preacher seeking to find a context for Jesus to do?

What most do is rely on earlier secondary sources, which themselves rely on yet earlier studies. In an academic version of the children's game of telephone, scholars quote other scholars who quote other scholars who at some point reference the rabbinic sources. Few go back to check the original. Even fewer make the effort to check the context of the quote. Fewer still look for counterevidence.

Were scholars to make the effort to see if "the rabbis" do talk with women, they would find a number of conversations, since the sources depict women as coming to rabbis for legal rulings and personal advice. Judith Hauptmann provides the following example from the Babylonian Talmud:

Judah and Hezekiah were twins. One was fully formed at the end of nine months [of gestation] and one at the beginning of seven [and so their mother gave birth to each one separately]. Judith, the wife of R. Hiyya [and the mother of the twins], suffered [agonizing] labor pains [and because of this unusual twin birth, wanted to stop having children]. She disguised herself, came before [her husband] R. Hiyya, and asked, "Is a woman obligated to procreate?" He answered, "No." She went and drank a sterilizing potion. After some time passed, it became known [that she was avoiding pregnancy]. Her husband said to her, "If only you had given birth to one more bellyful." (*Yevamot* 65b)[14]

In this story, not only does a "strange" woman (the wife in disguise) approach Rabbi Hiyya; she manages to obtain from him permission to use birth control. The point here is not that this anecdote tells us anything about the time of Jesus; it is that one text that advises men not to talk overmuch with women is not indicative of the entire corpus of rabbinic literature.

The one woman whose legal rulings the Talmud recognizes even seems to tease her fellow rabbis about their occasionally sexist attitudes. Again from the Babylonian Talmud, *Eruvin* 53b records how Rabbi Yosi the Galilean, while traveling, met the famous female sage Beruriah. He asks her, "By what road do I go to Lod?" She answers: "Foolish Galilean, did not the rabbis say 'Engage not in much talk with women'? You should have asked, 'Which to Lod?'" By continuing to speak to him, she forces him to engage in talk with her.

Jesus speaks with women in public, as did other Jewish men. But he is by no means anomalous for so doing. The New Testament itself shows that men and women spoke together in public. According to Luke, an elderly Jew named Simeon speaks directly to Mary in the Temple in Jerusalem (Luke 2:34); no scholar expresses surprise. Men would have been among the Jews who come to console Mary and Martha (John 11:19) upon hearing that Lazarus has died; they would not have been out of place. Peter speaks to Sapphira (Acts 5:8), and Paul speaks to Lydia (Acts 16:14–15).

The view that Jesus is anomalous in speaking with women derives from several factors. First, because, according to the Gospel of John, Jesus's own disciples "were astonished that he was speaking with a woman" (4:27a), commentators presume that the disciples had reverted to their Jewish default in which men did not talk with women. Ignored is the equally likely view that they were astonished to find *Jesus* talking with a woman: he was less than loquacious with his mother at the wedding in Cana, and he had not appointed any women to be with him among the Twelve. Additionally, the disciples may also have been surprised that he was talking to *this* woman, a Samaritan. Jesus had enjoined upon them no Samaritan mission, and the synoptic Gospels preclude any Samaritan mission. Mark does not mention the Samaritans; Luke reserves the Samaritan mission to a post-Easter event (Acts 8); and in Matthew Jesus instructs the Twelve: "Go nowhere among the Gentiles, and enter no town of the Samaritans, but go rather to the lost sheep of the house of Israel" (10:5b–6).

John's account of Jesus and the Samaritan woman lends itself to readings that offer the "bad Judaism" versus "good Jesus" mode of interpretation, for it fits the view that Jesus breaks down barriers between men and women, Jews and Gentiles. In this scenario, "Judaism" again becomes the system that erects and seeks to maintain those barriers, and the Samaritan woman represents the ultimate "outsider" who finds, with Jesus, her place on the inside. Jerome Neyrey summarizes the prevailing view. John has "concentrated in this one figure many of the characteristics of marginal persons with whom Jesus regularly deals in the Synoptic Gospels. She is an amalgam of cultural deviance. In terms of stereotypes, she is a non-Jew, who is ritually unclean; she is a 'sinner,' a publicly recognized 'shameless' person.... As a shameless woman, she embodies most of the social liabilities that would marginalize her in her society."[15] Neyrey then finds that the Samaritan woman "represents inclusivity in the Christian group in a most radical way."[16]

In the narrative itself, however, the woman is not an "outsider," ritually unclean, a sinner, shameless, or marginal. In the context of John 4, it is Jesus, the Jew in the Samaritan area, who is the "outsider," who behaves in a shameless way, and who is marginal to the community.

The argument that the woman's coming to the well at noon indicates her social ostracism, for the other women of the village would wait until the cool of the evening, falters by ignoring John's literary art. Nicodemus the Pharisaic elder, introduced in the previous chapter, comes to Jesus in the dark of midnight. The Samaritan woman, at noon, understands the "light" Jesus brings;[17] the Pharisee remains in the dark. The setting is symbolic of theological insight, not social ostracism. Nicodemus, who had had a very frustrating conversation with Jesus about being "born again," may never quite obtain belief. Rather, according to John's Gospel, he and Joseph of Arimathea bury Jesus under one hundred pounds of spices. That's a lot of spice for a body expected to be resurrected. The woman, on the other hand, is so fully integrated into and accepted by her Samaritan village that, as John states, "Many Samaritans from that city believed in him [Jesus] because of the woman's testimony, 'He told me everything I have ever done'" (4:39). Townspeople are not likely to believe the testimony of a marginalized, shameless sinner.

General cultural attitudes did separate Jews and Samaritans, a point John reinforces with the observation that "Jews do not share things in common with Samaritans" (4:9). The line is, like most stereotypes, exaggerated. Although by no means the most faithful of Jews, Herod the Great married a Samaritan, Malthace; she was the mother of Herod Antipas and Herod Archelaus. More of a problem, however, is the impression New Testament scholars give concerning the mechanisms by which this cultural antipathy was carried out. Following John's language that "the Jews" are the ones who do not share things in common with the Samaritans, they miss the mutual enmity between the two groups—Samaritans on the whole preferred to have no dealings with the Jews. For example, during the governorship of Cumanus (48–52), a Samaritan murdered Jewish pilgrims traveling from Galilee to Jerusalem. When Eliezer, a Jewish local leader (or "bandit," depending on who is telling the story), gathered a group of Galileans for a counterattack, Cumanus called out his own troops. Intervening, the Syrian legate Quadratus attempted to restore peace, and he sent both Jewish and Samaritan leaders to Rome, where the emperor Claudius sided with the Jews.

Nor does John's Gospel say anything about the Samaritan woman as being "ritually unclean" or about Jesus ignoring the laws of purity. Some New Testament scholars cite the Mishnah, *Niddah* 4:1, as evidence that Jesus, by talking with the Samaritan, is ignoring and so erasing Jewish views of female purity. The verse reads: "The daughters of the Samaritans are [deemed unclean as] menstruants from their cradle." What these scholars fail to mention is what follows in the Mishnah: "The daughters of the Sadducees, if they follow after the ways of their fathers, are deemed like to the women of the Samaritans" (*Niddah* 4:2). The passages reflect the worldview of the composers and not the sentiments of all Jews, and certainly not the views of the Sadducees. Scholars also fail to take the second step and see how the later sources understand the Mishnaic statements. Because the Mishnah goes on to describe how Samaritan women *do* observe the laws of family purity, the rabbis wonder how they could be unclean (Babylonian Talmud *Niddah* 31b). The Tosefta (*Terumah* 4:12) reads: "A Samaritan is like a non-Jew, according to the opinion of Rabbi [i.e., Judah ha-Nasi, the codifier of the Mishnah, ca. 200]. Rabbi Shimeon ben Gamliel [his father] says, 'A Samaritan is like Israel in all respects.'"[18] Ultimately, New Testament scholars reduce rabbinic *ambivalence* about the Samaritans to a singular, xenophobic, misogynistic Jewish hatred and then retroject this image back to Jesus's first-century context. The only Jew who escapes the retrojection is, of course, Jesus. The stereotype is much easier to repeat than is plowing through arcane Hebrew legal texts.

Next, despite the scholarly conclusion that the Samaritan woman is "sinful," John's Gospel also fails to say anything about the woman's sinful state. Although having been married to five husbands and currently living with a man who is not one's husband is by no means conventional, it need not be seen as sinful either. Sarah, the heroine of the book of Tobit, a text found in the deuterocanonical collection (Old Testament Apocrypha), was multiply married, for her husbands were all killed by a love-struck demon on the wedding night. In the synoptic tradition, the Sadducees pose to Jesus a question about a woman who is multiply married:

> "Teacher, Moses wrote for us that if a man's brother dies, leaving a wife but no child, his brother shall marry the widow and raise up children for his brother [so Deut. 25:5]. There were seven brothers; the first married and, when he died, left no children; and the second married her and died, leaving no children; and the third likewise; none of the seven left children. Last of all the woman herself died. In the resurrection, whose wife will she be?" (Mark 12:18–27)

The poor wife is unfortunate, but she is not sinful. Concerning the multiply married Samaritan, by living with a man not her husband, she violates no legal code. Jesus never says to her anything about her sinful behavior, and no one in the story seeks to stone her. The only ones who condemn her are the biblical scholars.

Johannine literary interests, not concern for sin, require her somewhat surprising sexual history. The meeting of Jesus and the woman at the well follows the convention well established in Scripture: Abraham's servant speaks to Rebekah at a well (Gen. 24); Jacob speaks to Rachel at a well (Gen. 29); Moses speaks to the seven daughters of a Midianite priest at a well (Exod. 2). The convention of the "woman at the well" is so firmly established that the author of 1 Samuel can trust readers to recognize the allusion in the story of Saul, the future king, who meets "some girls coming out to draw water" (1 Sam. 9:11). To fulfill the convention, Saul should marry one of these women and so make an alliance with her family. Instead, he asks for information on where to find a seer so that he might locate his father's lost donkeys. He fails to fulfill the convention, just as he fails to fulfill the goals of the monarchy; the scene, like his kingship, goes undeveloped. Had Jesus and the woman failed to have a conversation, the connection to the convention would have similarly failed and the allusion to the convention's anticipated end, namely, the joining of two families, would have been lost.

Moreover, John enhances the literary artistry of the scene through the use of banter spiced with what the Gospel's readers would have recognized to be sexually suggestive: references to wells and cisterns, fountains and living water, especially when made by a man and a woman at a well, are overflowing with innuendo. Proverbs advises young men: "Drink water from your own cistern, flowing water from your own well. Should your springs be scattered abroad, streams of water in the streets?" (5:15–16); Song of Songs refers to a woman as "a well of living water" (4:15). Whereas today readers might have more refined taste, in antiquity earthy humor, even in sacred Scriptures, was both recognized and appreciated.

Finally, the "shameful outsider" in this story is actually Jesus. He is the outsider in Samaritan territory; he is the one who orders the woman, "Give me a drink" (John 4:7) and so begins the conversation; he is the one who opens up the question of the woman's sexual background by commanding her, "Go, call your husband" and then by repeating her sexual history. However, concerning her "inclusivity in the Christian group in a most radical way," as Neyrey claims, actually at the end of the story she is dismissed rather than included. The Samaritans say to her: "It is no longer because of what you said that we believe, for we have heard for ourselves, and we know that this is truly the Savior of the world" (4:42).

There is much to be celebrated in the story of the Samaritan woman, not the least of which is the depiction of a successful female evangelist. John has offered an entertaining retelling of an ancient literary convention and in doing so has provided sublime teaching about what his Christ has to offer humanity. The unnamed Samaritan woman understands Jesus, while Nicodemus, the elite teacher, fails to get the point, and the unexpected result provides satisfaction to those outside the academy and the institutional church. With all this material to celebrate, the imposition of skewed comparisons to a monolithic Judaism not only gets in the way but promotes an anti-Jewish agenda rather than a pro-female one. Thus, everyone loses.

The Misogynistic Morass: Part II, The Forbidding of Divorce

A second example from the "Jesus was a feminist who liberated women from misogynistic Judaism" school concerns the Gospels' statements on divorce. In this example, apologetic interests are more evident, since Christian women entrapped in loveless or abusive marriages often seek some means of remaining faithful to both the Bible and their own experience. The response to this situation follows the same mechanism seen above: identify whatever the problem is as Jewish, and then depict Jesus as contravening the bad Jewish teaching. In this particular manifestation of the anti-Jewish argument, Jesus's injunction against divorce is regarded, not as condemning women to a life of abuse, but as protecting them from shame and poverty. This interpretation ultimately causes both suffering for women and an anti-Jewish attitude for those who hear it.

According to Mark 10:2, Pharisees seek to test Jesus by asking him, "Is it lawful for a man to divorce his wife?" The question is odd in a first-century Jewish context. The ability to divorce was not contested, since it is presumed by Deuteronomy 24:1–4. The Deuteronomic point is confirmed in the next two verses as Jesus asks his interlocutors, "What did Moses command you?" They reply, "Moses allowed a man to write a certificate of dismissal and to divorce her" (Mark 10:3–4). Jesus then contravenes Deuteronomy's granting of divorce: "Because of your hardness of heart he wrote this commandment for you," he tells the Pharisees. "But from the beginning of creation, 'God made them male and female.' For this reason, a man shall leave his father and mother and be joined to his wife, and the two shall become one flesh. So they are no longer two, but one flesh. Therefore what God has joined together, let no person separate" (10:5–9). Jesus thus forbids divorce.

Paul confirms the point. Writing to the Corinthians, he states: "To the married I give this command—not I but the Lord—that the wife should not separate from her husband [Paul here adds his own pastoral point that if she does, she should remain single or else return to her husband], and that the husband should not divorce his wife" (1 Cor. 7:10–11). The fact that Paul included the addition concerning separations shows both the authenticity of Jesus's statement and the need for the church to address those who could not, for religious or personal reasons, abide by it. Jesus said "no divorce," and Paul adapted that saying for the needs of his congregation.

Like Paul, Matthew repeats the injunction against divorce and then loosens it. In this retelling, Jesus states, "Anyone who divorces his wife, except on the ground of unchastity [*porneia*, unsanctioned sexual behavior], causes her to commit adultery; and whoever marries a divorced woman commits adultery" (Matt. 5:31; in 19:9, Jesus repeats: "Whoever divorces his wife, except for unchastity [*porneia*], and marries another commits adultery"). Thus, Jesus of Nazareth forbade divorce, and he similarly forbade remarriage after divorce.

Perhaps for Jesus's first followers the injunctions were not onerous. If they believed that the kingdom of heaven was about to break into the earth, and that when it happened, they would all be like "angels in heaven" who "neither marry nor are given in marriage" (Mark 12:25), then there was no need to go through the legal system of obtaining a divorce. They also had the option of remaining married but living separately from their spouses. The wife of Zebedee follows her sons into the movement, but Zebedee stays by the Sea of Galilee with his boats (Matt. 20:20–22; 27:56); Joanna, the wife of Herod's steward, Chuza, enters the community, but Chuza makes no appearance (Luke 8:3); Peter certainly has a wife, since Jesus heals his mother-in-law (Mark 1:30–31), but the wife does not appear in the Gospels.

The option of remaining married but separated, with no opportunity for remarriage, may have satisfied a number of Jesus's immediate followers, and it may have been especially appealing to those in the early church who promoted a celibate way of life. But for many Christians today, the option is often impossible economically, spiritually, and personally. In very conservative Christian circles, abused wives are still being counseled to "submit graciously" to their husbands and to be obedient to them. Ephesians commands: "Wives, be subject to your husbands as you are to the Lord. For the husband is the head of the wife just as Christ is the head of the church" (5:22–23); Colossians mandates, "Wives, be subject to your husbands, as is fitting in the Lord" (3:18); 1 Peter orders wives to "accept the authority" of their husbands, "so that, even if some of them do not obey the word, they may be won over without a word by their wives' conduct" (3:1). These injunctions *should* not be read as granting the husbands a domineering role in the household; on the contrary, the husband is to serve his wife and to love her. But when the husband refuses to hold up his part of the injunction, the wife suffers. For women in abusive relationships, a way out becomes desperately needed.

The easiest way of subverting Jesus's command against divorce is to resort to the old standby, the "misogynistic Jewish setting." In this argument, Jesus is not condemning women to impossible marital situations, but rather engaging in social engineering for their welfare. One popular Evangelical introduction to the New Testament states, for example, that Jesus "condemned casual divorce practices in which men took advantage of their wives (Mt 19:4–6)."[19] Although neither Matthew nor Mark says anything about "casual divorce practices" or men taking advantage of their wives, the Evangelical argument does have a practical value. If it can be shown that Jesus prohibited divorce in order to protect wives from being tossed out in the street, where they would be forced into either prostitution or begging, then his commandment could be ignored today, given laws protecting women. Again, select rabbinic citations support the apologia. The standard citation is the Mishnah, *Gittin* 9:10: "The House of Hillel says [that he may divorce his wife] even if she has merely spoiled his food.... Rabbi Akiva says, [he may divorce her] even if he finds another woman more beautiful than she is." Therefore, conclude the scholars, Jesus's injunctions against divorce protect the rights of women by curtailing Jewish patriarchal privilege.

There was, however, no general rule in the first century concerning the grounds on which one could obtain a divorce. The statements in the Mishnah are prescriptive rather than descriptive: they propose what, in the rabbis' ideal world, people should or could do rather than describing what people did do. In the case of divorce, the argument in *Gittin* 9 concerns what some rabbis found to be legally possible, not necessarily what they considered to be desirable or even socially sanctioned. Further, this particular Mishnaic citation is just as truncated and therefore just as skewed as the one used to show how "Jews" regarded Samaritan women as impure. The Mishnaic passage actually begins with a citation from the school of Shammai, the rival to the Hillelite branch, which unequivocally states, "A man should not divorce his wife unless he has found her guilty of some unseemly conduct." This version of the Law derives from Deuteronomy 24:1: "Suppose a man enters into marriage with a woman, but she does not please him because he finds something objectionable about her, and so he writes her a certificate of divorce." Almost never adduced in the

Christian apologetic contexts is the Talmudic commentary on the Mishnah, *Gittin* 90b, which quotes Rabbi Eleazar as saying, "If a man divorces his wife, even the altar sheds tears." Also going unmentioned are the rabbinic and even prerabbinic practices concerning the *ketubah*, the marriage contract, which guaranteed women some financial stability in case of divorce.

The selective appeal to Jewish sources is indicated as well by what the commentators do not address, namely, that women could also divorce their husbands. In this case, the idea of protecting women's rights becomes irrelevant. According to Mark's version of the injunction, Jesus forbids women to divorce their husbands (as some Jewish women, such as in the Herodian household, did). Josephus remarks, likely for the benefit of his Roman patrician readers, that "it is only the man who is permitted by us" to divorce (*Antiquities* 15.529; Deut. 24:1 presumes the male privilege, and the rabbinic texts follow this presumption), despite evidence to the contrary that he presents from the Herodian household: the divorces of Herod's sister Salome from Costabarus,[20] of Berenice, the daughter of King Arippa I, from Polemo of Cilicia, and of her sister Drucilla from Azizus of Emesa.[21] Josephus also indicates that Herodias fully participated in the dissolution of her first marriage and her subsequent relationship with Herod Antipas.[22] In his autobiography, he even mentions that his first wife deserted him.[23] Yet scholars who comment on Jesus's divorce pronouncements are not likely to claim that by forbidding divorce Jesus was concerned with those poor, abandoned, albeit royal husbands, forced to turn to prostitution or begging.

Despite the well-intended efforts of contemporary biblical commentators, Jesus's comments on divorce were not attempts to protect wives economically. That rationale is an excuse for modern readers to ignore what he actually said. Jesus does not forbid divorce to protect women; he explains his commandment not by quoting a distressed wife but, as noted above, by quoting Genesis. The disciples certainly recognize the harshness of the ruling, for they correctly observe that if divorce is prohibited, "it is better not to marry" (Matt. 19:10).

All this is not to say that Jesus required husbands and wives to remain together. According to Luke 18:29, Jesus states, "Truly I tell you, there is no one who has left house *or wife* or brothers or parents or children, for the sake of the kingdom of God, who will not get back very much more in this age, and in the age to come eternal life." Although arguments have been made that the verse is Luke's own editorial contribution—the inclusion of the wife in the saying is absent from the parallel references in Mark 10:29–30 and Matthew 19:29—the point is consistent with what the Gospels indicate about those following Jesus: none of the men is explicitly accompanied by a wife; none of the women is explicitly accompanied by a husband.

This last point confirms the fact that Jesus is not somehow liberating women from an oppressive, misogynistic Judaism. Mary Magdalene, Joanna, Susanna, and many other women who accompanied Jesus (see Luke 8:1–3) all had freedom to travel and access to their own funds. The women who provided him support, such as Mary and Martha (see Luke 10:38–42; John 11–12), not only had access to their own funds but could also own their own homes. Women frequented synagogue gatherings and the Jerusalem Temple, and neither place had balconies where the women were to be relegated.

Women followed Jesus then, and women follow him now, for the same reasons that men did: because they found something in his person and his message that spoke to their hearts. Perhaps single women were especially attracted to Jesus's new family, for the women who accompany him are not embedded in family systems. Mary and Martha, Mary Magdalene, the Samaritan woman, the adulterous woman, Anna, the Syro-Phoenician, Joanna, Susanna, Mrs. Zebedee—none is accompanied by a husband. In Jesus's family, relationship was determined not by marriage or biology but by faith: his "mother and brothers and sisters" are those who follow divine will (Mark 3:31–35).

Christian women can find much that is inspirational in Jesus's story, but they do not have to construct a negative view of Judaism in order to do so. To claim that Jesus "liberated" women from a repressive Judaism by forbidding divorce and so protecting women's rights is facile, wrong, and bigoted. One could, but should not, make an equally ugly claim about Jesus, namely, that he is a misogynist who appoints no women to his inner circle; rather, he appreciates them only when they pay his bills (Luke 8:1–3), attend to his body by anointing it (Mark 14:3–9; Matt. 26:6–13; John 12:1–8; cf. Luke 7:36–50), remain silent and at his feet (Luke 10:38–49), and stay home when their husbands follow him (Luke 18:29). Again, it is about time Jews and Christians stopped bearing false witness against each other's traditions.

Good Samaritans, Bad Jews, and Impure Corpses

The parable of the good Samaritan, unique to Luke's Gospel (10:25–37), begins with a lawyer who, seeking to test Jesus, asks, "Teacher, what must I do to inherit eternal life?" In a marvelously Jewish fashion, Jesus answers the question with another question: "What is written in the Law? What do you read there?" The lawyer gives the right answer. Citing Deuteronomy 6:5, he responds, "You shall love the Lord your God with all your heart, and with all your soul, and with all your strength, and with all your mind." Then citing Leviticus 19:18, he adds, "and your neighbor as yourself." Jesus acknowledges the response: "You have given the right answer; do this, and you will live."

Had the lawyer been smart, he'd have left at that point. Instead, "wanting to justify himself," he asks Jesus, "Who is my neighbor?" Jesus then tells him the parable of the good Samaritan:

A man was going down from Jerusalem to Jericho, and fell into the hands of robbers, who stripped him, beat him, and went away, leaving him half-dead. Now by chance a priest was going down that road; and when he saw him, he passed by on the other side. So likewise a Levite, when he came to the place and saw him, passed by on the other side. But a Samaritan while traveling came near him; and when he saw him, he was moved with pity. He went to him and bandaged his wounds, having poured oil and wine on them. Then he put him on his own animal, brought him to an inn, and took care of him. The next day he took out two denarii [silver coins], gave them to the innkeeper, and said, "Take care of him; and when I come back, I will repay you whatever you spend."

Jesus then asks the lawyer, "Which of these, do you think, was neighbor to the man who fell among the robbers?" The lawyer, not able to voice the hated name "Samaritan," answers, "The one who showed him mercy." Jesus responds, "Go and do likewise."

Across the Christian world, an increasingly common interpretation of the parable runs as follows. The priest and the Levite avoid the man in the ditch because they fear corpse contamination. Should they touch a corpse, they'll become ritually impure, and they were forbidden to do so by Law.

The parable thus breaks through the Jewish system that would prioritize purity over compassion, ritual over responsibility. The impression given of Judaism is appalling.

Rarely are sources cited in support of this claim, although commentators occasionally adduce Leviticus 21:1–3 and Numbers 19:11. The former teaches: "The Lord said to Moses, 'Speak to the priests, the sons of Aaron, and say to them: no one shall defile himself for a dead person among his relatives, except for his nearest kin: his mother, his father, his son, his daughter, his brother; likewise, for a virgin sister, close to him because she has no husband, he may defile himself for her.'" The problems with applying Leviticus to the parable begin with the fact that the man in the ditch is not dead. Next, the levitical Law is to the "sons of Aaron," not the "sons of Levi," so the application of the verse to the second passerby, the Levite, is not direct. Third, at times Laws are in tension with each other. For example, the people are not to work on the Sabbath, but priests have to work on the Sabbath. If one is to love one's neighbor as oneself, then the priest and the Levite are required, legally, to aid the man in the ditch. The concern for the neighbor even extends to the neighbor's corpse; the Mishnah reads: "A high priest or a Nazirite may not contract uncleanness because of their dead [kindred], but they may contract uncleanness because of a neglected corpse" (*Nazir* 7:1). Then again, the Mishnah postdates the parable, and the priest and the Levite might not have followed Mishnaic teaching.

As for the common claim that the priest and the Levite walk by the man in the ditch lest, because of corpse impurity, they be unable to perform their duties in the Temple, again, the evidence fails. Numbers 19:11 states that "those who touch the dead body of any human being shall be unclean seven days," but that specific concern would not be applicable to the priest or, probably, the Levite in the parable. The priest is definitively not going to the Temple; the Greek makes clear that he is going "down" (*katabaino*) from Jerusalem to Jericho.

The appeal to purity Laws for understanding the parable—an appeal the parable never mentions and Luke's Gospel never adduces—actually masks the narrative's surprising implications. All commentators agree that the Samaritan's compassion is a surprise. But they fail to find the behavior of the priest and the Levite surprising as well. It is just as likely that Jesus's Jewish listeners would have expected the priest and the

Levite to behave compassionately toward the man in the ditch. Insiders who are *expected* to provide aid do not; outsiders who are not expected to show compassion do.

Burying the dead was and remains a major *mitzvah* (literally, "commandment," but the term carries the sense of "good deed") in Judaism. It is the only service a person can render to another without any anticipation of reciprocation. The book of Tobit, in the Deuterocanonical Writings (Old Testament Apocrypha), emphasizes the titular hero's risk of death by the Assyrians for his burying corpses (1:18–19; Tobit resembles a comedic Jewish *Antigone*). When, according to John 19, Joseph of Arimathea and Nicodemus prepared the corpse of Jesus, they would have become ritually impure, although commentators tend to ignore this point. At the tomb of Lazarus, visitors would have become impure. Again, commentators ignore the point. And well they should, because impurity was a fact of life. From the Babylonian Talmud, *Gittin* 61a states: "Our rabbis taught, 'Give sustenance to the poor of the non-Jews along with the poor of Israel. Visit the sick of the non-Jews along with the sick of Israel. Bury the dead of the non-Jews along with the dead of Israel. [Do all these things] because of the ways of peace.'"

The emphasis on corpse contamination to interpret the parable of the good Samaritan does not follow from Luke's appeal to Leviticus or Numbers, for Luke makes no such appeal. It does not follow from Luke's references to purity, for the text makes no such reference. It stems, instead, from the popular academic argument that Jesus offers a "challenge to the purity system of the first-century Jewish social world" and advocates "the politics of compassion in a social world dominated by the politics of purity."[24] The construct is already faulty, since purity and compassion are hardly mutually exclusive. The opposite of compassion is not purity, but lack of compassion. Nor do the Gospels themselves indicate that Jesus's "social world" is "dominated by the politics of purity." The very introduction of the term "politics," a term coded negatively these days (as in the expression "politically correct"), already taints the concept of "purity." Thus, Jewish ritual practices that are designed to sanctify the body and its environment become, for the Christian interpreter, a system of marginalization, ostracism, and oppression.

The negative depiction of Jewish practice continues in the interpretation of the parable. The next move is to claim that purity is an effect of birth: "According to one purity map of the time, priests and Levites (both hereditary classes) come first, followed by 'Israelites,' followed by 'converts,'" and so on.[25] The point is true in terms of Temple-based functions. However, it tells only half the story. Priests and Levites could be and often were ritually unclean (that's how they produced little priests and Levites, since ejaculation makes one unclean, and since the priestly and levitical lines are transmitted by the father, not the mother). Conversely, converts could easily be in a state of ritual purity: they were required to be so in order to offer sacrifice in the Temple.

Then, extending the bad argument even further, scholars define purity by social class with the "worst of the nonobservant" being "outcasts." These "outcasts" included "occupational groups such as tax collectors."[26] In today's New Testament sermons as well as publications, the phrase "outcasts and marginals" has taken on a life of its own, although almost never articulated are the details. From what have these individuals been cast out? Who cast them out? What prompted them to be cast out? Again, the model lacks evidentiary support. To enter the Jerusalem Temple, indeed to enter any temple in antiquity, one needed to be in a ritually pure state. That tax collector in Luke 18 who beat his breast and asked for mercy may have been a sinner, but he was a sinner in a ritually pure state. The Gospels themselves demonstrate the artificiality of the categories. If women, children, tax collectors, the poor, and sinners are "outcast," then their presence in the Temple is inexplicable. Finally, this configuration skews its own categories. People choose whether to be observant or not; the nonobservant therefore are not "outcast" but rather are individuals, such as the various tax collectors who receive such praise in the Gospels, who deliberately choose to remove themselves from the community.

What priest and Levite have in common is not concern for ritual purity but, as already noted, common descent. One cannot be a priest or a Levite unless one's father was a priest or a Levite. The parable could have spoken of "priest, Levite, and Israelite," and so evoked the three major divisions of Jews. But Jesus, in good parabolic fashion, leaps from the convention to associate a *Samaritan* with a priest and the Levite. According to 2 Kings 17, Samaritans are the descendants of the Mesopotamians settled in the Northern Kingdom, Israel, by the conquering Assyrian army in the late eighth century BCE. Having a rival temple on Mt. Gerizim, a rival priesthood, and a rival Torah (the Samaritan Pentateuch) with its own comparable purity code, the Samaritans were the proximate "other" to the Jews. The rivalry lies behind the Samaritan woman's words to Jesus at the well of Sychar: "Our ancestors worshiped on this mountain [Mt. Gerizim], but you say that the place where people must worship is in Jerusalem" (John 4:20). Jesus responds, "You worship what you do not know; we worship what we know, for salvation is from the Jews" (4:22). Thus, the parable of the good Samaritan makes the genealogical "outsider" prove neighbor; the genealogical insiders fail. Were Jesus a Samaritan, he would have told the parable of the good Jew.

Along with misreading the parable by imposing on it concerns regarding purity, priests and pastors frequently misread it by making the Samaritan representative of the "oppressed minority" or "outcast group." The priest and the Levite almost inevitably become the evil people of privilege; the Samaritan is the saint who is compassionate to those who oppress his group. Such interpretations can be very effective in proclaiming a gospel that sees all people in the divine image: the priest and the Levite are the "conservative Christians who condemn homosexuality" and the Samaritan is the gay man; the priest and the Levite are the rich and the Samaritan is the homeless woman; the priest and the Levite are citizens and the Samaritan is the "illegal immigrant." But as appealing as the message is, it is not quite what the parable conveys, for there is no reason for the majority (or privileged) group to think that the gay man or the homeless woman or the illegal immigrant would harbor hatred against them. To recover the punch of the parable, readers need to see the Samaritans and the Jews as mutually antagonistic.

Luke helps readers to see this enmity by placing the parable of the good Samaritan right after Jesus's own negative experiences in a Samaritan neighborhood. According to Luke 9:51–56, Jesus had attempted to find lodging in a Samaritan village, but the locals refused him "because his face was set toward Jerusalem." Reacting to this lack of hospitality, the apostles James and John propose that they call down fire from heaven to destroy the village. Jesus has to explain that dropping the first-century equivalent of napalm is not a good response to lack of hospitality. The Samaritans are not the oppressed minority or outcasts; they are rather the ones who reject Jesus, and in turn Jesus's followers reject them.

To understand the parable in theological terms, we need to be able to see the image of God in everyone, not just members of our group. To hear this parable in contemporary terms, we should think of ourselves as the person in the ditch, and then ask, "Is there anyone, from any group, about whom we'd rather die than acknowledge, 'She offered help' or 'He showed compassion'?" More, is there any group whose members might rather die than help us? If so, then we know how to find the modern equivalent for the Samaritan. To recognize the shock and the possibility of the parable in practical, political, and pastoral terms, we might translate its first-century geographical and religious concerns into our modern idiom. The ancient kingdom of Samaria is, today, the West Bank. Thus, translated across the centuries, the parable retains the same meaning. The man in the ditch is an Israeli Jew; a rabbi and a Jewish member of the Israeli Knesset fail to help the wounded man, but a member of Hamas shows him compassion. If that scenario could be imagined by anyone in the Middle East, perhaps there might be more hope for peace.

The Temple Domination System

Mark 12:41–44 finds Jesus seated opposite the Temple treasury, where he observes people contributing funds. "A poor widow came and put in two small copper coins (*lepta*), which are worth a penny (*kodrantes*) [1/64 of a denarius]. Then he called his disciples and said to them, 'Truly I tell you, this poor widow has put in more than all those who are contributing to the treasury. For all of them have contributed out of their abundance; but she out of her poverty has put in everything she had, all she had to live on.'"

Numerous interpretations of the story are possible. Elizabeth Struthers Malbon suggests that the woman anticipates Jesus's own sacrifice: she gives her whole life, as he will do.[27] Pheme Perkins recognizes in the widow's story "a remote parallel to the story of the poor widow and the prophet Elijah, who asks for her last bit of food" (1 Kings 17:8–16).[28] From Josephus's retelling of Samuel's story in his *Antiquities of the Jews* (6.7.4), an even closer connection may be drawn:

> But the prophet Samuel replied [to Saul], "God is not delighted with sacrifices, but with good and with righteous men, who are such as follow his will and his Laws, and never think that anything is well done by them but when they do it as God had commanded them: that he then looks upon himself as affronted, not when any one

does not sacrifice, but when any one appears to be disobedient to him.... Nor does he require so much as a sacrifice from them, or if they do, though it be a small offering, he more gladly accepts this from poverty, than those that come from the richest men."

From a pastoral perspective, the passage from the Gospel insists that the poor have dignity, and that the value of a contribution is based not on the monetary amount, but on the spirit with which is it given. From the rabbinic tradition, *Midrash Rabbah* on Leviticus records:

It happened to a woman who brought a handful of fine flour, and there was a priest who mocked her and said: "See what they sacrifice, what is there to eat of it? What is there to sacrifice of it?" The priest dreamt: "Do not mock her; it is as if she sacrificed her soul."

Earlier in Mark's Gospel, Jesus advises the rich man, "Go, sell what you own, and give to the poor, and you will have treasure in heaven" (10:21); the woman who puts her coins into the Temple treasury enacts what Jesus told the rich man to do. One might even see the story of the poor widow as praising the Temple system in that it provides opportunities for the poor as well as the rich, women as well as men, Pharisee as well as tax collector to participate.

Despite all these positive readings, the story of the widow's mite has come to epitomize the evils of the Temple "domination system," which is, in turn, seen as epitomizing the practice of Judaism. The arguments range from select readings of Mark's Gospel to vague generalities about how temples function as institutions. The result of the scholarship is a socially conscious Jesus who opposes exploitative institutional religion and uncaring governmental systems; it's a lovely image that fits numerous twenty-first-century concerns. It is also poorly supported by the New Testament evidence and likely to promote an anti-Jewish agenda. The ends do not justify the means.

From Mark's narrative, some scholars find textual support for the Temple "domination system" in the depiction of the scribes. Prior to the presentation of the poor widow, Mark records Jesus denouncing scribes who "devour widows' houses" (12:40). Consequently, readers make the interpretive choice of concluding that the Temple does what the scribes do. True, the scribes of 12:38–40 are not a pleasant bunch. But there is no reason to presume that all scribes exploited widows or that the widow in the Temple was merely a pawn in the hands of the elite. The scribes who devour widows' houses are not connected to the Temple. On the contrary, the Temple seems to be the one place these nasty folks are not found. Mark reads: "As he [Jesus] taught, he said, 'Beware of the scribes, who like to walk around in long robes, and to be greeted with respect in the marketplaces, and to have the best seats in the synagogues and places of honor at banquets! They devour widows' houses and for the sake of appearance say long prayers. They will receive the greater condemnation.'" Mark locates these rapacious scribes in synagogues and streets and at banquets, but not in the Temple. Readers might therefore choose to praise the widow in the Temple, who did not allow the scribes to take her money, but who instead dedicated it as she saw fit. The scribes take; the widow donates.

The Gospel's own narrative arrangement reinforces this separation of rapacious scribe and generous widow. According to Mark 12:38–40, when Jesus utters the "widows' houses" saying, he is in the process of teaching his disciples. The account of the widow's mite takes place in a different location; there, Jesus is by himself, sitting opposite the treasury, and he has to call his disciples to him to direct their attention to the widow.

In fact, the one scribe who does speak to Jesus in the Temple gets it more or less right when he praises Jesus for citing Deuteronomy 6:4–5 on loving God and Leviticus 19:18 on loving neighbor. To this *Temple* scribe, Jesus states, "You are not far from the kingdom of God" (Mark 12:34).

Finally, if Jesus is so appalled by the Temple's encouraging the widow to contribute all she has—even after he's been telling his followers for ten chapters to do the same—then his failure to stop her from donating her coins becomes inexplicable. To condemn a practice as unjust while allowing it to be perpetuated is hypocritical. If Jesus can turn over the tables of the money changers and drive people out of the Temple, as he did back in Mark 11, surely he could whisper something to a widow. I doubt the ritual-purity police would fault him.

Along with citing rapacious scribes, Jesus's disruption of Temple activities (Mark 11:15–17; Matt. 21:12–13; Luke 19:45–46; John 2:14–16) is often read as a protest against Temple exploitation. The footnote to John 2:15–16 in the *New Oxford Annotated Bible* (third edition) epitomizes this interpretive move: "A public demonstration against the materialism that had become part of Temple worship services. Jesus's indignation was not toward those engaged in worship, but those detracting from it."[29] However, sacrifice was part of Temple worship, so the facile distinction between "engaged in" and "detracting from" does not quite work. Nor was worship carried out in the place where the business was transacted (one might think, although the analogy is not exact, of a church gift shop as opposed to the main sanctuary). The annotations for the Gospel of Mark in the same volume correctly identify the setting of the "cleansing" as the "Court of the Gentiles" and note that "commerce, including money-changing, was necessary in connection with sacrifices and offerings in the semi-monetarized economy."[30] But these notes too impose an interpretation not clearly warranted. It is asserted that "'den of robbers' is better translated 'bandits' stronghold,' conveying more the original sense of Jeremiah [7:11] that the rulers plunder the people like bandits and then seek refuge in the Temple." Mark, however, speaks of both buyers and sellers and people carrying things, so the plundering model does not completely fit.

Mark's account, which likely provided the basis for Matthew and Luke and possibly also John, reads:

> He entered the Temple and began to drive out those who were selling and those who were buying in the Temple, and he overturned the tables of the money changers and the seats of those who sold doves. And he would not allow anyone to carry anything through the Temple. He was teaching and saying, "Is it not written, 'My house shall be called a house of prayer for all the nations'? But you have made it a den of robbers." (11:15–17)

The problem Mark depicts is not exploitation or domination, plundering or robbing; it is the act of "doing business" itself. John's version accentuates the point; in it Jesus rages, "Stop making my Father's house a marketplace!" (2:16).

Whatever Jesus himself did or did not do in the Temple, the Gospel evidence does not suggest that his concern was to demolish an exploitative system. Bruce Chilton offers a viable alternative: Caiaphas had moved the vendors previously located on the Mount of Olives into the Court of the Gentiles, and some Jews, including Jesus, objected.[31] The issue then is not economic exploitation, but a change in the way the sacrificial system was run.

Jesus may also have expected a divine verdict against the Temple leadership or the destruction of the Temple at the end of days, just as did other Jews of the time. Mark quotes him as saying to the disciples: "Do you see these great buildings? Not one stone will be left here upon another; all will be thrown down" (13:2). That part of the Temple complex, the Western (or Wailing) Wall, still remains suggests that the statement attributed to Jesus has some historical validity. Had the church invented the saying, it would not have created the discrepancy between the prediction and what actually remained of the Temple. Josephus (*War* 6.5.3) recounts that during the governorship of Albinus in 62 CE (four years before the first revolt against Rome), Jesus son of Ananius came to the Temple during the Festival of Sukkot and began to cry out daily:

> A voice from the east,
> a voice from the west,
> a voice from the four winds,
> a voice against Jerusalem and the Holy House,
> a voice against the bridegrooms and the brides,
> and a voice against this whole people!

Despite being beaten on the governor's orders, he continued his cries. Albinus, concluding that the man was insane, released him. This Jesus continued his dirge for the next seven years and five months, until a Roman siege engine killed him. This Jesus also reveals that a prophetic prediction against the Temple need not indicate that the prophet found the institution exploitative. Jesus ben Ananius saw the Temple as no more exploitative than he did brides and grooms—the import of his cry was not economic, but eschatological.

Turning from internal evidence of scribes and cleansing and external evidence of Temple protests, Marcus Borg attempts to make the case for the exploitative system on the basis of the general business carried out in the Temple. He states: "It is Jerusalem, of course, not as the center of Judaism, but Jerusalem as the center of the native domination system, of that economically exploitative and politically oppressive system that radically impoverished peasants and drove them to an existence of destitution and even desperation. Jesus is killed because of his passionate criticism of that system and his advocacy of the Kingdom of God."[32] In this caricature, the Temple is primarily an elitist institution that imposes impossible demands on the people from extreme taxation to ritual practices that only the wealthiest can afford. Such treatments do not provide much guidance for readers to distinguish between "center of Judaism" and "center of the native domination system." The claim that Jesus is killed because he critiqued the "native domination system" sounds as if Rome is removed from any economic exploitation; only the "native" system (i.e., the Jewish Temple) is to blame. Nor in the majority of such studies of the Jerusalem Temple is the evidence given to show how it "exploited the peasants."

The Temple was the national bank; it collected tithes, and Jewish men age twenty and older did pay the Temple tax. But there is little evidence that people chose not to participate because they rejected the concept of the Temple itself. Some first-century Jews rejected the legitimacy of the priesthood; the analogy to this view would be: "I respect the office (e.g., bishop, president, judge), but not the person who presently holds it." Others would have agreed with the claim, attributed to Jesus, that the Temple had become a "den of robbers" (Mark 11:17), that is, a place where robbers store their ill-gotten gains, not a place where robbers do their robbing. The analogy here is the view that putting money in the collection plate on Sunday erases any concerns about improper business dealings. Rabbinic documents written after the destruction of the Temple say nothing about ongoing systemic exploitation by the Temple or popular rejection of it. Temples in antiquity could be "domination systems," but it is by no means clear that Jesus thought the Jerusalem Temple was such a system.

Both the New Testament and external sources indicate that the Jewish population in general considered the Temple not a "domination system" but the "house of God." The Gospels and Acts depict Jesus, his family, and his followers as worshiping in the Temple and participating in the Temple sacrificial system. Apparently, they didn't get the message that it was a "domination system." Nor, apparently, did the father of John the Baptist, who served as a priest in the Temple, or Simeon and Anna, the two aged Jews who, according to Luke's Gospel, greet the baby Jesus there. Whether Zechariah, Simeon, and Anna are Luke's inventions or actual historical figures does not matter for this conclusion; at the very least, their stories suggest that the Third Evangelist did not find the Temple an exploitative domination system. Not only Jesus and his family (as recorded by Luke), but also hundreds of thousands, if not millions, of Jewish pilgrims flocked to the Temple on the three pilgrimage holidays of Pesach (Passover), Shavuot (Weeks), and Sukkot (Booths).

The book of Acts records that Jesus's initial followers continued to gather in the Temple, which became the setting for several miracles. Acts 3:1–10 records:

> Peter and John were going up to the Temple at the hour of prayer.... A man lame from birth was being carried in. People would lay him daily at the gate of the Temple called the Beautiful Gate so that he could ask for alms from those entering the Temple. When he saw Peter and John about to go into the Temple, he asked them for alms.... He [Peter] took him by the right hand and raised him up; and immediately his feet and ankles were made strong. Jumping up, he stood and began to walk, and he entered the Temple with them, walking and leaping and praising God. All the people ... were filled with wonder and amazement at what had happened to him.

The people marvel at the healing and the man praises God; no one kvetches about the domination system.

Peter and John and their fellow believers continue daily to teach about Jesus in the Temple (Acts 5:42), and Paul also participates in the Temple system. Encouraged by "James and all the elders," he goes through the "rite of purification" with four men who had put themselves under a Nazirite vow (Acts 21:23–26). Again, the New Testament does not understand the Temple as a "domination system" that exploits the poor or the sick.

The Mishnah records: "There were two chambers in the sanctuary. One was called chamber of the silent.... [There] devout men secretly gave charitable gifts, and the poor of good family received there secretly their sustenance" (*Shekalim* 5:6). The "chamber of the silent" seems particularly well named, since it is almost never mentioned by those scholars and pastors who see Jesus condemning the Temple domination system.

According to Josephus, the mad emperor Caligula, who took himself to be divine and desired that everyone show their agreement with this idea by worshiping him, "extended his impiety as far as the Jews" by sending his officer Petronius with an army to Jerusalem to place his statues in the Temple. His orders were that "in case the Jews would not admit them, he should slay those that opposed it, and carry all the rest into captivity."[33] Josephus then records:

> The Jews got together in great numbers with their wives and children ... and begged Petronius first for their Laws, and in the next place, for themselves. And when they insisted on their Law and the custom of their country, and how it was not only not permitted for them to make either an image of God or indeed any man and put it in any lesser part of the country, much less in the Temple itself, Petronius replied, "And am I not also," said he, "bound to keep the laws of my own lord? For if I transgress his orders and spare you, I will perish ... for I am under command as much as you.... Will you then make war against Caesar?" The Jews said, "We offer sacrifices twice a day for Caesar and for the Roman people, but if he would place the images among them, he must first sacrifice the whole Jewish nation."

Petronius then intervened, as did King Agrippa I, Herod the Great's grandson and a friend of Caligula. Had the emperor not been assassinated, the statues would have been erected, Petronius would have been executed, and the revolt against Rome would have begun twenty years earlier. The passion of the people in this situation does not sound like the response of those broken by a "domination system."

When the first revolt against Rome did break out in 66 and the Zealot faction gained control of Jerusalem, they replaced the high priest but did not destroy the cult (although they did burn the tax records). During the second revolt against Rome (132–35), the Jewish leader bar Kokhba put images of the Temple on his coinage.

All this is not to say that all priests were saints or all Temple functionaries honest. Josephus (*Antiquities* 20.9.2–4) records, for example, that Ananias, the high priest during the governorship of Albinus (62), not only hoarded money given to the Temple but also took the priestly tithes from the threshing floors and so deprived these priests of their food. The Tosefta records that Abba Saul ben Botnit said in the name of Abba Jose ben Hanin: "Woe is me because of the house of Boethus; woe is me because of their staves [with which they beat the people]! Woe is me because of the house of Kathros; woe is me because of their pens [with which they wrote their evil decrees]! Woe is me because of the house of Ishmael the son of Phabi; woe is me because of their fists! For they are high priests and their sons are Temple treasurers and their sons-in-law are trustees and their servants beat the people with staves!" (*Menachot* 13:21; see also the Talmud *Pesachim* 57a). One might compare contemporary political discourse: the holders of certain offices are corrupt, but the offices themselves remain respected. The exploitation by some does not a "domination system" make.

Nevertheless, a number of scholars are wont to conclude that if it's the Temple, it's bad. It is a system that requires those who can afford it the least to give the most, that enforces unbearable purity legislation on the masses, that establishes and maintains an elitism that spreads throughout the entire Jewish world. Pity then the poor widow, compelled by this horrific, exploitative system that coerces her to spend her last coins. The Temple is no better than the televangelism program that tells senior citizens to sign over their Social Security checks to Jesus, in care of the well-dressed, well-coiffed, well-heeled Reverend Billy Bob.

Biblical scholars choose their reading of the story of the widow in the Temple in order to condemn the Temple as a domination system and then to divorce Jesus from it. Instead of recognizing the Temple as a place where even the poorest woman could feel that she was making a contribution, a place that the Jewish population risked their lives to preserve, and a place where the earliest followers of Jesus worshiped, academics, priests, and pastors make it a place that exploits the widow, oppresses the peasants, and steals from the population. This is all a mite strange, and a mite disturbing.

"Only to the Lost Sheep of the House of Israel"

Along with classifying Jewish purity practices and the Temple system as creating and reinforcing social divisions, scholars today often see Jewish attitudes as ethnocentric: insiders are welcome; outsiders are despised. For example, in its *The Jewish People and Their Sacred Scriptures in the Christian Bible*, the Pontifical Biblical Commission states: "The Church is conscious of being given a universal horizon. The reign of God is no longer confined to Israel alone, but is open to all, including the pagans, with a place of honor for the poor and oppressed." Thus, in comparison to Jewish exclusivity, the church is the universal system that erases difference and welcomes everyone.

Whether intended or not, the classifications serve an apologetic purpose. The church, commanded to "make disciples [or Gentiles] of all nations" and to baptize them "in the name of the Father and of the Son and of the Holy Spirit" (Matt. 28:19), becomes the universal model, despite the fact that it requires all to come under its umbrella. As Cyprian, a North African church father (d. 258), stated in his *On the Unity of the Catholic Church:* "You cannot have God for your Father unless you have the Church for your mother." Judaism, which on the whole did not think that Gentiles needed to become Jews in order to be in a right relationship with God, comes to represent exclusivity and ethnocentrism.

The evidence for such claims ranges from the contradictory to the incredible. Peter, having received a divine commission to baptize the gentile centurion Cornelius, announces, "You yourselves know that it is unlawful for a Jew to associate with [or hire himself out to, Luke 15:15] or to visit a Gentile" (Acts 10:28). The statement contradicts what Luke's own corpus teaches. Back in chapter 7 of the Gospel, Luke recounts how the "Jewish elders" asked Jesus to help another centurion with the sick servant, given that "he loves our people, and it is he who built our synagogue for us" (7:4). Clearly, some association has taken place. When Jesus teaches in the "Court of the Gentiles," the very setting indicates that Jews and Gentiles will be in close proximity.

Later, in Acts 16, Luke introduces readers to Timothy, child of a Jewish mother and a gentile father. There is no suggestion that their relationship was "forbidden" (although the grandmother may have wondered why her daughter could not find a nice Jewish boy). If association between Jews and Gentiles were forbidden, then the presence of God-fearers in synagogues becomes incomprehensible and Nicolaus, the proselyte from Antioch introduced in Acts 6 as one of the seven Hellenists appointed to wait tables, could not have existed. There is no Law forbidding contact between Jews and Gentiles; there is no Law forbidding Jews to work for Gentiles. Indeed, the royal house of Adiabene (the area now known as

Kurdish Iraq, Armenia, and northern Iran) is converted when a Jewish merchant describes to the queen mother the traditions of Judaism (*Antiquities* 20.2.1–5).

The Jewish system was, however, "ethnocentric." Jews could go farther into the Temple than Gentiles; Jews had certain roles in the synagogue that Gentiles could not play. But it was no more exclusivist than the church, which restricted its roles to Christians. Jews welcomed converts, as did the church.

Ironically, when Jews in the New Testament are seen as wanting to preserve their own traditions, of diet and circumcision, of synagogue practice and forms of worship, Christian readers are sometimes inclined to regard these efforts as retrograde or exclusive. Today, when any other ethnic or religious group seeks to maintain its own integrity despite cultural pressures to assimilate, it is regarded positively as promoting identity, resisting colonialism, and celebrating its heritage.

The Jewish texts *Seder Eliyyahu Rabbah* and *Seder Eliyyahu Zuta* insist: "The Prophet Elijah said, 'I call heaven and earth to witness that whether it be Jew or Gentile, man or woman, manservant or maidservant, the Holy Spirit will suffuse each in proportion to the deeds he or she performs.'" The proclamation resembles Paul's insistence that "there is no longer Jew or Greek, there is no longer slave or free, there is no longer male and female … in Christ Jesus" (Gal. 3:28). Whereas the synagogue's statement keeps all six categories and Paul's seeks to erase them, the point that in the divine purview distinctions in gender, religion, ethnicity, and class do not matter is one that both groups can affirm.

The Judenrein *New Testament*

Whether John's Gospel is "anti-Jewish" or not, as the previous chapter notes, is not the correct question. Some readers see it as anti-Jewish; others do not. However, because the text has been interpreted in an anti-Jewish manner, some scholars have attempted to remove the prompts that lead to anti-Jewish readings by eliminating Jews from the narrative. In the *Bauer-Arndt-Gingrich Lexicon for New Testament Greek (Koine)*, the editor, Frederick Danker, suggests in the entry for *Ioudaios*, the Greek term usually translated "Jew," that "incalculable harm has been caused by simply glossing *Ioudaios* with 'Jew,' for many readers or auditors of Bible translations do not practice the historical judgment necessary to distinguish between circumstances and events of ancient time and contemporary ethnic-religious-social realities, with the result that anti-Judaism in the modern sense of the term is needlessly fostered through biblical texts."[34] Philip Esler, in his recent commentary on Paul's Letter to the Romans, makes a related point: using "Jew" or "Jewish" "encourages the anti-Semitic notion of 'the eternal Jew' who, it is alleged, killed Christ and is still around, to be persecuted if possible."[35] Therefore, these and other scholars suggest that, in most if not all New Testament uses, *Ioudaios* should be translated "Judean," and the term should be understood as referring to the group rooted in Judea.

The Jew is replaced with the Judean, and thus we have a *Judenrein* ("Jew-free") text, a text purified of Jews. Complementing this erasure, scholars then proclaim that Jesus is neither Jew nor even Judean, but Galilean. As John H. Elliott put it in his "call to arms" at the 2004 plenary lecture to the Catholic Biblical Association in the paper entitled "Jesus Was Neither a 'Jew' nor a 'Christian'": "Let us entirely avoid the name 'Jew' or the term 'Judaism' when speaking of the people defined by Temple and Torah in the first three centuries of the common era."[36]

Before delineating my concerns with the de-Judification of John's Gospel, I begin, in good "Jewish" fashion, with a story. A few years ago I was invited to a Methodist-affiliated university in one of the southern states to give a lecture on the New Testament and Judaism. The school had obtained a grant to introduce students to Jews and Judaism; the goal was entirely commendable. I opened the talk by noting that various churches over the past few decades have manifested grace in repenting from their sins of anti-Judaism and in seeking a greater knowledge of Jesus within his Jewish context. I went on to mention how important it is to see Jesus as a Jew, given contemporary politics. Specifically, I was concerned about Islamists who have adopted the anti-Judaism of which the church has repented.

As I began the talk, I noticed out of the corner of my eye, far on the left in the front row, a young bald man with his hand raised. I assumed that he was unfamiliar with professional lecture etiquette and told him that we'd have plenty of time for questions and answers later. I returned to my notes but had not uttered more than a few words, when he called out, "You're not saying Jesus was a Jew, are you?" Now my first thought was,

"Hello? Yes, that's exactly what I'm saying." Several people near him told him to hush, but he continued: "What about the Idumaeans? What about the Khazars? What about the Ashkenazim?"

My host, who was on the other side of the auditorium, got up to ask the man to leave. While this was happening, I stepped away from the podium and sought a better look. As I put my glasses on, I noticed what I had not seen previously. First, I saw that the man was not just bald—his head was shaved. Then I noticed that he was wearing jackboots. Then I saw the swastika on his jacket. And then it occurred to me that he was not raising his hand; he was doing a Nazi salute. This young man is part of the new breed of the old hatred. Like many major German New Testament scholars of the Nazi era—including people whose works are still being read in New Testament studies—he believes that Jesus was Aryan. It is the Aryan Christian who is heir to the biblical tradition, not the Jew (and heaven knows, certainly not anyone who is not white). The Idumaeans, for example, were a gentile population converted to Judaism a century prior to Jesus.

My point—the need for the church to recover Jesus as a Jew—was made that evening in a way I neither anticipated nor desired. Thus, my agenda in this discussion of how to translate the Gospel of John's use of the term *Ioudaios* is more than a historical-critical exercise; it is also driven by political considerations.

The translation of *Ioudaios* as "Judean" does have some historical credibility. As Robert Doran argues in his forthcoming commentary on 2 Maccabees: "It is tempting to translate *Ioudaios* as 'Judean,' as this word has the connotation of one from the land of Judea and it reflects the Ptolemaic practice of identifying non-citizens by their point of origin, whether Macedonian, Lycian, Athenian or Judean, even if sometimes the original city-state no longer existed and those so designated had lived in Egypt for generations."[37] Fair enough.

However, the geographical designation downplays the significant shift in Jewish thought at least by the second century BCE, if not earlier, when the "ethnic-geographical self-definition [of Judean] was supplemented by religious (or 'cultural') and political definitions, because it was only in this period that the Judean *ethnos* opened itself to the incorporation of outsiders."[38] Such evidence includes, for example, Josephus's use of *Ioudaios* to describe the converted members of the royal house of Adiabene (*Antiquities*

20.38–39); it includes 2 Maccabees 6:6, which states that "people could neither keep the Sabbath, nor observe the festivals of their ancestors, nor so much as confess themselves to be *Ioudaioi*." In these cases, the ethnic designation does not apply very well, whereas the "religious" one fits perfectly. The term *Ioudaismos* also first appears in 2 Maccabees (2:21; 8:1; 14:38); Cohen suggests that it might be translated as "Judeanness," but the term must be more than just an ethnic or geographical marker.[39] The better translation would be "Judaism."

The *Bauer-Arndt-Gingrich Lexicon*, although promoting the translation "Judean," observes that *Ioudaios* includes "one who identifies with beliefs, rites, and customs of adherents of Israel's Mosaic and prophetic tradition." The translation "Judean" will not convey to modern readers anything regarding practice or belief. The translation "Jew," however, signals a number of aspects of Jesus's behavior and that of other "Jews," whether Judean, Galilean, or from the Diaspora: circumcision, wearing *tzitzit*, keeping kosher, calling God "father," attending synagogue gatherings, reading Torah and Prophets, knowing that they are neither Gentiles nor Samaritans, honoring the Sabbath, and celebrating the Passover. All these, and much more, are markers also of traditional Jews today. Continuity outweighs the discontinuity. To translate the New Testament term as "Judean" rather than "Jew" will lose, for today's readers, the specific sense of religious affiliation and religious practice. Doran concludes, correctly: "In modern English 'Judean' retains only the connotation of geographical origin, without maintaining the religious and cultural significance that a point-of-origin term would have retained in antiquity. I have therefore opted to keep the traditional translation," that is, "Jew."

Elliott, who prefers "Judean," argues from a social-science perspective, and several of his arguments have merit. For example, the terms "Judean" and "Galilean" have different connotations with regard to regional loyalties and some cultural concerns, just as in the United States "Yankee" and "southerner" have different connotations. However, rather than just claiming Jesus is a Galilean as opposed to a Judean and so losing any connection to the term "Jew," preferable is to see Jesus as a "Galilean Jew" and Josephus as a "Judean Jew." The "both/and" model is clearer to modern readers than the "either/or."

Elliott is also correct that, according to the New Testament, Jesus's primary designations are "Israelite" and "Galilean." He observes, "Outsiders used the term *Ioudaios*; insiders designated themselves as 'Israel.'"[40] That point still holds today: in worship contexts, Jews today refer to themselves as "Israel." However, in communication with non-Jews (and note the term "non-Jews"), they use the term "Jew." The scholar has a choice of using the insider identification or the outsider terminology, and when it comes to a description of Jesus and his contemporaries today, neither "Israelite" nor "Galilean" is a helpful primary designation for Jesus, for neither the scholars nor the readers are insiders. To Elliott, Jesus would have identified himself as a "Jew," and were Elliott living in the first century, he would have seen Jesus as such. The Samaritan woman who calls Jesus a *Ioudaios* (John 4:9) was not thinking "Judean," but rather "Jew." Elliott suggests that she would have perceived his movement northward, back to Galilee from Judea, and so, by implication, she is suggesting that she thinks he is from Judea, but the Gospel doesn't suggest that. On the contrary, Jesus is not on the move but sitting down when she encounters him.

Elliott also draws a distinction between Jews today and whatever "Jew" or "Judaism" meant in the first century. He states, again correctly: "Jesus was neither a 'Jew' nor a 'Christian' in the sense that these terms are used in ordinary discourse today" and so concludes that to call Jesus a "Jew" would be "anachronistic and misleading." As another recent work concludes: "From a religious point of view, all modern Jews belong to traditions developed largely after the time of Jesus and compiled in the Babylonian Talmud (sixth century CE)."[41] To speak of Jews, then, means to speak of a post-Talmudic phenomenon.

The question of continuity and separation presents the expected problems of determining what to emphasize and at what point the break occurs. The argument about what is "anachronistic and misleading" begs the question: anachronistic and misleading to whom? Christian teaching changed because of the Council of Nicea in 325 and the Council of Chalcedon in 451. Catholic teaching, and so Catholic attitudes, have changed since Vatican II, for the liturgy is now in the vernacular rather than in Latin, the College of Cardinals has substantial representation from Asia and Africa, the faithful no longer pray for the "perfidious Jews," and in some parishes altar girls can be found serving at the Mass. But scholars should have no difficulty calling Pope Pius XII or Francis of Assisi Catholic. Nor should they have difficulty calling those followers of the Way described by Luke in Acts 11 "Christian," for, as Luke tells us, the name

"Christian" was first applied to this group. So too Jews see continuity from the Bible to the Maccabees to the Mishnah to Maimonides to my synagogue today, as the *siddur*, the prayer book of the synagogue, indicates on almost every page. The connections outweigh the distinctions.

Even less convincing is the social-science argument that seeks to restrict the use of the term "Jew" to central European Jews (called Ashkenazi Jews), who, this argument claims, "largely trace their origin to Turkic and Iranian ancestors who comprised the Khazar Empire and converted to Judaism in the eighth century CE." Thus, this approach concludes, "given the sixth-century CE [Talmudic] origin of all forms of contemporary Jewish religion, and given the U.S. experience of Jews based largely on central European Jews, themselves originating from eighth-century CE converts, it would be quite anachronistic to identify any modern Jews with the 'Judeans' mentioned in John's Gospel or the rest of the New Testament."[42] On the Internet, the major proponent of this view, Bruce Malina, extends his argument to claim

> an even greater anachronistic and ethnocentric agenda for Central European Jews ("Ashkenazi") for their claiming the name "Jew." They retroject the label even to the patriarch Abraham, now the mythological founder of 5th–6th century Talmudic Jewishness. Again, the fact is that most of those Central European Jews and hence most U.S. Jews from Central Europe are descended from Khazars, a people who accepted the Jewish religion in the 8th century AD.... Thus most U.S. Jews are essentially Khazar Americans rather than "Jewish" Americans. The same is true of the majority of people living in the Jewish State.[43]

Malina's point about the retrojection of the term "Jew" to Abraham is correct. Abraham is no more the first "Jew" than he is the first "Christian" or the first "Muslim." All three terms are anachronistically applied to him, for all three developed after his time. The rest of his claims, however, are either overstated or irrelevant. In terms of ethnicity, his focus eliminates Sephardic Jews in Italy and Greece, Hamburg and Amsterdam, Tunisia and Spain, Yemen and Syria, and of course Iraq, where the Babylonian Talmud was compiled, let alone those who remained in Israel/Palestine. The focus on Khazars ignores the Karaites, a Jewish movement that is not based on the Talmud and that is, albeit in small numbers, still around today. As for the argument that all Jews are descended from the Khazars, this argument presumes that those Jews responsible for the conversion then disappeared. Ironically, whereas Malina argues for using "insider" language to identify Jesus not as a Judean but as an Israelite or Galilean, here he uses outsider language—"Khazar Americans"—to identify Jews. The Khazar Web site itself, which Malina cites, offers a variety of perspectives on the origin of eastern European Jews; it also includes references to South Asian and sub-Saharan African Jews.[44] The site mentions how it "gathers available evidence on genetics and shows that Ashkenazi Jews have substantial roots in the Middle East."

The historical aspects of this argument are flawed; its political implications are worse. The argument that Jesus is not a Jew but a Galilean and then the severing of Jews today from any connection to the people of Israel in the late Second Temple period lead to the inevitable conclusion that Jews have no connection—historically, ethnically, spiritually—to the land of Israel. Jesus the Jew becomes Jesus the Galilean, and Jesus the Galilean becomes Jesus the Palestinian.

And whereas Danker and Esler imagine a monolithic modern reader, incapable of seeing both continuity and discontinuity between Jews of the first century and Jews today, there is some evidence of what modern readers are capable of concluding. And so I return, reluctantly, to that night I encountered the neo-Nazi. The argument that Jesus should be called a "Galilean" rather than a "Judean" because it will eliminate anti-Semitism in fact has the opposite effect. The argument is featured on the Web sites of such hate groups as Stormfront White Pride, the New Covenant Church of God, the Christian Separatist Church Society, Jew Watch, the Zundelsite, and so on. Once Jesus is not a Jew or a Judean, but a Galilean, it is also an easy step to make him an Aryan. So much for the elimination of anti-Semitism by means of changing vocabulary.

The discussion to this point has followed those who work in social-scientific arenas. But the translation and interpretation of texts is not primarily a science; it is an art, and it requires some sensitivity to aesthetics. To translate the New Testament uses of *Ioudaios* as anything but "Jew" loses the Evangelists' art. The *Ioudaioi* at the end of Matthew—the one and only time that the narrator uses the term as a group designation—who insist that the disciples stole Jesus's body are surely to be understood not as "Judeans" but as "Jews." This is Matthew's indication of the distinction between *ekklesia* (the church) and the *Ioudaioi* (the Jews). Nor did the Gospel writers think of Jesus only as "king of the Judeans" when they recorded the words on the *titulus*, the inscription tacked onto the cross.

Jesus Wept

Viewing Jews and Judaism in terms of a burdensome Law, a militaristic messianic speculation, an intense misogyny, an obsession with purity, a Temple domination system, and a pervasive xenophobia will misconstrue Jesus's context and so both misunderstand his message and foster anti-Judaism. Removing Jews from the New Testament does a disservice to Jews, Jesus, church, and synagogue.

By all means, scholars should indicate that first-century *Judaisms* are not the same as twenty-first-century ones. By all means, scholars should engage in linguistic rigor. But by all means, as well, when we write or teach, we might think about that young man with the swastika and the jackboots. What sins of commission have we made in the classroom, in the pulpit, in the religious education bulletin that could have made his move to Nazi ideology easier? And what sins of omission might we have committed such that we failed to keep him on the path of love rather than of hate?

The task of biblical scholarship is not merely one of arid academic exercise. It is one with potential import for politics, for justice, and for the spirit. The various classifications noted in this chapter of a "bad" Judaism have spread, mostly in a crass, unnuanced form, from the classroom and the professional journal to the pew and Bible study. Scholars who would be appalled to be thought of as anti-Jewish wind up spreading anti-Jewish views among themselves, to the rest of academia, and to the broader Christian world beyond the ivory tower. Again, Jesus wept.

FIVE

With Friends Like These ...

The negative images of Judaism—legalistic, purity obsessed, Temple dominated, bellicose, greedy, anything distasteful to Christians—appear not only in biblical interpretation but also in theological education, from theology to pastoral care. Moreover, they span the globe. Anti-Jewish teachings at the start of the twenty-first century should have been corrected by several decades of good biblical scholarship and several decades of churches expressing regret for past prejudice. They should have been stopped by the rise of various interpretive methods, from feminist studies to postcolonialism to autobiographical approaches, which are designed to show how all readings have subjective elements and how all readings inevitably promote certain agendas. Even the recent interest in multiculturalism should have at least chipped away at the negative stereotyping of particular Jewish practices, if not encouraged respect for them.

Alas, what should have been is not what is. As our discussion turns from biblical studies in the Western academy and classroom to liberation theology and postcolonial interpretation, it finds Christian education, broadly construed, still marked by anti-Judaism. But in these settings, the bad scholarship has mutated into a particularly vicious disease. Negative comments about Jews and Judaism become the means of showing how Jesus is in solidarity with the poor, with women, with the Palestinian population, and with any group oppressed by "the West." The goals of such readings are commendable; the means are deplorable.

Liberation Theology

"Liberation theology" is the rubric under which individuals, reflecting on (usually personal) experiences of systemic evil—racism, colonialism, poverty, and the host of human sins—turn to their religious tradition's resources to find words of hope and catalysts for change. In its Christian form, liberation theology appeals to Jesus as the one who preaches good news to the poor and proclaims the release of captives. Beginning with the presupposition that Jesus redeems from oppression, liberation theologians turn to the two pressing questions, "Redeems how?" and "Redeems from what?" The answers are found in the social realm: Jesus redeems from political and economic, sexual and racial oppression by challenging any force that represses human wholeness. So far, so good. But then come the details. Jesus needs to redeem from something *tangible;* the theology has to have a practical payoff. It's not enough to discuss how Jesus redeems from "sin" and "death" when children are starving and there is no clean water or access to health care. Thus, the liberation theologian looks at redemption in practical terms, and the focus becomes not sacraments and soteriology, but empire and economics.

When the theologians turn to the Gospels, they find not only Jesus the liberator, but also the "oppressor." In much liberation-theological interpretation, however, the oppressor is seen not as Roman imperialism or colonialism. Taking their cues from the New Testament and nurtured by centuries of the church's anti-Jewish teaching, these theologians instead find Judaism and Jews to epitomize systemic evil. In the New Testament itself, Jesus has little to say directly about the Roman Empire, despite the fact that he dies as a political criminal on a Roman cross. The Gospels had already begun to shift the blame for Jesus's death from Rome to the Jewish leadership: poor Pilate emerges more as a dupe manipulated by the crowds who call for Jesus's blood to be on them (Matt. 27:25) and by the high priest who threatens him with the charge of treason if he fails to execute the (pretend) king (John 19:12). First Thessalonians 2 speaks not of the Romans but of "the Jews, who killed the Lord Jesus"; the speeches in Acts blame the Jews for the cross, not the Romans. Jesus's controversies are not with Pilate but with the Pharisees or, in John's Gospel, the Jews; his major act of protest was not against Pilate in Caesarea, but against the Temple in Jerusalem. Thus, liberation theology sees the oppressor as Pharisaism, the Jewish priesthood, or, more often, just "Judaism" itself—its laws, beliefs, traditions, and practices. The fathers of liberation theology, themselves influenced by the standard academic presentations of "bad" Judaism, recast some of the standard anti-Jewish materials into a liberation-theological mode.[1]

In effect, much of the anti-Judaism found globally today is substantially a colonial product. Theologians and biblical scholars from Africa and Asia, seeking to make their work relevant to their own countries and congregations, absorb from Western academic scholarship anti-Jewish impressions. Writing from their own social locations, they allow the anti-Jewish stereotypes to inform their understanding of Jesus, Paul, Mary and Martha, and the other figures from the New Testament whom they establish as role models. Next, such works are then published by Western presses and disseminated around the globe. In seminary libraries in Manila and Tokyo, Lagos and Soweto, such works then threaten to poison the next generations.

The poison had already begun in the founding documents of liberation theology. One of the fathers of the movement, Gustavo Gutiérrez, stated in 1973 in an Orbis Books publication that the "infidelities of the Jewish people made the Old Covenant invalid."[2] Leonardo Boff observed in an Orbis Books publication in 1987: "In the world as Jesus found it, human beings were ... under the yoke of absolutization of religion, of tradition, and of the law. Religion was no longer the way in which human beings expressed their own openness to God. It had crystallized and stagnated in a world of its own, a world of rites and sacrifice. Pharisees had a morbid conception of their God."[3] This rhetoric should sound familiar: it echoes standard New Testament scholarship of the 1970s. Yet these works, classics in their field, are still being assigned to students of theology and still being read across the globe. In their wake comes anti-Judaism. I have myself recommended these early works to my students in part because there is much of value in what Gutiérrez and Boff have to say, and I would not want to throw out the baby with the bathwater. But, sadly, when I ask my students whether they have any critique of the theology itself, not all notice the anti-Jewish rhetoric.

Sadly as well, these anti-Jewish obscenities are still produced by those who in fact know better. The presses that publish such materials—the World Council of Churches (WCC) press in Geneva; Fortress Press, which is connected to the Evangelical Lutheran Church of America; the Catholic (Maryknoll, NY) Orbis Books, and so on—are all affiliated with groups that have splendid statements on Jewish-Christian relations.[4] But the evil of anti-Jewish biblical and theological interpretation is so pernicious, so omnipresent, that it affects even those who seek its eradication. Just as racism and sexism and the host of other human sins affect us all, so too anti-Judaism is promoted even by the best of institutions, the most progressive of theologians, and the most sensitive of those who work for justice and peace.

The World Council of Churches

The World Council of Churches presents an excellent example of the problem. This organization sponsors a number of laudatory programs. A focus on HIV-AIDS education and prevention, efforts on behalf of refugees, attention to the needs of women and children, and work at reconciling oppressors and the oppressed are just a few of its entirely commendable efforts. Further, the WCC models a concern for the integrity of diverse cultures with which it works, and it does not expect all of Christianity to fit into one mold. On the interfaith front, the WCC has published several progressive statements on Jesus in his Jewish context, the relationship between anti-Semitism and the Holocaust, and the need for interfaith conversation. Its Web site even posts the report of the Christian Peacemaker Teams' Steering Committee entitled "A Letter to Our Churches About Anti-Semitism." This courageous document does not deny that the member churches of the organization have been guilty of perpetuating anti-Semitic ideas but rather acknowledges that within their organization are

> many adherents who use theological arguments to support their anti-Semitism. We have encountered simplistic characterizations of the Hebrew Bible as vengeful and ungraceful, beliefs that Jesus' criticisms of some Jewish leaders of his day apply to all Jews then and now, and Christian Zionism, in which Jews become pawns with magical power in an end-times drama.[5]

Yet the WCC, along with Orbis Books, Fortress Press, numerous university presses, and others, also distributes the "teaching of contempt" for Judaism and Jews.[6] The organization's formal pronouncements stand in contradiction to what its press publishes and what its officers and clergy write.

My search through the WCC publication record was somewhat serendipitous. For the August 2005 meeting of the International Council of

Christians and Jews (ICCJ), I was invited to present a plenary speech. Because the meeting's theme was "globalization" and because the opening plenary was to be delivered by the president of the WCC, I chose to explore the WCC's record on Jewish-Christian relations by looking at both its official statements and its publications. In a search of approximately ninety publications available in the Vanderbilt Divinity School library, I found much to celebrate. I also found new manifestations of old problems: a view of Judaism not only as misogynistic but also as filled with "taboos," particularly uninformed understandings of rabbinic literature, a version of multiculturalism that praises all distinct practices except for those associated with Judaism, and a theology that intimates the ancient heresy known as Marcionism by distinguishing the God of Judaism from the God of Jesus.

In this search, I deliberately avoided anything concerning the Middle East. In February 2005, the WCC praised the Presbyterian Church USA for its decision to put economic pressure on Israel and hailed its "process of phased, selective divestment from multinational corporations involved in the occupation." It also urged its 346 other member churches—which adds up to about 500 million Protestant and Eastern Orthodox Christians in approximately 120 countries—to consider doing the same. The targeted companies make equipment the Israeli army used to demolish homes belonging to the families of homicide bombers and by the Israeli government both to build what the churches consider illegal settlements and to construct the "security fence" designed to block off terrorist access to Israel. The WCC insisted, as have all the churches that recommend divestment, that its "criticism of the policies of the Israeli government is not in itself anti-Jewish."

Criticism of Israeli policy need not indicate an anti-Jewish motivation. However, I include Palestinian liberation-theological writings in this chapter because the effect of this work is much the same as the effect of the writings from the WCC publications: Jesus becomes divorced from Jews and Judaism, and the impression given is that "the Jews" in the biblical account who persecuted Jesus and his followers become associated with the Israeli army. If the goal of Christian liberation theology includes bringing about peace, the method in which this work is done will not succeed in the goal.

Misogynistic and Taboo-Ridden Judaism: The Global Version

The old Western feminist argument that Jesus redeems women from Judaism and eliminates Jewish "taboos" that create outcasts takes on a particularly ugly form in WCC publications. For example, in a 1995 essay, "Challenges for Feminist Theology in Francophone Africa," Marguérite Fassinou, the "President of the Union of Methodist Women of Benin and a member of the WCC Commission on Faith and Order," states: "Two thousand years ago Jesus Christ gave women their rightful place despite the heavy yoke of the Jewish culture weighing on them. For women in general and Jewish women in particular the coming of Jesus meant a revolution." She goes on to insist that "being a Christian cannot mean relinquishing our culture; we must remain genuinely African while still being good Christian men and women."[7] Similarly, Ruth M. Besha, a professor of linguistics at the University of Dar Es Salaam, Tanzania, writes in "A Life of Endless Struggle: The Position of Women in Africa" that "Christ never compromised with injustice and acted and spoke against the oppression of women in traditional Jewish society."[8] In a collection from 1986, *New Eyes for Reading: Biblical and Theological Reflections by Women from the Third World*, Grace Eneme, a Presbyterian and representative of the Federation of Protestant Churches in Cameroon, writes, "Christ was the only rabbi who did not discriminate against the women of his time."[9] And in this same volume, Bette Ekeya, a Kenyan Roman Catholic, states, "In his own relationship with women, he [Jesus] chose to ignore the traditional Jewish attitudes and instead treated women with compassion and complete acceptance."[10]

Phrases such as "the heavy yoke of Jewish culture" presume that for women Judaism was oppressive and repressive and suppressive. The argument follows from the Western academy's early feminist steps. It does not follow, however, from the Bible itself, in which the New Testament records numerous rights that Jewish women had in the first century: home ownership, patronage positions, access to their own funds, the right to worship in synagogues and in the Temple, freedom of travel, and so forth. Women did not join Jesus because "Judaism" treated them poorly; nor did they stop being Jews, any more than did Jesus himself, once they joined.

The most common Gospel text cited to prove Jesus's anomalous views of women is the account of the hemorrhaging woman and the framing narrative of the dead girl, which appears in all three synoptic Gospels: Matthew 9:18–26, Mark 5:21–43, and Luke 8:40–56. Matthew's version begins as Jesus is teaching; suddenly a "ruler" (*archon*; Mark, Matthew's source, specifically identifies the man "Jairus," a "synagogue ruler") "came in and knelt before him, saying, 'My daughter has just died; but come and lay your hand on her, and she will live.'" Matthew intensifies the situation, for in Mark's version the girl is only ill. "Jesus got up and followed him, with his disciples." Then, interrupting the story of the dead girl, Matthew recounts that "a woman who had been suffering from hemorrhages for twelve years came up behind him and touched the fringe of his cloak" in hopes of receiving a healing. Jesus turns, sees the woman, and says, "Take heart, daughter; your faith has made you well." Matthew provides the happy announcement: "And instantly the woman was made well." Resuming the story of the desperate father and the dead daughter, the narrative picks up with the notice that "when Jesus came to the leader's house and saw the flute players and the crowd making a commotion, he said, 'Go away; for the girl is not dead but sleeping.' And they laughed at him. But when the crowd had been put outside, he went in and took her by the hand, and the girl got up. And the report of this spread throughout that district."

Christian feminists tend to love this story for, selectively interpreted, it plays perfectly into the argument that Jesus rejects any religious practice that would keep women from being equal to men. The problem with the argument is that it rests on faulty historical reasoning, and bad history cannot lead to good theology. Although no version of the story cites Leviticus, mentions impurity, expresses surprise at a bleeding woman in public, finds odd Jesus's touching a corpse, or portrays Jesus as abrogating any Law, New Testament scholars import all this and more.[11] Thus we read of the "woman's courage in breaking with crippling cultural taboos imposed on her so as to reach Jesus directly and be fully restored and integrated as a person with full rights in her society."[12] The inevitable conclusion of this reading is its practical payoff for women in the church today: "To continue to exclude women from certain Christian ministries on the basis of outmoded Jewish taboos is to render null and void the liberation that Jesus won for us."[13] The end, the liberation of women today, does not, however, justify the means, the false portrait of Judaism.

The term "taboo" is already loaded; "crippling cultural taboos" much more so. Both are unwarranted. There is no reason why the woman would not be in public; there is no reason why she should not seek Jesus's help. No crowd parts before her with the cry, "Get away, get away, hemorrhaging woman!" No authorities restrict her to her house or require her to proclaim herself "Unclean, unclean." And, finally, Jesus abrogates no Laws concerning any "crippling cultural taboos," for there is no Law forbidding the woman to touch him or him to touch her.

Concerning ritual-purity practices, John Meier correctly states:

> The purity Laws of the Pentateuch (Lev 15:25–30) do not explicitly state that a *zaba* [woman with a uterine or vaginal discharge] communicates ritual impurity simply by touching someone—or, *a fortiori*, in the case of Jesus, someone's clothing. Unless we suppose that ordinary Galilean peasants knew and observed the more rigorous rules of the Essenes or anticipated the *halachah* of the later Rabbis, there is no reason to think that either the woman or Jesus thought that impurity was being communicated by her touching his garment.[14]

Noting Jesus's silence about corpse, menstrual, and ejaculatory impurity, Meier concludes that "Jesus was simply not interested in the questions of ritual purity that consumed the interests of many pious Jews of his time."[15]

The point can be made in a stronger manner, for absence of evidence is not the same thing as evidence of absence or lack of concern. The historical default would be that Jesus was no more, *and no less*, concerned with ritual purity than were the majority of his fellow Jews and that he and his followers practiced what his fellow Jews did. Jesus kept the purity Laws, as did his earliest followers. His dining with tax collectors and sinners (as well as with Pharisees) need not have transgressed any purity regulations. Purity Laws are not mentioned in this passage concerning the hemorrhaging woman and the dead girl, because they did not need to be; they are not relevant to the story. In like manner, they are also not mentioned in connection with the burial of the corpses of John the Baptist and Jesus himself.

Such readings that speak of Jesus's breaking or violating purity Laws rest on the misunderstanding and so misrepresentation of Jewish practices. Interpreters describe these practices not as *halakhot*, or *mitzvot*, or even commandments, but with the negative term "taboos." In this classification, Jewish tradition is always retrograde, and Jesus or the church liberates people from it. The point is the opposite of multiculturalism: rather than celebrating cultural difference, theologians first misinterpret Jewish cultural practices and then condemn them.

Musimbi Kanyoro, a member of the Evangelical Lutheran Church, is a Kenyan who lives in Geneva, where she serves as the General Secretary of the World YWCA. In her 1996 *Turn to God: Rejoice in Hope,* she states that Jesus "broke the taboos that marginalized people, above all the unclean, the sinners, women and children."[16] She lists no such "taboos," nor could she, since none exist. Jesus heals lepers, but his doing so breaks no Laws. For example, immediately after the Sermon on the Mount, Matthew records that a leper came to Jesus. Already the scene challenges the conventional view that lepers were not allowed in public or were placed "outside the camp" (Num. 5:1–4) in the first century. The leper kneels before Jesus and says, "Lord, if you choose, you can make me clean." Jesus stretches out his hand, touches the man, and says, "I do choose. Be made clean." There is no Law forbidding him to touch a leper. Then Jesus instructs the man, "Go, show yourself to the priest, and offer the gift that Moses commanded, as a testimony to them" (Matt. 8:1–4; on the presentation to the priest, see Lev. 14).

There is no "taboo" that "marginalizes" a sinner; sinners (those who deliberately ignore Halakhah) and "the righteous" (those who remain within the covenant) appear in both Temple and synagogue, village and town. "Women" were no more or less "marginal" to the Jesus movement than they were in the greater society. As for children, the Gospels continually show the care Jewish parents express toward their children. Already noted is Mark's story of Jairus, the "synagogue ruler" (5:35) who entreats Jesus to heal his twelve-year-old daughter. An equally desperate father, who had already sought the disciples' help in healing his son, begs Jesus, "I believe; help my unbelief" (Mark 9:24). Jesus rebukes the unclean spirit afflicting the child: "You spirit that keeps this boy from speaking and hearing, I command you, come out of him, and never enter him again!" (Mark 9:25). This is no indication of a system in which "taboos" kept children "marginalized." Kanyoro also does not detail any stories about children in the Jesus movement; she could not, for there are none.

Like Kanyoro, Deborah Malacky Belonick of the Orthodox Church
in America, writes in her 1999 essay in *Orthodox Women Speak* that "Jesus
broke many Jewish rabbinic prohibitions.... There are many other in-
stances in which Jesus rebuffed rabbinic taboos and returned to authentic Mosaic tradition. He touched dead bodies ..."[17] Belonick goes on:
"Jesus' example elevated woman to her proper place in creation. Woman
regained her status as co-equal with man in regard to her union and relationship with the Creator. ... The husband could no longer issue a
divorce decree for minor irritations or out of displeasure with his
wife (Matt. 19:9)."[18] She concludes: "Through Jesus' actions, women
were emancipated from rabbinic rigidity."[19] In the same volume Dimitra
Koukoura, of the Church of Greece, states:

> The callous view of women and for their position which prevailed
> in the Graeco-Roman world was reinforced by the curse of the
> Mosaic law, in which sin, evil and women acquired the same negative
> connotations, making it impossible for women to play a creative role
> in social life. Women's position was determined by reference to the
> man, who ruled over her, oppressed her, used her and approached or
> rejected her according to her menstrual cycle.... In the New Testa-
> ment we see all the marginal and stigmatized groups of the society
> finding a place near Christ: prostitutes, tax-collectors, Gentiles, chil-
> dren, those possessed by demons, lepers, bandits. For the first time,
> women find their place.[20]

These words should sound familiar: they invent a bad Judaism, provide
no support for their claims, and then explain how Jesus abrogates this bad
system. Distinguishing between "authentic Mosaic tradition" and its subsequent interpretation, Belonick recapitulates the old argument that "late
Judaism"—that is, the Judaism of the Second Temple period (one won-
ders, then, what contemporary Judaism would be, if third century BCE
Judaism is "late")—is a fossilized version of the truth that Jesus comes to
reveal.

There is no law forbidding Jesus to touch a corpse; on the contrary, the
book of Tobit, which is in the Eastern Orthodox canon, hails Tobit precisely because he buries corpses. Belonick gives no indication of how Jesus
"restores" women, because she cannot list how women *qua women* are in

need of such restoration. Regarding divorce, Jesus states (in the starker, Markan version, Mark 10:11–12): "Whoever divorces his wife and marries another commits adultery against her; and if she divorces her husband and marries another she commits adultery." First, nothing is said about "elevating women." Second, the Markan Jesus forbids women divorcing their husbands, but Belonick says nothing about men being elevated to their "proper place." Third, she omits any reference to the *ketubah,* the woman's marriage contract. Fourth, she fails to note that the lenient divorce legislation is the opinion of only one rabbi. Finally, the Gospel says nothing about divorce practices at the time, either in Jewish or gentile households. Ms. Belonick has picked up this information about Jewish divorce practices from some other Christian Bible study and repeated it. And so the negative portrait of Judaism continues.

As for the Mosaic Law in which "sin, evil and women acquired the same negative connotations," again, no "Law" or commentary on it is cited. The same points can be applied to the New Testament. First Timothy 2:11–15 explicitly connects women, sin, and evil: "Let a woman learn in silence with full submissiveness. I permit no woman to teach or to have authority over a man; she is to keep silent. For Adam was formed first, then Eve; and Adam was not deceived, but the woman was deceived and became a transgressor. Yet she will be saved through childbearing [i.e., by bearing children], provided they continue in faith and love and holiness, with modesty." The New Testament also offers numerous statements that hail women's contributions to the church. To generalize from select materials in the Old Testament and then to set Jesus up in opposition to the generalization is bad apologia, not scholarship.

Finally, the Laws of family purity, still practiced by some Jews today, do not speak of men "rejecting" women who are menstruating. Rather, it is the woman who is responsible for determining when she is sexually available to her husband. Thus she controls permitted sexual intercourse, not the husband. He no more "rejects" her than she "rejects" him. Today, ultra-Orthodox Jewish men will not touch women who are not related to them, but this is not an indication that they find women dirty or that they harbor misogynistic views. Their wives, sisters, and daughters will not touch men not related to them either, yet no one seems to think that they keep this concern for purity because they are radical feminists who hate men.

"The Rabbis"

The second type of anti-Jewish reading overlaps with the first. In this manifestation, anything in the New Testament that the writer finds problematic is explained as a vestige of "rabbinic" tradition (again, no sources are cited, let alone dated or discussed with regard to whether they are prescriptive or descriptive) or as a concession to Jewish demands. In cases where readers might have a problem, such as Paul's restrictions on women's roles (e.g., 1 Cor. 14.33b–36), a bad Judaism is invented to make Paul look progressive.

For example, S. Wesley Ariarajah, a Sri Lankan Methodist minister and former deputy secretary of the WCC, states in his 1996 volume *Did I Betray the Gospel? The Letters of Paul and the Place of Women* that Paul's sexist views are products of his "rabbinic" training. The term is anachronistic: Paul was not a member of a rabbinic school, and the rabbinic documents, as we have seen, date to the period after Paul. According to Ariarajah, Paul "advocated admonitions and prohibitions ... to satisfy the Jewish Christians who would otherwise have chosen to leave the fellowship."[21] Given that Paul is writing to Gentiles, this would be at best an odd concern. As for the specific (negative) "admonitions and prohibitions" concerning women, Ariarajah mentions not a one.

Nirmala Vasanthakumar, director of the women's program for the National Council of Churches of India, provides another example of this approach. In her 1997 article "Rereading the Scripture: A Hermeneutical Approach," she writes: "Women did not have a positive role to play in the Judaism of Paul's time.... Paul advocates such a positive role for women against the background of Judaism, where women's role was passive."[22] Ironically, in the same volume, Brazilian theologian Wanda Deifelt writes in her "Power, Authority and the Bible": "There is growing evidence that within Judaism and Christianity women were not uniformly excluded from religious studies and practices."[23] In the same volume as well, Elisabeth Schüssler Fiorenza, a German Roman Catholic who teaches at Harvard Divinity School, comments that taking select Pauline material out of context for apologetic purposes "often justifies Christian at the cost of Jewish tradition, has engendered anti-Jewish attitudes and interpretations, although its apologetic intent is to reclaim the Bible as a positive support for wo/men's emancipation."[24] In this volume, the right hand of noxious stereotypes apparently did not know what the left hand of historically informed readings had to contribute.

Bärbel von Wartenberg-Potter, bishop of the Northelbian Evangelical (Lutheran) Church, Germany, and director of the Women's Department of the WCC, offers a variant on these Pauline texts. She avers in her *We Will Not Hang Our Harps on the Willows: Engagement and Spirituality* that "when Paul abolished circumcision as an initiation rite into the religious community (Gal. 5:1–6), he did two things: first of all he opened up the new faith to the gentiles, women and men, in that he went beyond the narrow ethnic, racist understanding of election.... Secondly—and for this we need feminist exegesis—he abolished a rite that venerated male fertility."[25]

Von Wartenberg-Potter's readings are problematic in two respects. On the one hand, she does not note that baptism, a symbol of rebirth, can be interpreted as replacing the birth by the biological mother with a birth into the church. That is, baptism can be just as much a problem symbolically as circumcision when it comes to questions of gender. She also fails to mention that Jewish women fully saw themselves as part of the covenant community. On the other, she introduces categories that are inaccurate and, given post-Shoah concerns, particularly disturbing. For von Wartenberg-Potter, the old "faith" (in contrast to Paul's "new faith"), i.e., Judaism, has a "narrow ethnic, racist understanding of election." Judaism, then and now, welcomed converts, from Nicolaus the proselyte to the royal house of Adiabene to the numerous pagan women whose conversions are attested by Josephus and in inscriptional remains. To introduce categories of "race" for Judaism—a movement then and now—is inappropriate. Finally, as for narrow understandings of election, Reverend von Wartenberg-Potter neglects to mention the similarly narrow understandings in some New Testament texts and in later Christian history in which belief in Jesus was the requisite for salvation.

Multicultural Selectivity

A related move places Jesus as the representative of whatever "culture" finds itself marginalized. In his "Reading the Bible as Hispanic Americans" in the popular *New Interpreter's Bible*, published by a United Methodist press, Fernando F. Segovia describes the *mestizaje* theology of Roman Catholic priest and theologian Virgilio Elizondo. His liberationist readings, which have made an enormous impact on Hispanic religious thought, emphasize Jesus's Galilean identity as marked by a mixture of races and cultures. Segovia then summarizes the inevitable conclusion: "This place of mestizaje is rejected by Gentiles and Jews alike as impure and inferior, with the Galileans as a clear example of a marginalized and oppressed people."[26] This reading distinguishes "Jews" from "Galileans" and thereby creates the false comparison between a regional identification (Galileans) and one with a religious import (Jews). It separates Jesus from Judaism, even as it depicts "Judaism" as a program designed to create marginalization and oppression. It is also historically incorrect, for it ignores the archaeological evidence that reveals Galilee to be not a "mixed" area but one fully Jewish, as shown by many factors from the presence of ritual baths to the absence of pig bones.[27]

Theologically and pastorally, Christian identification of Jesus with and by any who find themselves marginal, oppressed, or otherwise deprived of right and dignity is appropriate, even necessary. Yet when this identification defaults to an anti-Judaism, wherein the oppressive system or the oppressor becomes "the Jews," the process is poisoned.

Once "Judaism" becomes the trope for that which marginalizes and oppresses, the liberationist reading has a proverbial field day with the rest of the New Testament. Chan-Hie Kim, in his "Reading the Cornelius Story from an Asian-Immigrant Perspective,"[28] which appeared in a Fortress Press publication, writes: "Most of the mainline U.S. Protestant churches do not seem to realize that these [new immigrants] are the 'gentile' Christians who do not know and are not willing to accept 'Jewish' laws and practices." The article argues for Peter's, and our, "recognition of multiplicity of our cultures" but in the next sentence claims that "the Jewish regulations about clean and unclean are not valid, indeed that they contradict the nature of God as the Creator of all living things." Commenting on how U.S. churches seek to acculturate rather than enculturate Asian émigrés, Kim classifies the "Jewish" system as the negative. In his configuration, Jews ironically represent the "melting pot" cultural model of America, which seeks to turn all people into Jews, whereas (good) Christianity is more the "salad bowl" model, which recognizes the value of distinct cultural modes.

While celebrating their own distinct identities and cultures, Kim and others deny value to Jewish identity. Insisting on enculturation—on celebrating the unique practices of African, Asian, Hispanic, or Eastern Orthodox Christianities—he and his fellow theologians refuse to accord value to the practices that mark Judaism as unique: its traditions concerning diet, Sabbath observance, respect for Torah, and laws of family purity. This is a common trope in multiculturally oriented biblical studies or reading from one's "social location."

The God of Judaism, Again

Of these various types of anti-Jewish models, the worst is the assertion that Jesus introduces a new and different deity than the one revealed in Torah and worshiped in the synagogue. This is the liberation-theological spin on that old canard of the Old Testament "god of wrath" versus the New Testament "God of love." The false god is now the "god" (lowercase *g*) of Pharisaic Judaism or the god of the Jewish tradition.

Kwok Pui-lan, an Anglican from Hong Kong who now teaches at the Episcopal Divinity School in Cambridge, Massachusetts, identifies the "God who cried out from the cross" and the one who "suffered under the oppressive Jewish tradition."[29] The Reverend Louise Kumandjek Tappa, from the Union des églises baptistes du Cameroun, draws out the implications of this theological distinction:

> Jesus died as the result of the clash between his God [capital G] and the god [lowercase *g*] of Pharisaic Judaism. Judaism had encaged God in its laws and tradition and its ministers could not accept a concept of God that went beyond their own limits.... Jesus' cruci-fixion marked the temporal triumph of the patriarchal god of Juda-ism. His resurrection, however, proved that his God is the true God. But alas, Christianity has fallen back to the patriarchal god of Juda-ism with even greater zeal. The god of the institutional church now yields more power because the "clan" has become more powerful. The god of the clan will sanctify anything including militarism, war, sexism, apartheid, as long as it serves the interests of the clan.[30]

In a 1990 Orbis Books volume, we find again Mexican American Catholic priest Virgilio Elizondo, now speaking of the jars for the "Jewish rites of purification" mentioned in John's account of the wedding at Cana

(John 2:1–11): "From that time on, religion will no longer be based on the law and constant ablutions (a sign of their uselessness) or on the observance of precepts followed under the fear of punishment and guilt. The presence of Jesus is the epiphany of this new and different God—not a God of fear and punishment, distant from us and delighting in sacrifice."[31]

Utilizing a bit of everything—bad Jewish Laws; oppressive purity system; sexist, racist Jewish culture; different images of the deity; Jewish responsibility for killing Jesus because he was nice—John Bluck, an Anglican priest from New Zealand and communication director for the WCC, writes in *The Giveaway God: Ecumenical Studies on Divine Generosity* that Jesus's

> vision of the world ... refused to divide people by gender or race or religion; [it was] a vision that created no outsiders. It was driven by generosity, forgiveness and room to start over again when we fail. It valued love above everything, and justice, which is love spread around evenly. In first-century Palestine, this vision was translated into a ministry of hospitality and healing and teaching that got Jesus crucified, such was the threat it posed.... Maybe he [Jesus] deliberately set about showing that God was very different from the official version being promoted by the culture and religion of the day. For God had become tied up and tied down in a system of ritual purity and cultural honour and social roles that divided the world into insiders and outsiders, the clean and the contaminated, the honourable and the shameful.

He concludes (in a discussion of the Sadducees' question of resurrection): "It's a clash of systems and values: the old law of Moses reserved for some versus the new law of grace and love open to all."[32]

To repeat, liberation theology, the World Council of Churches, the various Christian churches that sponsor the presses that publish this material—these are all, on the whole, splendid, praiseworthy institutions that do not intend to promote anti-Jewish views. On the contrary, they formally stand against this sort of prejudice. The vast majority of their works are not only innocent of bigotry but go out of their way to prevent it. Thus, the lines I am quoting are selective. But a single line is enough to create or reinforce prejudice; a single line is too much.

The Palestinian Jesus

Movies and television shows about Arab or Muslim terrorists solidify anti-Arab and anti-Muslim bigotry already heightened because of the events of September 11, 2001, and they convey messages that necessarily influence Western political views. Similarly, the message that Judaism is a monolithic, taboo-ridden, xenophobic, sexist, vengeful tradition necessarily impacts how one views the "Jewish state" of Israel. When forms of Palestinian liberation theology appropriate Jesus for political ends, the messages conveyed about the Middle East to churches there and abroad become even more complicated. Any writing that separates Jesus and his first followers from Jewish identity, associates these proto-Christians with the Palestinian population, and reserves the label "Jew" for those who crucified Jesus and persecuted the church is not only historically untenable but theologically abhorrent.

A few comments from Naim Ateek, an Anglican priest and founder of the "Sabeel Ecumenical Liberation Theology Center" in Jerusalem, are indicative of this rhetoric.[33] At Notre Dame in 2001, Ateek preached on "The Zionist Ideology of Domination Versus the Reign of God"; he identified "Jesus Christ, living in our country as a Palestinian under occupation" and declared that "Israel has placed a large boulder, a big stone that has metaphorically shut off the Palestinians in a tomb. It is similar to the stone placed on the entrance of Jesus' tomb." That same year, for his Easter message, he proclaimed: "In this season of Lent, it seems to many of us that Jesus is on the cross again with thousands of crucified Palestinians around Him.... The Israeli government crucifixion system is operating daily." At a worship service in Jerusalem in April 2002, he stated: "Palestinians have been condemned as a nation by Israel, and sentenced to destruction. The accusations of people in power are strikingly similar throughout history to the charges leveled against Jesus in this city—terrorist, evildoer, or rebel and a subversive person. Palestinians are being crucified today for refusing to succumb to Israel's demand for greater concession on land."

The rhetoric is overblown. Jesus did not advise his followers to blow up Romans (and Ateek is not advising his followers to blow up Jews, but by lumping all Palestinians into one category, he risks that impression); Palestinians have not been sentenced to destruction. Ateek is hardly silenced.

On the contrary, he continues to hold international conferences at his center and give talks and sermons at Notre Dame, the Center for Jewish-Christian Relations at Cambridge University, the Lutheran School of Theology in Chicago, and elsewhere.

Ateek's rhetoric is also slippery, since its anti-Jewish impact is often more a matter of perception. For a convocation at the Episcopal Divinity School in Cambridge, Massachusetts, he preached concerning Jesus's messages:

> They reflect an inclusive commitment to one's fellow humanity and a ministry that has depth and breadth of scope—a commitment to the poor, a commitment to the ministry of healing, a commitment to justice and liberation of the oppressed, a commitment to jubilee which involves economic justice for all. I believe that these words constituted a *paradigm shift* at the time of Jesus, and they provide us with the basis of a paradigm shift for ministry in the twenty-first century.[34]

In making this claim, he erases Jesus's Judaism. If concern for the poor originated with Jesus, then the church might follow that ancient heretic Marcion and jettison the entire "Old Testament."

In the well-respected series *Reading from this Place*, Ateek's article begins with the standard, and false, view that Judaism is particularistic and Christianity is universal: "Membership was no longer seen as confined to one ethnic group of people, but rather in terms of a renewed covenant that included people of all races and ethnic backgrounds."[35] Given his social location, it becomes both particularly pernicious and particularly ironic. Israeli citizens are by no means just of one ethnic group; on the contrary, Israel is the most multiethnic and indeed multicultural state in the Middle East. The article then focuses on John 20, an account describing how the followers of Jesus hid "for fear of the Jews." In this piece, the "Jews" seeking the lives of Jesus's followers become the Israeli army. Ateek goes on to compare the Intifada to Pentecost, the descent of the Holy Spirit on the Christians. Needless to say, the series does not include a piece by an Israeli Jew describing how Lamentations is understood by parents in Jerusalem or Natanya whose children are killed by Palestinians.

Such slippery rhetoric continues to mark pockets of Palestinian-Christian discourse. Palestinian spokeswoman and Anglican Hanan

Ashrawi announced, for example, that the "first Christians were Arab."[36] According to the book of Acts (11:26), the term "Christian" was first applied to followers of Jesus, both Jewish and gentile, in Antioch. However, her audiences do not recognize the subtlety of the point; they hear, rather, that Peter and Paul, Mary Magdalene and James were all "Arab" and so, by definition, not "Jews."

My point is not to play the obscene game of "who is most victimized," and it is not to dismiss the legitimate claims of the Palestinian people. Nor am I arguing that there is no comparably ugly rhetoric on the part of those who would oppose the Palestinian state. It is to state that any prejudicial commentary that divorces Jesus from Judaism and then uses the story of Jesus to condemn all Jews is not a "Christian" message. It is, rather, a recycled anti-Judaism that depicts Israel as a country of Christ killers. The goal of Palestinian statehood is good; these particular means of achieving it are not.

Origins of Evil

How did we come to such a situation? The causes are several.

First, although these particular comments stem more from the modern academy—postcolonial theory, enculturation, and feminism are not the hallmarks of the nineteenth century—clergy, professors, preachers, and religious educators have fertilized the fields of anti-Jewish readings for centuries. The "teaching of contempt" is hardly a new invention. When missionaries brought the gospel to all parts of the globe, they brought their own normative anti-Semitic beliefs with them and left them with their converts. Several years ago a Kenyan student entered Vanderbilt's Ph.D. program in New Testament. The first semester, she was, at best, distant toward me despite my best efforts to engage her in conversation. Finally, toward December, she knocked on my door. Her comments were honest, and tragic. She noted that in her native language, the word for "Jew" means someone who deceives or betrays. It had taken her a semester to be able to see me as an individual and to be able to challenge her own prejudices. The legacy of the missionary dies hard. Thus, although these present readings do not stem directly from traditional church teachings in Europe or the missionary legacies of those teachings, they did prepare the way.

Second, for some of these authors Jews are not real people; Jews are inventions constructed of select Old Testament readings, New Testament polemics such as Matthew 23, and an occasional reference to the state of Israel. Thus for much of the world the Jew is either a bathrobe-clad Old Testament patriarch (or his taboo-fearing, marginalized wife), an evil Pharisee, or a member of the Israeli army carrying a gun aimed at a Palestinian child. Jesus and his followers have all become (proto-)Christian, or, in liberation-theological terms, they have been appropriated by the local culture. Jesus then is African, Asian, Aleut, a blue-eyed blond, and so on, but in few, if any, cases of such appropriation does he retain any "Jewish" identity by ethnicity, theology, or practice. No other possibilities exist, save possibly for a local production of *Fiddler on the Roof*.

In the Philippines in the summer of 2004, I gave a series of lectures at Roman Catholic seminaries. On one occasion, in a talk designed for the public, I asked the audience if they had ever seen a Jewish person aside from me. Only a few of the several hundred raised their hands. This is not surprising: there are only about two hundred Jews (if that) in the country of eighty million. Yet I was standing directly in front of a crucifix. I turned, pointed to Jesus, and simply noted that they had been looking at a Jewish person all their lives. The idea had not occurred to them.

Third, anti-Jewish, Marcionistic, and just plain unhelpful comments appear in almost all aspects of Christian liberation-theological education, regardless of the global location. The majority of the authors of these liberationist materials are administrators, ethicists, or theologians; they are not biblical scholars, and what they write is therefore more than the residue of a poor education in Bible. As I was compiling the WCC information, a Vanderbilt student mentioned to me a quote he found in a required text for a pastoral care course: "The God who, from the peak of Mt. Sinai, issues detailed regulations for the management of life ... is a tempting model for ministry and counseling, managing others' lives—for their own welfare of course—from aloofness and with detailed regulation. But the New Testament portrays a very different kind of God, a God ... who renounced being God for the sake of being God, a God who could heal and save and make whole and holy."[37]

Pastoral care specialists and religious ethicists in (usually liberal) Ph.D. programs do not typically take courses in biblical studies or interfaith dialogue. Thus they rely on whatever they learned in their undergraduate or divinity school classrooms, which is usually not much more than the basics about content and, in some cases, a course or two on hermeneutics. Thus they may know something about reading from their own social locations or how the Bible has been interpreted for evil as well as good ends. But since the Bible is not necessarily firmly integrated into their program, it is easier to fall back on stereotype. A little knowledge can be a dangerous thing.

Further, given the scarcity of up-to-date books in seminaries outside the West—many libraries in Asia and Africa are filled with outdated volumes bequeathed by Western pastors—there is little means by which correction can be made. The writers do the best they can with what they have. Even for Western writers, the lack of appropriate resources remains a problem, for often church libraries are replete with equally outdated materials. Moreover, what is being promulgated in some New Testament classrooms would not be of much help.

Kwok, whose comment about the God who "suffered under the oppressive Jewish tradition" is cited above, states about her essay, which was written in Hong Kong around 1984: "I was not aware of the anti-Jewish criticism in the United States and I was certainly influenced by the work of Bultmann and other scholars, which I now see as deeply biased toward [*sic*] the Jewish people." She continues: "I was surprised to find that the editors of the publishing house have changed [my original] 'long Jewish tradition' to 'oppressive Jewish tradition' without my knowing when reprinting the article."[38] She even notes that this "is not a single incidence, for other Third World women have told me that their poetry or writings have been used, cited, excerpted, or edited without their permission." Although the phrase "suffered under the long Jewish tradition" is not much of an improvement on "suffered under the oppressive Jewish tradition," her points about both how her education misled her and how her words were changed provide helpful contextualization of the unfortunate material.

In her excellent volume *Postcolonial Imagination and Feminist Theology*, Kwok not only directly grapples with the anti-Jewish tendencies found in liberationist work but also adds the important point that "the critique of patriarchy in Jewish culture may have served as a rhetorical device not just to make Jesus look good, but also to bring into sharp relief patriarchy in their [the Third World women's] own cultures.[39] The charge, then, to theologians, ethicists, and others becomes that of finding new models for making liberationist points or at least more careful means of expressing them.

Fourth, teachings about the impossibility of the Law, the pervasiveness of Jewish xenophobia, and Jesus's feminist impulse were part and parcel of the biblical studies classrooms in the 1960s and 1970s, and their vestiges have yet to be fully uprooted. When I heard it in my New Testament courses and read it in the books I found in the university library, I believed it. Ph.D.s told me it was true, and surely they knew. The tragic thing was that I was (and still am) a Jew, a part of this system, and I believed all this nonsense. Then, finally, what is called the "hermeneutics of suspicion" kicked in. Going back to the primary sources, I found the correction to much of the prejudice that had passed for historical rigor.

Yet as historical-critical work becomes only one of numerous approaches to the Bible, this corrective may disappear. In some classrooms, history is reduced to a series of tropes such as "honor and shame" or "challenge and riposte"—valuable tropes to be sure, but, like structuralism before or certain forms of deconstructive or liberationist readings today, in continual danger of being reduced to mechanical templates. In like manner, the historical-critical approach—an approach that remains viable, albeit recognized to be contaminated by subjective concerns both ancient and modern—has in some classrooms been ousted in favor of readings "in front of the text" or by "cultural criticism." No more attempting to determine the community to which Luke was written or how Jesus's statements would have sounded to their original audiences; better to have a reader-response study (preferably one, to use the current term, "from the margins"). The focus shifts from the text, and so the text's first-century context, to the reader. The utilitarian anti-Jewish views thus become reinforced rather than questioned.

Fifth, as Kwok suggests, the fault for this material to some extent lies with the gatekeepers, the editors of the volumes and the presses that publish them. Worse is when the gatekeepers deny that the problem exists. I had previously published, in the *Journal of Feminist Studies in Religion,* an article on liberation theology, postcolonialism, feminism, and anti-Semitism in which I cited a number of problematic comments in publications by African women.[40] Responding to this earlier work, Kanyoro writes:

Reading anti-Semitism in the writings of the Circle [of African] Women is a preoccupation of Levine and her context rather than the agenda of the African women.... African women critique African cultures vehemently and those of the Old Testament Hebrew people which allowed women to only go through their lives obeying customs and fearing taboos. It is in this respect that they call upon Jesus of the New Testament to save them from their indigenous cultures and their Biblical heritages as well as the ills of modernity. Jesus is understood as having saved other women, the New Testament women whom he healed from cultural taboos or physical illness.

She concludes, "I think that Levine's pain as a Jewish woman can make her see anti-Semitism where it does not exist."[41]

On one level, Kanyoro is correct. In 1998, the WCC published *The Theology of the Churches and the Jewish People: Statements by the World Council of Churches and Its Member Churches.* The introduction indicates that the sources for the statements are principally "the World Council of Churches and member churches of the World Council, [which are] solely from the so-called North Atlantic churches." They go on to note: "That does not mean ... that churches in Asia, Africa and South America are unaware of the Jewish people or are unaffected by anti-Semitism. But it does mean that they have not, as official church bodies, taken theological positions relative to the Jewish people."[42]

Ignorance, however, is no excuse. Kanyoro's response takes a step backward when it perceives pain to be *only* a projection on the part of the person hurt. It stumbles when general charges are levied, but no specifics are attached. It becomes paralyzed when problems are acknowledged, but then excused. One respondent to the *JFSR* article, who provided some of the more juicy examples of anti-Judaism, stated that she could not possibly be anti-Jewish because she respects the Old Testament. Another sought to excuse her anti-Jewish views by saying she spent two weeks in a Palestinian refugee camp. A third said that she couldn't be anti-Jewish because she did not *intend* to be.

These various responses do not advance the conversation. The "Old Testament" is not the same thing as Judaism. Nor do events in Palestine summarize what "Judaism" is (any more than a Muslim blowing up an

Israeli pizza parlor or the Pentagon summarizes Islam). The argument that non–North Atlantic work cannot be anti-Semitic because anti-Semitism is not on the radar in Ghana or Benin or Hong Kong is specious. Moreover, the authors from the World Council of Churches and numerous others are from Great Britain, Germany, the United States, and other Western contexts as well as from Africa and Asia. Regardless of anti-Jewish intent, the materials are problematic. Movies depicting Africans as savages in order to show how the white man (Tarzan, the European doctor, the missionary) represents wisdom, civilization, or salvation are racist, although I doubt the producers intended them to be so. When American parents of Italian or Polish or Kenyan background tell their children to "stop acting like wild Indians," they are not intending to promote bigotry, but they are promoting it nonetheless. And when parents in rural areas of the Philippines tell their children to "stop acting like Jews," anti-Judaism is the unintended result. Disease cannot be cured when those infected are in denial.

It is now almost sixty years since the ICCJ and the WCC published their documents on the importance of interfaith relations, but prejudices remain, in Germany and the United States, Ghana and Hong Kong, Sri Lanka and Tanzania. The major issues in interfaith conversation remain the Shoah and the Middle East, but the anti-Judaism (whether intended or not) underlying the first and infecting the second remains too often ignored or insufficiently addressed. These prejudices are not idiosyncratic; they are systemic and they are global. They begin in the academic classroom and the Sunday school, they are passed along to pastors and priests, and they are taught to congregations under the labels of justice, compassion, and respect.

Frequent inoculations, consistent warnings, and solid vigilance will help sort the liberationist wheat of this material from the anti-Jewish chaff. The World Council of Churches is to be commended for choosing to make the effort, for it has decided to publish my critique of their earlier publications. A few courageous scholars such as Kwok have begun the self-critique needed to advance liberationist readings in a global context. More, of course, needs to be done, but at least the problem is now named, and the first steps have been taken.

SIX

Distinct Canons, Distinct Practices

Anti-Jewish and potentially anti-Jewish rhetoric goes unnoticed in so much Christian scholarship because the authors are not attuned to how their words sound to different ears. The symptom is part of a larger problem in any interfaith or multicultural conversation. Jews and Christians, although using the same language, imbue the terms with different connotations and so talk past, rather than with, each other. In like manner, although they read the same texts, they take different messages from them. Efforts at harmonizing or reaching a theological consensus tend rather to blur the distinct messages synagogue and church proclaim and thus do a disservice to both. Nevertheless, those very distinctions might provide a fruitful means for fostering interfaith conversation—once freed from the compulsion to reach common ground, together church and synagogue can celebrate their different voices and different practices and so both educate each other and, perhaps, foster a bit of holy envy.

How Not to Read Scripture

In the second century, a Christian named Justin wrote a treatise called *Dialogue with Trypho*. Throughout this long and frequently tedious document, Justin tries to convince his interlocutor, Trypho, a Jew, that the Scriptures of the synagogue predict the coming of Jesus the Christ. In chapter 67, Justin finally gets around to discussing Isaiah 7:14, a verse he translates: "Behold, the virgin shall conceive ..." He takes this verse, as did the Gospel of Matthew before him, to be a prediction fulfilled by the conception of Jesus within the womb of the Virgin Mary.[1]

Historically speaking, the idea that Isaiah, sometime at the end of the eighth century BCE, predicted a virgin birth to occur seven hundred years later strains credulity. Isaiah's oracles, like the other prophetic works in the canon, such as Amos, Hosea, and Jeremiah, concerned not the far future, but rather the time at hand. For a modern analogy, one might think of a prophet today who predicts that in seven hundred years there will be an end to disease. Some may find comfort in the news; others, particularly those now suffering, might find the idea that God will act, but not for more than half a millennium, at best unhelpful.

On the other hand, there is a sense in which both Matthew and Justin have correctly interpreted Isaiah. They are both reading from a Greek translation of Isaiah's Hebrew text. The translation, developed for Jews in the Diaspora whose abilities in Hebrew were weak, if not absent, describes the young woman in question as a *parthenos*. The Greek term has a primary meaning of "virgin," as seen, for example, in the term "Parthenon," the temple dedicated to the virgin goddess Athena. The term could also mean "young woman," with no connotations concerning her sexual experience, but this is not the translation the New Testament, or Justin, prefers.

Trypho the Jew responds, "The Scripture does not say, 'Behold, the virgin shall conceive and bear a son,' but 'Behold, the young woman shall conceive and bear a son.'.... And the whole prophecy refers to King Hezekiah." Thus for Trypho, Isaiah's oracle concerns political advice for the reigning king. The problem for interfaith conversation is that Trypho is also reading correctly. The Hebrew text of Isaiah refers to an *alma*, a young woman; the term need not connote "virgin." The Hebrew term more often used for "virgin," *betulah*, appears elsewhere in Isaiah (23:4; 23:12; 37:22; 47:1; 62:5), but not in chapter 7. The Hebrew participle describing the woman's condition could be translated either "will conceive" or "is pregnant." Consequently, Trypho the Jew sees no messianic prediction and no miraculous idea. There is no pre-Christian messianic interpretation accorded Isaiah 7:14, nor need there be.

Justin, the author, gets the last word: "Your teachers ... have altogether taken away many Scriptures from the [Greek] translation." In other words, "You Jews changed the text." Trypho grants the possibility of tampering but gives it little credence: "Whether the rulers of the people have erased any portion of the Scripture, as you affirm, God knows, but it seems incredible."[2] Again, Justin has some support for his claim, for later Greek versions of Isaiah, dated after the rise of Christianity, translate the Hebrew term *alma* not as *parthenos*, "virgin," but as *neanis*, "young woman." Justin and Trypho thus have mutually exclusive readings and mutually exclusive interpretations, but given the evidence available to each, neither has read incorrectly.

Whereas the vast majority of Old Testament versions printed in English today translate Isaiah 7:14 according to the Hebrew and so read "The young woman is with child," splinter groups use the distinction to preach hatred of Jews. For example, the Christian Separatists state on their Web site: "It has long been the firm position of true Christians that the only legitimate source for what is called the Old Testament is the Greek Septuagint.... And this Hebrew [of the Masoretic text, used in the synagogue] had been edited, changed, and in some cases rewritten entirely by Talmudic, atheistic, mongrel Jews."[3] I cite this site not only because it is indicative of the hate against Jews still festering among some who call themselves Christians, but also because a Google search for "Masoretic text" yields their site as the first reference.

But this example from Isaiah also reveals the new possibilities of interfaith conversation. By recognizing their use of separate texts and different theological interpretive traditions, Jews and Christians today are in a better position to advance interfaith discussion without having to resort to charges of falsification or foolishness.

Different Canons

In the 1970s, the language of biblical studies changed in the academy and in liberal churches. Instead of studying the "Old Testament," students and congregations were now to speak of the "Hebrew Bible," "Hebrew Scriptures," "First Testament," or even "Jewish Testament." Those who promoted this shift in vocabulary did so with the best of intentions. They recognized that for many students in the classroom and worshipers in the pews, the term "Old Testament"—with an emphasis on "old"—connoted something outdated, useless, and needing to be replaced. Thirsty teenagers purchase not "Old Coke," but "Classic Coke"; shoppers buy "vintage" clothes and "antique" cars, not "old" ones. "Gray Panthers," "The American Association of Retired Persons (AARP)," "senior citizens"—all fine terms; "old folks" is insulting. Further, because a number of Christian (and a few Jewish) readers associate the "Old Testament" with Judaism (hence the alternative designation "Jewish Bible"), revisionists promoted alternative designations lest anyone conclude that Judaism too was outdated or replaced. Changing the label might stop "supersessionism," that is, the claim that the church supersedes and therefore replaces the synagogue. Moreover, a more "neutral" label like "Hebrew Scriptures" might lead to the respecting of religious diversity in the classroom. Some Jewish students resisted the term "Old Testament," since the very name conveys a Christian view: there can be no "Old Testament" apart from a "New Testament."

Consequently, "Old Testament" was relegated to the trash heap of terms that fail to meet the goals of interfaith acceptance or current scholarly fad. "Hebrew Bible," "First Testament," "Jewish Scriptures," and even "Literature, Religion, and Faith of Ancient Israel" courses popped up across the country, along with their counterparts, for no longer could "New Testament" be used. Students instead began to register for courses in "Christian Scriptures," "Second Testament," or "Literature, Religion, and Faith of Early Christianity."

As with many well-intended efforts, the attempt to relabel the Bible does more harm than good. "Hebrew Scriptures" or "Hebrew Bible" is inappropriate for several reasons. First, the Old Testament of some churches, such as Greek Orthodoxy, is not the "Hebrew Bible," but the Greek translation of the Hebrew. The new vocabulary thus relegates Orthodoxy, a multifaceted tradition that too often falls off the radar when public discourse addresses "Christianity," to oblivion. Greek Orthodox students in the classroom were told that their language of "Old Testament" was insensitive; their occasional protest that shifting the terminology to "Hebrew Bible" erased their tradition went unheeded.

Second, Roman Catholic, Anglican, and Eastern Orthodox communions consider the Deuterocanonical Writings part of the Old Testament. This collection, written by Jews and preserved in Greek, includes the history of the Maccabees, the well-known story of Susanna and the elders, the books of Judith and Tobit, Additions to the book of Esther, the Wisdom of Jesus ben Sirach (Ecclesiasticus), and the Wisdom of Solomon. For Protestants, the collection, known as the "Old Testament Apocrypha"—that is, "hidden books"—lacks canonical status. The shift in vocabulary to "Hebrew Bible" thus creates a Protestant default. In attempting to avoid anti-Semitism, the shift in terminology promoted a generally unacknowledged anti-Catholicism. Finally on the "Hebrew Bible" label, some of the canonical material included in the books of Ezra-Nehemiah and Daniel is not in Hebrew, but in Aramaic.

The shift in terminology creates problems rather than resolving them. In the academy, I found that "Hebrew Bible" confused the students. A few hesitated to sign up for the course because they thought they needed to know Hebrew (conversely, every year at least one student would ask, "In what language is the Hebrew Bible written?"); a few had never heard of the "Hebrew Bible" but did want an "Old Testament" course. Two or three Christians complained that by rejecting the term "Old Testament" I was erasing their own religious vocabulary, and their Jewish counterparts wanted to know why I wasn't using the term "Tanakh," which is the term preferred by the synagogue. "Tanakh" is an acronym for the Torah (Pentateuch), Nevi'im (Prophets), and Ketuvim (Writings).

The alternatives to "Hebrew Scriptures" or "Hebrew Bible" are even less helpful. "First Testament" fails to eliminate supersessionism or confessionalism, for "first" implies a "second" and perhaps a "third" or "fourth." Christians may well find the equivalent "Second Testament" demeaning. If "Old" as in "Old Testament" connotes something outdated, then "Second" as in "Second Testament" has even worse connotations: second place, secondhand, second-rate. Moreover, the term "First Testament" or "First Covenant"—the Greek word *diathteke*, meaning "Testament" as in "New Testament," is the term also used for "covenant"— appears in the New Testament's Letter to the Hebrews in a negative way. Hebrews 8:13 states: "In speaking of 'a new covenant,' he has made the first one obsolete. And what is obsolete and growing old will soon disappear." "First Covenant" could also be translated "First Testament." Whereas Hebrews is talking about the covenant made between God and Israel at Sinai and not about the canon of the synagogue explicitly, the phrasing blights the term "First Testament."

A few scholars opt for the label "Jewish Scriptures," perhaps in the hope that it will increase Christian students' recognition that the text is not just the Old Testament of the church. Unfortunately, "Jewish Scriptures" conveys the message that the material is of no relevance to the church. In some cases, "Jewish Scriptures" reinforces the idea that the text is *equivalent* to Judaism. Nor is the linguistic equivalent, "Christian Scriptures," an appropriate designation for the New Testament; to call the New

Testament "Christian Scriptures" implies that the Old Testament is not part of the Christian canon.

By seeking a common term that would not offend anyone, well-meaning scholars thus erased not only Judaism's distinct use of the canon but also the Catholic tradition, or relegated Christianity to second-class status, or confused a number of people.[4] The problem with the expression "Old Testament" lies not in the labeling, but in a combination of cultural attitudes and Christian education. "Old" need not mean "bad." One speaks of "golden oldies," not "golden newies." Bob Seger observed, "Still like that old time rock and roll, that kind of music just soothes my soul." The "old time religion" is still "good enough" for many. Little Christian children do not grow up thinking that "Old Testament" means "'less good' or 'not good' Testament." It is not the terminology that needs to change: it's Christian education. Instead of using the falsely neutral, Protestant, linguistically inaccurate term "Hebrew Bible," Christians might simply use the title "Old Testament," which is the title found in most family and pulpit Bibles. Jews should continue to use "Tanakh."

The separate labels of "Tanakh" and "Old Testament" prevent the canon of one group from being subordinated by or subsumed into the canon of another; they have the added benefit of indicating that synagogue and church each has its own story, told in its own order. The church's narrative starts with Genesis, and Part One (skipping the deuterocanonical works, which are often printed at the end of the New Testament) ends with the prophet Malachi. This conclusion makes abundant sense. First, it follows the order of the earlier Greek translations, created before the finalization of the material in the "Writings," or Ketuvim, section. Further, Malachi predicts the coming of the prophet Elijah before the "great and terrible day of the Lord" (4:5). Elijah was the ninth-century BCE prophet for whom, as the song goes, the sweet chariot swung low: he ascended to heaven (see 2 Kings 2:11–12), where he awaits his future role as forerunner of the messianic age. Malachi states that Elijah will "turn the hearts of parents to their children and the hearts of children to their parents" (4:6) in the process of preparing for the messianic age.

The first document in the New Testament, the Gospel According to Matthew, functions almost like a précis of Israel's history. Opening with the genealogy of "Jesus the Christ, the son of David, the son of Abraham" (1:1), the first two chapters offer seven citations from the prophets that Jesus is said to fulfill. The most famous of these appears in Matthew 1:22–23: "All this took place to fulfill what had been spoken by the Lord through the prophet: 'Look, the virgin shall conceive and bear a son, and they shall name him Emmanuel,' which means, 'God is with us.'" Even for Joseph, Mary's husband, connections are drawn to Israel's past. Unlike the Gospel of Luke, which identifies Joseph as the son of Heli (Luke 3:23), Matthew 1:16 lists Joseph's father as Jacob and so connects Jesus's adoptive father to that earlier Joseph, son of Jacob. When the first-century Joseph receives prophetic dreams and takes his family to Egypt for protection, connections to the first Joseph are confirmed. Matthew thus sets out a model whereby the story of Jesus echoes the stories of the Old Testament.

For Matthew, John the Baptist, the forerunner of Jesus, fulfills Elijah's role. Jesus states: "For all the Prophets and the Law prophesied until John came, and if you are willing to accept it, he is Elijah who is to come" (11:13–14). The Gospel of Mark opens with John the Baptist, who here as well assumes the role of Elijah. Not only does John the Baptist herald the coming of the messianic age—as he states, "The ax is lying at the root of the trees" (Matt. 3:10); he also announces the coming of the one more worthy than he (Mark 1:7). In Mark 9, Jesus cryptically identifies John the Baptist with Elijah: "I tell you that Elijah has come, and they did to him whatever they pleased" (v. 13).

Luke's Gospel offers yet a third means of demonstrating how the Christian message fulfills the promises to Israel. The Gospel starts not with the annunciation of the angel Gabriel to Mary but with the miraculous conception of John the Baptist by the aged Elizabeth and Zechariah (Luke 1). The story recapitulates the numerous special births of the figures of Israel's past, starting with the birth of Isaac to the aged Abraham and his infertile wife, Sarah (Gen. 18; 21). Genesis records that this same Isaac would later pray "to the Lord for his wife, because she was barren; and the Lord granted his prayer, and Rebekah his wife conceived" (25:21). The infertile Rachel begs her husband Jacob, "Give me children, or I shall die" (Gen. 30:1); ironically, she dies giving birth to Benjamin (35:16–19). Hannah, unable to conceive, prays for a child and, after bearing her son Samuel and then dedicating him to God, sings a hymn of liberation that will be echoed in Mary's Magnificat. Hannah sings, "The bows of the mighty are broken, but the feeble gird on strength. Those who were full have hired themselves out for bread, but those who were hungry are fat with spoil.... The Lord makes poor and makes rich; he brings low, he also exalts. He raises up the poor from the dust; he lifts the needy from the ash heap, to make them sit with princes and inherit a seat of honor" (1 Sam. 2:4–5, 7–8). Mary echoes in her song, "He has brought down the powerful from their thrones, and lifted up the lowly; he has filled the hungry with good things, and sent the rich away empty" (Luke 1:52–53). When the book of Judges introduces Manoah and his "barren" wife (13:2), readers immediately know that they will have a child, and they do—Samson. When the prophet Elisha seeks to thank the wealthy woman of Shunem for her hospitality, his servant Gehazi notes, "She has no son, and her husband is old." One does not need to be a prophet to predict what will happen next (2 Kings 4:8–17).

Finally, the Gospel of John provides its own anchor into the earlier material even as it moves into the notice of fulfillment. John's famous opening, "In the beginning was the Word, and the Word was with God, and the Word was God" (1:1), recollects the opening lines of the book of Genesis: "In the beginning, when God created the heavens and the earth, the earth was a formless void and darkness covered the face of the deep."

The rest of the New Testament continues to evoke the ancient materials. Taking a universal scope, Paul suggests that the errors made by Adam find their correction in the Christ (Rom. 5), and the book of Revelation promises that "everyone who conquers" and remains faithful during times of intense persecution inherits Eden (2:7). Because of this history of interpretation, not only does the church present itself as the continuation of Israel's history; it also reimagines the Old Testament as a Christian book.

This is not Judaism's canonical story or way of reading Scripture. The Tanakh ends not with Malachi, for this prophet comes in the Nevi'im, the middle section in the canon. Rather, the last passage in the Tanakh is 2 Chronicles 36. The chapter introduces the edict of King Cyrus of Persia, the ruler who conquered the Babylonian Empire in 538 BCE and whom Isaiah called "God's anointed" or "God's messiah" (Isa. 45:1 reads: "Thus says the Lord to his anointed [messiah, Christ], to Cyrus, whose right hand I have grasped to subdue nations before him, and to strip kings of their robes, to open doors before him—and the gates shall not be closed"). According to the Chronicler, Cyrus proclaims: "The Lord, the

God of heaven, has given me all the kingdoms of the earth, and he has charged me to build him a house at Jerusalem, which is in Judah. Whoever is among you of all his people, may the Lord his God be with him! Let him go up" (2 Chron. 36:23).

Judaism's Scriptures thus have as their goal the return to Israel; in modern terms, this would be "making *aliyah*" or, literally, "going up." A few medieval Hebrew manuscripts end not with Chronicles but with Ezra-Nehemiah. But the same message of return to one's origins prevails, since Nehemiah's language of "God" and "good" harkens back to the Genesis creation in which "God" (*Elohim*) saw that everything was "good" (*tov*). The Tanakh thus ends not with a promise to be fulfilled by something new but with an injunction to return to one's home, to one's roots. For a modern analogy, sports metaphors prove helpful. Christianity is football (and not just because of possible "pigskin" references). There is a linear sense to the Christian canon; one moves from the promise of the line of scrimmage to the goal of the (eschatological) end zone. Judaism, at least as understood by the canonical order, is baseball. The concern is to return to Zion, to go home.

Different Interpretations

In addition to distinct translations and canonical orders, church and synagogue also maintain distinctive understandings of biblical figures and events. The problems such interpretations create in interfaith conversation are particularly acute in Protestant-Jewish relations. What for Jews and Catholics are the delights of multiple meanings are for many Protestants a gilding of the pure text. As some Protestant scholars see it, they have the pure text; Catholics and Jews have layers of fluff along with numerous thought-up rituals.

The synagogue and the Catholic and Orthodox communions read Scripture through traditional commentaries. For the churches, these include the allegorical interpretations of the church fathers, such as Augustine (354–430) and Jerome (ca. 340–420); they also include texts from a collection now known as the New Testament Apocrypha. These works, resembling folktales or Hellenistic romances, provide details ignored by the canon. What was Jesus's childhood like? See the *Infancy Gospel of Thomas*, which offers charming images of Jesus's turning mud pies into birds and horrific images of Jesus's striking dead playmates who don't play nice. What about Mary's childhood? See the *Protevangelium of James*, which describes, not surprisingly, Mary's birth to aged and righteous parents.

From the Jewish side, the rabbis told stories, called midrashim, in part to fill in gaps in the biblical text. How did Moses develop his speech impediment? One midrash explains that when Moses was an infant, a soothsayer in Pharaoh's court predicted that the baby would challenge Pharaoh's empire. To test the child, the Egyptian ruler put before him two plates, one filled with hot coals and the other filled with jewels. He rationalized that if the baby reached for the jewels, his throne would be in danger. The baby, attracted to the shiny stones, reached out for the jewels, but at the last minute an angel intervened (this sort of thing happens in midrashim as well as in the occasional text from the New Testament Apocrypha) and pushed the child's hand to the coals. Baby Moses, burning his finger, touched it to his lips; his lips too became burned—hence, a speech impediment.

Among the best known of the distinct interpretations are the understandings of the opening pages of Genesis. In his study of the story of Adam and Eve, Augustine, the bishop of the North African city of Hippo, declared that "the deliberate sin of the first man is the cause of original sin."[5] For Augustine, original sin is transmitted biologically, through the "seed of Adam," and it indicates that all humanity exists in a state of sin, which is a state of alienation from God. Only the water of baptism can remove this stain. The origin of the idea of original sin is Paul's Letter to the Romans: "Just as one man's trespasses led to condemnation for all, so one man's act of righteousness leads to justification and life for all" (5:18).

Because of their different understandings of shared stories, Jews and Christians also misunderstand why they come to different understandings of Jesus and of messianic ideas. For example, Judaism does not have a teaching of "original sin" per se; it does not presuppose a negative anthropology in which humanity exists in a state of alienation from God. Thus it does not require the sacrifice of the Christ to rectify the original breach. This is not to say, however, that Jewish tradition ignores Eden. One early midrash records: "After Adam sinned, the Holy One deprived Adam of six things: splendor of visage, lofty stature, life without death, perfection of the earth's fruit, the Garden of Eden, and brilliance of the luminaries in heaven. In the time to come, the Holy One will restore them."[6] A later legend from the Jewish mystical text the *Zohar* suggests Adam and Eve were originally covered in the substance that fingernails and toenails are made out of. Thus it explains why in the celebration of Havdalah, the ceremony separating the end of Sabbath from the rest of the week, Jews look at their fingernails in the light of the double-wicked candle: they are reminded that during the next six days of labor they carry with them a piece of the Sabbath and a piece of Eden.

Distinct understandings, also with theological implications, are had of the story of Abraham. Both Judaism and Christianity agree that the story of Abraham begins with a divine call in Genesis 12. For Paul, Abraham is called without having done anything to deserve it; he is, as Paul puts it, "justified by faith" (Rom. 4). Paul further asserts that the promises to Abraham that his people will be as numerous as the sand on the seashore and as the stars in the heaven bypass Abraham's descendants "according to the flesh" (i.e., the Jews) in favor of Jesus and those who follow him (so Galatians).

Jewish tradition fills in the details of Abraham's past, just as Catholic tradition tells us of Mary's childhood. One well-known midrash explains that Abraham worked in the idol shop of his father, Terah. Charged by his father with tending the store, young Abraham accidentally breaks one of the idols. Quickly realizing that creations made from stone and wood are not divine, he smashes all but one of his father's wares. His father, returning home, is understandably upset. "What did you do?" he screams at his son. "It wasn't me," responds little Abe. "It was that idol in the corner." Abraham came to the realization that since the idols were not gods, there must be a single divine authority. Thus the first move is that of Abraham to God, not God to Abraham. This charming story is also known in Islamic tradition, and a version appears in an early Christian text called the *Apocalypse of Abraham*.

Another midrash states: "When our father Abraham was born, a star rose in the East and swallowed four stars in the four corners of heaven. Nimrod's wizards said to him: 'To Terah, at this hour, a son has been born, out of whom will issue a people destined to inherit this world and the world to come. With your permission, let his father be given a house full of silver and gold, on condition that his newly born son be slain.'"[7]

The account echoes not only the story of Moses, whose life was threatened by Egypt's pharaoh, but even more closely the story of Jesus as told in Matthew 2.

As for Moses himself, a number of midrashim go out of their way to prevent the view that Moses is divine. The Babylonian Talmud (*Menachot* 29b) recounts how Moses receives God's permission to see the great teacher Rabbi Akiva. Seated in the last row of Akiva's school, Moses is so distressed by his inability to follow the discussion that he grows faint. Yet when Akiva's students inquire, "Master, where did you learn this?" Akiva responds, "It is a Law given to Moses at Sinai." In other words, Moses could not understand the interpretation of the Torah that he himself received. The story not only highlights Moses's limited knowledge but simultaneously praises those who continue to interpret the text and celebrates the text's own ability to speak to each generation.

This same praise and celebration mark not only the synagogue's understanding of narrative, but also its understanding of the Torah's legal material. According to the rabbinic tradition, at the same time Moses received the written Torah, he received the "oral Torah" or "oral Law" as well; this tradition of interpretation Moses passed on to Joshua, who delivered it to his successors, and on to the rabbis and their heirs today. *Pirke Avot*, a tractate of the Mishnah, details the transmission of the tradition.

Because of oral Law, one cannot read a text from the written Torah and claim to know what Judaism teaches. A number of Christians believe, primarily because of Jesus's statement in the Sermon on the Mount, "You have heard that it said, 'An eye for an eye and a tooth for a tooth.' But I say to you, do not resist an evildoer" (Matt. 5:38, citing Exod. 21:23–24; Lev. 24:19–20; Deut. 19:21; the next verse in Matthew speaks of turning the other cheek), that Judaism teaches justice without mercy and Jesus invented the mechanism to stop the retributive system. But Jewish tradition has its own gloss on that earlier legal material. The rabbis noted that there could never be certainty that the punishment was not worse than the crime, so they determined that, in the case of injury, the one causing the injury does not surrender a body part. Instead, they worked out a legal system that requires compensatory payment determined on the basis of damages, pain, medical expenses, loss of work due to injury, and anguish or embarrassment.[8] Thereby, the rabbinic tradition also refuses to repay evil with evil, even as it prepares anyone who studies it for law school.

When it comes to the legal or paraenetic material in their respective canons, both Christian and Jewish communities claim the right of interpretation, just as today in the United States judges provide interpretations of the Constitution and the Bill of Rights. Does the "right to bear arms" mean that one can carry a concealed gun into a church? Does the clause prohibiting Congress from establishing religion extend to the states? Is execution in the electric chair "cruel and unusual punishment"? The current debates over these issues show that interpretation of legal material is often both controversial and complicated.

For Jesus, interpretation of legal materials seems to have developed on an ad hoc basis. Someone would inquire about the legality of a particular issue, and he would offer a response. To the question of healing on the Sabbath, he said, "Absolutely." That he healed miraculously would not have transgressed Sabbath Laws. However, most physicians who follow Jesus today do not practice medicine on Sunday, in church, for people with chronic, nonpainful conditions. Jesus arrogated to himself the right to interpret Torah, and he did so in what the Gospels record was a remarkable way. At the end of the Sermon on the Mount, Matthew states: "Now when Jesus had finished saying these things, the crowds were astonished at his teaching, for he taught them as one having authority, and not as their scribes" (7:28–29). That is, he spoke without citing his teachers and without always offering scriptural precedent or justification.

In the Babylonian Talmud, the synagogue's arrogation to itself of the power to interpret Torah is discussed in a famous passage concerning the relatively mundane question of whether a particular oven is kosher. The protagonist, Rabbi Eliezer, argues that the oven is ritually pure, although his fellow rabbis disagree:

> Rabbi Eliezer related all the answers of the world and they were not accepted. Then he said, "Let this carob tree prove that the *Halakhah* agrees with me." Thereupon the carob tree was torn a hundred cubits out of its place (others affirm, four hundred cubits). They answered, "No proof can be brought from a carob tree."
>
> Again he said to them: "Let the spring of water prove that the *Halakhah* prevails." Thereupon the stream of water flowed backwards. They answered, "No proof can be brought from a stream of water."

Again he said to them: "If the *Halakhah* agrees with me, let the walls of the study house prove it," whereupon the walls were about to fall. But Rabbi Joshua rebuked them, saying: "When the sages of this study house are engaged in a *Halakhic* dispute, what (right) do You have to interfere?" They did not fall, in honor of Rabbi Joshua, nor did they resume the upright (position), in honor of Rabbi Eliezer; and they are still standing this way today.

Again he said to them: "Let it be announced by the heavens that the *Halakhah* prevails according to my statement!" A voice from heaven [*bat qol*, literally, "daughter of the voice"; the voice that speaks at Jesus's baptism is a *bat qol*] cried out: "Why do you dispute with Rabbi Eliezer, seeing that in all matters the *Halakhah* agrees with him?" But Rabbi Joshua arose and exclaimed: "The Torah is not in heaven." [See Deut. 30:12–14: "It is not in heaven, that you should say, 'Who will go up to heaven for us and get it for us so that we may hear and observe it?' Neither is it beyond the sea, that you should say, 'Who will cross to the other side of the sea for us, and get it for us that we may hear it and observe it?' No, the word is very near to you; it is in your mouth, and in your heart for you to observe."]

Rabbi Jeremiah [explaining this comment] said, "The Torah had already been given at Mount Sinai; we pay no attention to a voice from heaven [*bat qol*], because You have written that 'one follows the majority'" [Exod. 23:2].

Rabbi Nathan met Elijah [the prophet] and asked him, "What did the Holy One, Blessed be He, do in that hour?" He replied, "He laughed [with joy], saying, "My sons have defeated [or overruled] Me, My sons have defeated Me." (*Baba Metzia* 59a)

The passage teaches that because God has given Israel the Torah, it is now Israel's role to interpret it; in so doing, Israel honors both the Scriptures and God. The passage also indicates the responsibility of the communal voice: neither miracles nor individual charismatic authority can drive community practice. For the rabbinic tradition, no matter how honored, wise, or holy the individual rabbi, the "sages," speaking for and as the community, make final determinations on legal matters.

Conversely, church teaching often promoted the individual voice: first

Jesus, then Peter the "rock," then Paul. Although it did hold councils, such as Nicea in 325 and Chalcedon in 451—both under the sponsorship of the emperor—to ensure orthodoxy, the church's early literature tends to focus on the thoughts of individuals. Paul already establishes his own voice in 1 Corinthians 7 in the discussion of whether members of the congregation can divorce. First he cites Jesus (either recalling a teaching Jesus gave initially to his followers or one received through prophecy), and then he gives his own opinion: "To the married I give this command—not I but the Lord—that the wife should not separate from her husband.... To the rest I say—I and not the Lord—that if any brother has a wife who is an unbeliever, and she consents to live with him, he should not divorce her" (7:10–12). Similarly, although Acts 15 records a discussion about the entry of Gentiles into the church apart from their first converting to Judaism or at the very least submitting to circumcision, James makes the decision on policy.

This distinction between communal versus individual determination should not be overstressed. Within Judaism today, certain commentators, such as Maimonides and Rashi, prevail over others; within the church, councils and synods and presbyteries all contribute a communal voice. Nevertheless, the general sense in the Jewish tradition is that one argues with the text and with fellow Jews about the text, and that in some cases multiple meanings are possible. Jews are more inclined to say, "I'm right, and you may be right too." Christians, more familiar with the word from the pulpit, the hierarchy, or the individual (not just Jesus, but Paul, Augustine, Aquinas, Luther, Calvin, Wesley, etc.), may be more prone to seek a single response.

Concerning where these interpreters, either communally or individually, focus, again synagogue and church have different scriptural emphases. What is of major import to one community is irrelevant to another. Adam plays a much more central role in Christian theology than in Judaism; whereas for the church Jesus heals the breach Adam created between humanity and divinity, in Judaism there is no inherited irreparable breach. The church attends more to the prophets and the covenants with Abraham and David, while the synagogue focuses on the Torah, the covenant between God and the people Israel. Most churches pay little attention to the book of Esther, and Martin Luther wanted to remove it from the canon because it seemed "too Jewish" to him (the church's standard reference to Esther seems to be on the Sunday dedicated to the women of the congregation, when Mordecai's insistence that Esther had been chosen "for such a time as this" serves as the catalyst to describe the contributions of the women's guild). Conversely, Jews accord Esther's rescue of her people a holiday, Purim, on which the entire Megillah (literally "scroll," with the connotation of the book of Esther as *the* scroll) is chanted. The tradition developed in the rabbinic period that on Purim men would become so intoxicated that they could not tell the difference between the book's hero, Mordecai, and its villain, Haman. Churches tend not to promote this sort of thing. Ironically, the text of Esther in its Greek version preserved by the church makes the heroine a much more pious Jew than the Hebrew text read in the synagogue. Church and synagogue agree, however, that the Psalms are central to worship.

Different Practices

Sharing Psalms is one thing; sharing rituals is something else entirely. Jesus of Nazareth lived and died a faithful Jew. That does not mean, however, that his followers today should see themselves as "faithful Jews," or even that the members of the Pauline churches of the 40s and 50s of the first century should have seen themselves as such. There are certain elements of Jesus's Jewishness that the church, today a gentile institution, should not claim.

Across the United States and Canada, Christian churches are celebrating the Passover holiday by participating in the Jewish *seder*, that is, the ritual meal that recalls the exodus of the Hebrew people from Egyptian slavery (for the scriptural details, see Exod. 12:1–20; Lev. 23:5–8; Num. 28:16–25). The *seder*, meaning "order," is a choreographed celebration in which participants eat special foods (including a bitter herb; unleavened bread, called matzo; a green vegetable dipped in salt water; and charoset, a mixture of fruits, usually apples, spices such as cinnamon and ginger, nuts, and wine), drink four cups of wine, and tell the Passover story. Christian rationales for celebrating this ritual range from the desire to connect with Old Testament roots to the goal of following Jesus through his last week by celebrating the Passover as he did, for according to the Gospels of Matthew, Mark, and Luke, the Last Supper was a Passover meal, to an interest in learning about Jewish customs. Churches typically celebrate their *seders* on Holy Thursday, the day before Good Friday; the meal is often concluded with a Communion (or eucharistic) celebration.

The interfaith as well as spiritual benefits of this practice are substantial. First, Christians regain connection with the exodus event and so can enhance the meaning of Easter not only by celebrating the freedom from sin and death purchased by the cross but also by remembering that freedom from slavery is a precious gift still out of the reach of some even in the twenty-first century. Second, introducing Christian congregations to Jewish practices helps break down ignorance and enhance knowledge. During Passover time, beginning in 1144, Jews were, sporadically throughout Europe—in England (Norwich, Winchester, London, Lincoln), France (Blois), Germany (Ravensburg, Überlingen, Lindau), Austria (Vienna), Spain (Saragossa, La Guarida), Italy (Trent), Syria (Damascus), and Russia (Saratov)—accused of killing Christian children and using their blood to bake matzo. The last "blood libel" trial, the infamous "Beilis case," on which Bernard Malamud based his book *The Fixer,* took place less than a century ago, in Kiev in 1911–13. The custom at the *seder* of opening the door for the prophet Elijah—who, like Jesus in John 20, does not need to have the door opened for him in order for him to make an appearance—began as a protection against accusations of blood libel; it demonstrated to Christian neighbors that no child was being slaughtered. Blood-libel accusations remain a prominent part of Christian separatist, neo-Nazi, and Islamist rhetoric. Therefore, by learning about *seders* from Jews, Christians gain understanding of their neighbors and, at the same time, learn to combat such hateful teachings.

Understanding the traditional Jewish *seder* will also prevent confusion when Christians encounter a *seder* sponsored by messianic Jews, Jews for Jesus, and other groups that combine the proclamation of Jesus as Lord and Savior with Jewish identification and practice. The Christianized *seder* translates the various symbols of the meal—the matzo, the cups of wine, the hiding of a piece of matzo called the *afikomen* (ironically, a Greek term meaning "dessert")—into Christian terms. The perforations on the matzo symbolize the wounds Jesus suffers; the hidden piece represents Jesus's time in the tomb; and so forth. The New Testament already began the practice of transposing Jewish practices and texts into a new Christological key; the Christianized *seder* is another example of this retention and extension of a beloved ritual (if one approves of the practice), appropriation (if one is neutral), or co-optation (perhaps the nicest label, if one finds the practice illegitimate).

Yet the problems with the practice may outweigh these benefits. If the rationale for celebrating the *seder* is to "get back" to what Jesus did, then the goal necessarily fails. For Jesus, the Passover meal would have been consumed in Jerusalem, and it would have consisted of a lamb sacrificed in the Jerusalem Temple. Further, at the time of Jesus, while the Temple still stood, participation in the Passover sacrifice was restricted to Jews. Christian churches today that have a "closed table" for eucharistic celebration—that is, only those baptized in and in good standing with the church can participate in the fellowship meal—carry over that same ancient sacrificial model. The *seder* today is substantially a rabbinic tradition, which then developed over the centuries.

Nor is it certain that the Last Supper was a Passover meal. The synoptic Gospels set the Last Supper on the first night of Passover. However, they do not mention matzo or bitter herbs at the table; there is no discussion of the exodus from Egypt. Although absence of evidence does not preclude the Last Supper's being a *seder*, and although the term used for "bread" serves as a catchall term for all bread products, including "unleavened bread," the silence coupled with what is presented makes the Passover date unlikely. The synoptic Gospels suggest that the entire Jewish council, the Sanhedrin, met on the first night of Passover to determine Jesus's fate—this would be tantamount to gathering all the members of the Supreme Court, Congress, and the White House press corps together late on Christmas Eve to debate a minor case of law. If the story of Barabbas, the insurrectionist released from custody, has any credibility (see above, pp. 99–100), then the story makes no sense given the Synoptics' timing: he would have been released too late to celebrate the Passover.

John sets the Last Supper on the day before the holiday and thus dates Jesus's crucifixion to the "Day of Preparation," the time when the Passover lambs are being sacrificed in the Temple. The symbolism perfectly complements another unique aspect of the Fourth Gospel, namely, John the Baptist's identification of Jesus as the "Lamb of God who takes away the sin of the world" (1:29). Thus John's Gospel connects the death of Jesus to the paschal lamb whose blood saved the firstborn of Israel on the night of the tenth plague (Exod. 12). It may also suggest a connection of Jesus to Isaiah's suffering servant: "He was oppressed, and he was afflicted, yet he did not open his mouth; like a lamb that is led to the slaughter and like a sheep that before its shearers is silent, so he did not open his mouth" (53:7). "When you make his life an offering for sin, he shall see his offspring, and shall prolong his days; through him the will of the Lord shall prosper" (53:10). Increasing the paschal imagery, the Johannine Jesus is offered hyssop on the cross, and the text specifically mentions that Jesus's legs were not broken. Hyssop was used to dress the paschal lambs, and the sacrificial animal could not have a broken limb.

John also uses the Passover dating to demonstrate the hypocrisy of the Jewish leaders. "The Jews" bring Jesus to an interrogation before Pilate, but they refuse to enter Pilate's praetorium "to be able to eat the Passover in a state of ritual purity" (18:28b). They are willing to execute an innocent man, but they do not want to become impure. The dating of the Last Supper is thus symbolically exquisite.

It may also be historically credible, for John's description of Jesus's last hours makes more historical sense than the Synoptics' versions. John depicts not a Sanhedrin trial but a hearing before Annas, the father-in-law of the current high priest, Caiaphas. A Galilean upstart would not warrant a full hearing. Further, although it is difficult to determine the extent to which the Mishnaic material reflects events that occurred before 70 CE (it is difficult to determine the extent to which the Mishnah reflects social practice even at the time the document was written!), at least John's Gospel does make more sense in light of Mishnaic reflection. For example, *Sanhedrin* 4:1 forbids the trying of a capital case on either the start of the Sabbath (Friday night) or the eve of a festival day. John's dating does not violate the Mishnaic teaching; the Synoptics' does.

Theological arguments against churches celebrating *seders* are even stronger than the historical ones. For the church, the *seder* is replaced by the Eucharist, as the Gospel of John intimates when it speaks of Jesus as the "Lamb of God" or, even more definitively, when Paul states in 1 Corinthians 5:7: "Clean out the old yeast, so that you may be a new batch, as you really are unleavened. For our paschal lamb, Christ, has been sacrificed." If the Christ *is* the paschal lamb, then it would be not only historically inaccurate but also theologically unwarranted for Christians to celebrate the *seder*.

Even the food served at the *seder*, compared with the traditional Easter dinner of numerous Christians, reinforces the theological point. Jews mark the Passover with special food, even as Christians mark Holy Week gastronomically. In Europe, for example, the custom developed of eating ham on Easter. One might have thought that lamb would be the more appropriate symbol. But the consumption of ham signaled that the Christian was *not* a Jew, that the covenant with the Jews had been replaced by the covenant with the (gentile) Christians. Ludwig Feuerbach coined the expression, "You are what you eat," and he was right. Supersessionism in the Middle Ages was sealed with a pork chop.

Interfaith Possibilities

Once the differences between church and synagogue are acknowledged, Christians and Jews are in a better position to determine how far their mutual relations can go. On the matter of building bridges, the majority of the efforts toward interfaith biblical interpretation have come from the Christian side. Numerous church groups have recognized the benefits of conversations between Christians and Jews about the Bible. The Evangelical Lutheran Church in America asserts, "We as Christians share deep and common roots with Jews, not least books of Scripture revered by both communities. There is much to be gained in exploring those common roots, as well as the reasons for the 'parting of the ways' during the first generations of the followers of Jesus."[9] Similarly, the Presbyterian Church (USA) 199th General Assembly adopted "A Theological Understanding of the Relationship Between Christians and Jews," which, citing the prophet Isaiah, affirms: "We are willing to ponder with Jews the mystery of God's election of both Jews and Christians to be a light to the nations."[10]

On the subject of Jewish-Christian conversation on the Bible, the Roman Catholic Church has made the most extraordinary efforts. In December 2000, Joseph Cardinal Ratzinger, then prefect of the Congregation for the Doctrine of the Faith and now Pope Benedict XVI, stated in the Vatican's official paper, *L'Osservatore Romano:* "The faith witnessed to by the Jewish Bible (the Old Testament for Christians) is not merely another religion to us, but is the foundation of our own faith. Therefore, Christians—and today increasingly in collaboration with their Jewish sisters and brothers—read and attentively study these books of Sacred Scripture, as a part of their common heritage." In continuity with this assertion, in December 2001 the Pontifical Biblical Commission published *The Jewish People and Their Sacred Scriptures in the Christian Bible*.[11] This remarkable text makes the following assertions.

First, it insists that supersessionist readings are illegitimate. The church rejects any claim that it supersedes or replaces the synagogue as either a "new Israel" or a "true Israel."

Second, it recognizes that Christological interpretations of the "Old Testament" are made retrospectively; that is, readers should not be expected to find references to Jesus in the pages of the Old Testament unless they presuppose that those references are there. Christians see a reference to Jesus in Isaiah's description of the "man of suffering" who "was wounded for our transgressions, and crushed for our iniquities," who, "like a lamb that is led to the slaughter, and like a sheep that before its shearers is silent," was "stricken for the transgression of my people … although he had done no violence, and there was no deceit in his mouth" (53:3–9). In the New Testament, 1 Peter 2:21–25 alludes to Isaiah's words: "He committed no sin, and no deceit was found in his mouth.… He himself bore our sins in his body on the tree." For Christians, Jesus is thus the incarnation of Isaiah's suffering servant. Jews traditionally see Isaiah 53:3–9 as referring not to a single, future figure but to God's servant, the people Israel, redeemed from exile. Isaiah 41:8–9 reads: "But you, Israel, my servant, Jacob, whom I have chosen, the offspring of Abraham, my friend; you whom I took from the ends of the earth, and called from its farthest corners, saying to you, 'You are my servant, I have chosen you and not cast you off.'"[12] The Vatican document would allow for both interpretations.

Not only does the Pontifical Biblical Commission recognize the retrospective aspect of the church's interpretations; it acknowledges that Jewish readings of Scripture are viable, even when they disagree with Christian claims. The commission affirms: "The Old Testament in itself has great value as the Word of God. To read the Old Testament as Christians then does not mean wishing to find everywhere direct reference to Jesus and to Christian realities."

Because the document acknowledges the legitimacy of Jewish readings, it logically moves to the next point and in so doing advances Jewish-Christian dialogue far beyond where it had been:

Jewish messianic expectation is not in vain. It can become for us Christians a powerful stimulant to keep alive the eschatological dimension of our faith. Like them, we too live in expectation. The difference is that for us the One who is to come will have the traits of the Jesus who has already come and is already present and active among us.

For the Roman Catholic Church to consider kosher Jewish messianic expectation—expectation that does not relate to Jesus of Nazareth—is graciously generous.

Finally, the commission advises, "Christians can learn much from Jewish exegesis,"[13] that is, from Jewish understandings of the texts shared by church and synagogue. Thus, the connection drawn between the two communities extends beyond the Scriptures to the history of their interpretation.

Whether Jews would respond similarly to these Roman Catholic readings is an open question. For Christians to acknowledge Jewish interpretations is not quite the same thing as for Jews to acknowledge Christian ones. Christians should have little difficulty seeing Isaiah's suffering servant as referring *both* to Israel and to Jesus; Jews may find it impossible to take a "both/and" rather than "either/or" approach to the same passage. Nevertheless, given the grace that the Pontifical Biblical Commission's document shows toward Jewish biblical interpretation, Jews might at the very least consider the extent to which reciprocation is warranted. If the Roman Catholic Church can reject supersessionism, perhaps some synagogues might grant that the church is also under its own covenant with God. If the Vatican can sanction Jewish messianic hope and biblical interpretation, perhaps Jews might acknowledge that Christian hopes and interpretations are legitimate, at least for the church. Finally, Jews can certainly learn Christian biblical interpretation.

There is a difference, of course, between the church's reaching out to Jews and Jews' reciprocating with an acknowledgment of Christian covenantal roles. Jews are already part of the biblical tradition of the church, and the divine covenant the Bible describes between God and Israel is therefore a necessary component of Christian theology, whether it is seen as superseded or not. The New Testament is not, conversely, part of the Jewish tradition. However, both church and synagogue (as well as mosque) claim to be children of Abraham, and both claim a future vision premised on the idea that the God of Israel is the God of the world.

Whereas the past and the future hold the commonalities, today church and synagogue have different canons, different vocabularies, different understandings, and different practices. We might then return to the railroad analogy discussed above in relation to Paul's gospel but reconfigure the design. Synagogue and church may be pictured as railroad cars traveling on parallel tracks. The cars look the same from a distance: they both have wheels marked "Genesis" and "Isaiah"; they both have dining areas; they both have conductors. On closer inspection, the differences become more apparent. The synagogue also has wheels marked Talmud and midrash, and the church has wheels inscribed Gospels and Letters. The dining car of the synagogue has matzo-ball soup, whereas the specialty of the house for the church is ham. The conductors for the synagogue include Rashi and Maimonides; for the church, Augustine and Aquinas share driving duties. And the conductors drive on parallel, but separate, tracks. They and the passengers are aware that if one car gets derailed, the other will likely be damaged.

But this is only the immediate view. If we follow those parallel tracks back toward one horizon, we see that they meet. Skeptics call this an optical illusion; theologians call it God's-eye view. In that far past, there was only one track, that of Jesus and Hillel, James and Akiva, for all the passengers were Jews. They might have sat in separate rows, but they were all on the same track. There was no distinction between "Christian" and "Jew"; there were only Jews. If we look then to the other horizon, we see that the tracks meet once more. As different as they are, church and synagogue have the same goals, the same destination, whether called *olam habah*, the kingdom of heaven, or the messianic age. The two cars pull into the same station, and they have the same stationmaster there to welcome them.

SEVEN

Quo Vadis?

How, then, do we travel in the meantime, so that neither synagogue nor church gets derailed?

Jews and Christians are too often afraid to engage each other in interfaith conversation. We fear sounding ignorant. We fear giving the impression that we are trying to proselytize. Perhaps we fear that we might find something attractive about the other tradition and so question loyalty to our own. Worse, sometimes we do not even know what our own tradition teaches. Today these fears are exacerbated by stereotypes. We presume we already know what our neighbor will say: the Jew will advocate a pro-Israel agenda; the Christian will advocate an anti-abortion stance. In all these cases, defensive walls go up, and the result is ignorance at best, if not fear and even hate.

The following alphabet of suggestions addresses the major pitfalls that prevent church and synagogue from traveling together safely and smoothly and offers some suggestions for getting the journey under way.

A. Be cautious of any statement beginning "All Jews think ..." or any stereotype that asserts "All Jews are ..." Judaism in the first century and Judaism in the twenty-first are as diverse as was the early church. Similarly, it is historically untenable to state that "all Christians" follow the same orthodoxy or orthopraxy. The best we can do is talk within somewhat generous parameters. All interpreters come to the text first as individuals: informed by the past, but with distinct experiences and interpretations. Thus, none of us can fully speak for our community.

   a. Similarly, because diversity exists not only within the wider categories of Judaism and Christianity but also within individual congregations, do not claim "All Southern Baptists think ..." or "All Reform (not, by the way, "Reformed"; that is a designation for a set of Christian traditions) Jews think ..." Whereas the New Testament and Jesus of Nazareth hold Christian communities together, how Christians understand the text and the Jesus that text proclaims are as myriad as are Jewish views of God and Torah. If possible, Christians should attend different types of Jewish services. Just as Roman Catholic services differ from Southern Baptist ones, so Orthodox Judaism's worship differs from what is found in Reform congregations. When visiting, it is advisable either to go with a member of the congregation or to call the synagogue to arrange an escort. The same point holds for Jews. When visiting churches, Jews need not kneel or sing, pray, or participate. All that is required is respect; sit when the congregation sits, stand when it stands.

B. Recognize that Jewish sources and Christian sources both contain ugly, misogynistic, intolerant, and hateful material. Dialogue partners need to be able to acknowledge the bad as well as the good, and they should try to keep their levels of defensiveness under control. At the same time, try to avoid romanticizing the other.

C. Avoid selective use of rabbinic sources, especially if they are used as a negative foil for something in the New Testament. The general claim "The rabbis say ..." should set off alarm bells, as might today the comments "Christians say ..." and "All ministers say ..." It would be splendid if all citations to the rabbinic sources gave text, chapter, and verse. If such citation is lacking in a secondary source, be forewarned: the author may not have looked up the source directly (scholars tend to crib from other scholars without double-checking the footnoted references), and the quotation may have been yanked out of context or broken off without any conflicting information that might have accompanied it. The same point applies to citations of biblical sources and the church fathers.

D. Avoid comments that create the picture of a Jesus divorced from his own people. Jesus is not speaking against Jews and Judaism; he is speaking to Jews from within Judaism. However, also recognize that his words, put into the literary context of the Gospels and then put into the canon of the New Testament, may well take on problematic connotations. To understand Jesus, he must be seen as provocative enough both to prompt some to leave their homes and families and to follow him and to prompt others to regard him as insane or demon possessed. This means, at the very least, that his message is not an easy one to follow. Jesus demanded of his followers an economic overhaul and a nonviolent response to injustice. The former is at best impractical; the latter is psychologically difficult. Neither is beyond the competencies of most individuals, but Jesus asked for even more. A domesticated Jesus whose primary role is to make one "feel good" or "feel saved" is not a Jewish Jesus—and not a historical Jesus.

    a. Christians should be clear that Jesus and his immediate followers were Jewish by practice and belief, but they should also be cautious in determining how much of this practice can transfer into a Christian context.

E. Avoid the immediate association of Judaism with the Old Testament. Judaism is based on ever-evolving interpretations of the Tanakh; therefore Leviticus and Ezekiel do not necessarily provide readers any information about what Jews in the first century, or subsequently, do or think. The same point holds, mutatis mutandis, for the study of Christianity. The immediate problem that beset the church in Galatia—namely, whether the men should undergo circumcision—is not likely to be occupying Methodists in Memphis or Presbyterians in Pittsburgh. To understand Judaism and Christianity today, one must know not only the biblical material but also the history of its interpretation.

F. Recognize that history is a messy business, and religious competition makes it even messier. The Gospels are products of this process. They are not objective reports; rather, they are the stories passed down from the eyewitnesses to the later followers. The Gospel writers adapted the received traditions to fit the needs of their congregations, just as priests and pastors adapt the stories of the New Testament to address congregational concerns today. Part of this adaptation includes the separation between the majority Jewish body and the members of it who chose to follow Jesus. Like most sectarian movements, the nascent church needed to define itself over and against the synagogue majority. It also needed to explain why Jesus's own people did not follow him. Animosity had already developed during Jesus's lifetime between him and other Jews who rejected his message.

a. Few were willing to do what Jesus required: leave "house or wife or brothers or parents or children for the sake of the kingdom of God" (Luke 18:29); "sell all you own and distribute the money to the poor" (Luke 18:22); be "eunuchs for the sake of the kingdom of heaven" (Matt. 19:12). This is why we speak of those able to enter the religious life as possessing a spiritual gift or vocation.

b. As the church grew increasingly gentile, the Jewish followers of Jesus became a minority, and their practices eventually marked them as heretics. In deciding who it was, the church defined itself over and against the synagogue, and the synagogue reciprocated.

c. The majority of Jews, of course, had very good reasons for refusing the invitation. Those reasons included the lack of a messianic age: that heavenly banquet had not yet been set out. Those Jews who did believe that a messiah was coming—and not all did—put the messiah together with the messianic age; it was a package deal. The messianic age meant that the dead would rise, justice would prevail, and war, famine, disease, and death would stop. Clearly, that hadn't happened. Nor did the Jews believe, for the most part, that they needed Jesus's death to save them from sin or death. They believed, rather, in a compassionate God who always forgave the repentant sinner, and they did not believe they needed an intermediary. They had always prayed to their God directly.

d. But these were not the answers the church cared to promulgate. Rather, they came up with their own views. Most benignly, Paul explained Israel's "failure" by stating that a "hardening" had come upon the Jews until the gentile mission could be completed. The passage is not altogether a model of good Jewish-Christian relations (here the terms are anachronistic), since Paul does identify those hardened Jews as "enemies of God" and as lopped off the root of Israel (Rom. 11). Matthew suggests that the Jews were misled by their leaders. Ultimately, however, the people as a whole are responsible as well, for they chose to follow the Pharisees and scribes rather than Jesus. John asserts that the Jews were "children of the devil" who were not predestined to join the elect. "Jesus said to them, 'If God were your Father, you would love me, for I came from God.... Why do you not understand what I say? It is because you cannot accept my word. You are from your father the devil, and you choose to do your father's desires'" (8:42–44). If the Jews were on the side of the devil, then it followed that Jesus could not be on the side of the Jews, and so the long hatred began.

e. The time has come to agree to disagree, to recognize our connection, and to treat each other with respect and generosity. The animosity that marked the church's process of self-definition need not define Jewish-Christian relations today.

G. Be careful lest misunderstanding come about because Jews and Christians are not using words the same way. The "Bible" of the church is not the "Bible" of the synagogue; the "Messiah" proclaimed by Christianity, Jesus of Nazareth, is not the messiah proclaimed by Judaism; the church celebrates the Sabbath on Sunday; the synagogue celebrates the Sabbath from Friday evening until Saturday evening. Even our customs differ. For example, Jews traditionally do not handle money on the Sabbath and would never take out money in the synagogue on that day, for the Sabbath is a day of rest, not of trade. Conversely, Christians on Sunday, the church's Sabbath, pass a collection plate. What is unthinkable in one tradition is normative in the other.

H. Do not seek artificial connections, and do not be afraid of disagreement. For example, rather than considering interfaith dialogue to be about the "Judeo-Christian tradition," think rather of the contributions Judaism and Christianity separately make to the understanding of the Bible, the God of Israel, and the love of neighbor. "Judeo-Christian" is a politically expedient phrase that really means the "Old Testament" as interpreted by the church, plus Christianity. After the first few centuries CE, there is nothing distinctly "Judeo" about Christianity (Constantine, Luther, Calvin, Billy Graham, and James Dobson were or are not following rabbinic rulings, wearing *tzitzit*, keeping kosher, praying in Hebrew, or calling themselves "Jews"). "Christian" is not an appropriate adjective for Rashi, Rambam, the Baal Shem Tov, or Barbra Streisand.

I.   Watch out for the heresy known as Marcionism, named for Marcion, a mid-second century Christian who distinguished between the God of the Old Testament (and Judaism) and the God of the New (and so Christianity). The most common manifestation of Marcionism today is the false juxtaposition of the "Old Testament God of wrath" to the "New Testament God of love."

J.   Christians and Jews both need to know more about their own history before we can have any great success in interfaith conversation. Ideally, the conversation will then send the participants back to the resources of each tradition.

    a.   The need for both self-knowledge and knowledge of the neighbor is particularly important for clergy, because they are the ones who can convey information to congregations. Thus, all congregations should encourage the seminaries and divinity schools connected to their particular tradition to require students to learn interfaith sensitivity.

K.   If possible, read the Scriptures in an interfaith setting. Individuals do not always recognize the impact a text can have until they read it in the company of those directly affected. In other words, engage in "conversational theology."[1]

    a.   Similarly, learn to hear with each other's ears, for sermons and homilies can also inculcate anti-Judaism where none is intended. For example, the "Letter to the Eighth Assembly of the World Council of Churches from the Women and Men of the Decade Festival of the Churches in Solidarity with Women" speaks of the various organizations (SISTERS, ENYA) "which seek to honour the biblical vision of a world where 'there is no longer Jew or Greek.'"[2] The last line is a reference to Galatians 3:28: "There is no longer Jew or Greek, there is no longer slave and free, there is no longer male and female, for all of you are one in Christ Jesus." But to my ears and perhaps to other readers of this appeal, I hear a desire that my people, that Jews, cease to exist. Heaven forbid that we would find the "biblical vision" to be a world where there is no longer a Jew (I suspect those of Greek descent might feel the same way). In like manner, synagogues might make clear what they mean by "chosen people." In other words, we need to be able to listen with the ears of our neighbors.

L. Speak out when you hear negative comments about the neighbor and, if necessary, speak out in a public forum. When I presented the material from the World Council of Churches' publications to the International Council of Christians and Jews, a few people chided me for doing so. They said the way to eliminate anti-Semitic and anti-Jewish materials is to speak directly to the authors. This is a naïve view. Personal contact will not remove the material from the bookshelves in Manila, Seoul, or Chicago. Further, unless people who work in interfaith relations are aware of what is on the bookshelves, they will have no reason to seek to counter it. Nor does private communication always work. My privately contacting some of the writers cited as presenting material that could be seen as anti-Jewish resulted not in correction but in denial: they did not "intend" to be anti-Jewish; I was projecting my own psychological concerns; and so on.

M. Note that anti-Judaism may arise in the hymnal. The best example of this is "Lord of the Dance," which is sung to a fairly bouncy Shaker tune. In the third verse, the voice of Jesus trills: "I danced on the Sabbath, and I cured the lame. The holy people said it was a shame. They whipped and they stripped, and they hung me on high; and they left me there, on a cross to die." Tra-la-la. Congregants and the choir will not think that the "holy people" refers to the Romans. There is no need to reintroduce the idea that Jews are Christ killers in a major key.

    a. Anti-Jewish impressions can also be delivered by the spiritual guides and daily devotionals found in a number of church foyers. At an Episcopal church in Memphis, I picked up the small booklet *Forward Day by Day*, in which I read in the entry for Saturday, June 25: "The belief that the Messiah would raise an army, retake the land, and restore the kingdom of David was deeply engrained in the cultural consciousness and in their [the disciples'] minds and hearts. A military solution was what the world understood."[3] The reading did not "intend" to be anti-Jewish. When I asked a few of the parishioners what they thought about the paragraph, they all stated something to the effect that "the Jews" wanted a "military messiah" or a "warrior messiah."

N. Notice as well that anti-Jewish impressions can be conveyed by lectionary readings, that is, the practice some churches have for set readings from the Old Testament, the Psalms, the Gospels, and the Letters. Homilists need to be alert for the slippage that sometimes occurs between what the texts say and the impression that can be conveyed to the congregation.

O. Address why Jesus died, because far too prevalent are explanations that rely on negative stereotypes of Judaism and Jews. Jesus did not die because he taught that the poor would have an easier time getting into heaven than the rich; he did not die because he rejected Torah; he did not die because he preached love of God and love of neighbor. He died because a man being proclaimed "king" in Roman-occupied Jerusalem was a political liability. He died under the criminal charge of sedition: "Jesus of Nazareth, king of the Jews."

P. Park guilt and entitlement at the door before engaging in interfaith conversation. Some Christians come to the interfaith table so aware of their history of supersessionism, anti-Semitism, and violence against Jews that they avoid claiming that Jesus is the Messiah, for to do so would be telling Jews that Judaism is wrong. They refrain from stating that Jesus is divine, that his crucifixion and resurrection defeated the powers of sin and death, and that "no one comes to the Father" except through him. Conversely, aware of the tragic history of supersessionism, anti-Semitism, and violence against Jews, some Jews come to the table with a sense of entitlement: they seek apologies rather than engagement. Neither approach is useful. Christians today are not responsible for the sins of the past; Jews today are not in the position to grant forgiveness for those sins. Neither Judaism nor Christianity has a pristine history, and victimization is not something to be celebrated.

Q. A similar situation prevails with public prayer. Some Christian ministers resort to a watered-down, generic invocation that satisfies few. Some insist on praying in the "name of Jesus," which prevents Jews and other non-Christians from saying "Amen." Atheists are ignored in any case. More cynical biblical readers, finding dissatisfactory public prayer ranging from high-school students gathered around flagpoles to senators representing the American people in Washington, might cite the Sermon on the Mount. Jesus states: "Whenever you pray, do not be like the hypocrites, for they love to stand and pray in the synagogues and at the street corners [and around flagpoles, and at legislative assemblies, and on television broadcasts ...], so that they may be seen by others. Truly I tell you, they have received their reward. But when you pray, go into your room and shut the door and pray to your Father who is in secret; and your Father who sees in secret will reward you" (Matt. 6:5–6). But since public religiosity is not going to go away, then the person offering the prayer needs to find a way of invoking the deity in a way that both affirms distinct confessions and recognizes the existence of alternative truth claims. Ending a prayer "in the name of Jesus" keeps the prayer parochial. Ending it "as I pray in the name of Jesus" is a bit of an improvement. "As I pray in the name of Jesus, and we all pray to the God who has many names and many children" is even better. The fundamentalist Christian should have little objection, since the God of the Bible does have many names: El Shaddai, El Elyon, YHWH, Elohim. In turn, Jews may choose to pray in Hebrew, but then they should provide a translation so the people in attendance know to what, exactly, they are saying "Amen." Atheists, of course, are still left out, but at least the theists in the group are all included.

R. Do not bear false witness against the neighbor. For example, the argument that Jesus set up his "new Jewish charismatic movement that departed in certain key ways from biblical authenticity" in Galilee, since "it would be much easier to pull off such a thing there, among the relatively simple folk, than in the south, in Judea and its metropolis, Jerusalem, with its rabbis, its priests, who would know better,"[4] both overstates the historical evidence and manages to insult Christianity. Regardless of what the fishermen and tax collectors knew or didn't know about what the folks in the south did, the movement nevertheless became based not in Galilee, but in Jerusalem. Apparently, those Galilean peasants did not find much appealing about Jesus, and he recognized their rejection of him: "Woe to you, Chorazin! Woe to you, Bethsaida!... And you, Capernaum,... will be brought down to Hades" (Matt. 11:21–23). Even if these harsh lines come not from Jesus himself but from his followers, the point still holds: the decision

to follow Jesus was not a matter of ignorant Galileans versus sophisti-
cated and better-informed Judeans. Some Judeans followed Jesus;
some Galileans did not. Today, some intellectual, well-informed Jews
choose to convert to Christianity, and some intellectual, well-
informed Christians choose to convert to Judaism.

S. Christian missionaries who seek to bring Jews the "good news of
Jesus" do not do so because they hate Jews; they do so because they
love Jews. On the other hand, the message that Jews are not "complete" or "fulfilled" unless they accept Jesus as the Messiah is not
likely to be received by most Jews with great warmth; it is tantamount
to telling Christians that their religion is incomplete or erroneous
without acceptance of the Qur'an. Thus, again, Jews and Christians
need to listen with each other's ears. Jews need to hear the sincerity in
the Christians' message; Christians need to respect the integrity of the
Jewish position.

    a. For Jews who are concerned about missionaries seeking to
        convert their children, the best way of preventing the tempta-
        tion is not to bash the church or to point out inconsistencies
        in Christian understandings of their Old Testament. The best
        way to prevent missionaries from making inroads among Jews
        is to teach Jews about Judaism: its ethical code, its theology,
        its messianic teaching, and its history. Judaism cannot afford
        to be a reactionary religion.

    b. For Christians who feel compelled to evangelize—as they are
        commanded to do in Matthew 28:19, "make disciples of all
        the nations"—the best means of evangelizing is to act, rather
        than to preach or go door-to-door. Thus, Christians might
        consider stepping up to the front lines of work for justice,
        and when they are asked why they are seeking health-care cov-
        erage for the poor, taking in foster children, or visiting people
        in prison, they can respond, "Because the love of Christ com-
        pels me."

T. Be particularly careful when engaging in conversation about the Middle East. Prepare for conversation by exploring the history of the
conflict, and do so by looking at a variety of sources. Do not equate
Israel's relationship to the Palestinians with the Nazi treatment of the
Jews (if this were the case, there would be, after sixty years, no "Pales-

tinian question"); do not state that all Palestinians left their homes in 1948 "voluntarily"; do not equate all Palestinians with the violent few, and do not dismiss the suffering that they face. Finally, do not equate "Jew" with "Israeli," and then "Israeli" with "hard-liner." On the positive side, seek suggestions on how Israeli citizens might be secure from terrorism, and do not adopt the naïve belief that if Israel simply pulls back its borders to the 1967 line all will be fine. The Gaza pullout has occurred, and bombers are still trying to blow up Israelis. Participate in this conversation, but also obtain information about Palestinian teaching and textbooks where not just anti-Israeli but anti-Semitic comments abound. Similarly, obtain information about how the ultra-Orthodox portray Palestinians. According to the book of Genesis, Ishmael and Isaac came together, in peace, to bury Abraham. If the younger generation is already poisoned, then another generation of killing is almost inevitable.

U. Double-check that your Hebrew school, Sunday school, and religious education teachers are informed about both the history of their own tradition and the history of the other. Untrained but well-meaning teachers tend to implant a great deal of religious bigotry. Just as parents today do well to check the assignments given in the regular school system, so too should they check the assignments for religious education.

V. If possible, learn Hebrew and Greek and read the primary texts in the original. To take Scripture seriously should mean taking seriously what it might have originally conveyed. If possible as well, read the other sources of the period: the Dead Sea Scrolls, the Apocrypha and Pseudepigrapha, Josephus and Philo, early rabbinic literature, and the various gentile writers who provide a context for the times. Even more, read the archaeological studies of life in Galilee and in the Diaspora as well as in Judea. The first century is not our world, and we need to catch ourselves before we impose our own lifestyles and values on the ancient sources.

W. Be wary of Internet sites. Anti-Jewish and anti-Semitic groups have flooded the Internet with selective citations from Jewish sources designed to make Judaism look uniformly evil (often these sites then explain why the "Christian" way is better). There are similar sites dedicated to anti-Catholic and anti-Muslim views. Distinguishing the harmful and hateful from the helpful is not always an easy task. The best place to start on interfaith relations is the Center for Christian-Jewish Learning at Boston College (http://www.bc.edu/research/cjl/).

X. Practice holy envy: look at the other tradition with generosity and seek to see the good.

Y. Finally, if all else fails, psychological manipulation may prove effective. At Vanderbilt, I have been known to bring my son to my class. I introduce him to my students, and then I say: "When you speak of Jews, picture this kid in the front pew. Don't say anything that will hurt this child, and don't say anything that will cause a member of your congregation to hurt this child." I grant that the move is theatrical and manipulative; it's also remarkably effective.

Z. And just in case that doesn't sink in, I also tell them to imagine me sitting in the back of the church. Twice, I have found myself on my feet, literally, during a sermon, because I simply could not refrain from reacting to a proclamation of hate (one was a sermon using Jews as negative foils; the other devolved into gay bashing).

Today's interfaith conversations are at a critical point. We have acknowledged the problems of the past; we have realized the major points of contention for the present; the next step is to see what solutions we can bring to the concerns of the future. But as we begin to highlight the differences, the aspects of our traditions that cannot be shared, the need to compromise in some cases and the refusal to do so in others, we might note that both church and synagogue have an ultimate focus on peace discovered through a combination of action and belief.

Judaism follows *halakhah*, the "way" or the "path"; alternatively, Jews speak of *derekh eretz*, literally, the "way of the land," but with the connotations of appropriate behavior. Jews do this not to earn a place in heaven (this is already part of the covenant between God and Israel), but because this is our role as human beings, made in the divine image and in relationship with God. We see Jesus doing this in the New Testament; as he puts it, he comes not to abolish Torah, but to fulfill it. The church follows what the book of Acts calls *hodos*, the "way" (as in the English "odometer"), with good works prompted by divine grace. The goal of both traditions, then, is a combination of belief and action, with the hope that the future will be one of peace and sanctity.

Epilogue

In the summer of 2004, I was sent to the Philippines by the Catholic Biblical Association of America to give a series of lectures on Jesus and Judaism. In the Maryknoll Convent in Project 4, Quezon City, Manila, where I was staying, Sr. Helen Graham handed me a volume by the Catholic writer Megan McKenna, in which I found the following rabbinic story:

> In a dream, a devout disciple of the master was permitted to approach the Temple in Paradise where all the great old sages who had studied the Talmud all their lives were now spending eternity. He gazed in at them, and to his amazement, they were all sitting around tables, just as they had done on earth, studying the Talmud still! The disciple watched them passionately exclaiming and arguing and reverently fingering the text. He wondered, "Is this really Paradise? It seems like the earth." But then his thoughts were interrupted by warm laughter. "You are mistaken. This is not Paradise. The sages are not in Paradise. Paradise is in the sages."[1]

I immediately thought of Luke 17:20–21. Some Pharisees inquired of Jesus when God's kingdom would come. He answered, "The kingdom of God is not coming with things that can be observed; nor will they say, 'Look, Here it is!' or 'There it is!' For in fact the kingdom of God is among you" [or even "in your midst!"].

In these days of interfaith relations, a Catholic woman can teach me a midrash, and I can respond to her by citing a Gospel text that she does not mention.

The Pontifical Biblical Commission's document states: "In the past, the break between the Jewish people and the Church of Christ Jesus could sometimes, in certain times and places, give the impression of being complete. In the light of the Scriptures, this should never have occurred. For a complete break between the church and the synagogue contradicts Sacred Scripture." The connections church and synagogue share, not only in the recognition of the same sacred stories, but also in the similar interpretive understandings, necessarily hold the two movements together. If Isaac and Ishmael, and Jacob and Esau, can learn to live together in peace, there is hope not only for the responsible and the prodigal; there is hope for church and synagogue as well. And if the church and synagogue both could recognize their connection to Jesus, a Jewish prophet who spoke to Jews, perhaps we'd be in a better place for understanding.

Acknowledgments

I wish to acknowledge the support, encouragement, and critiques of numerous friends. To Professor Ben Witherington III, Dr. John Dominic Crossan, Rabbi Micah D. Greenstein, Dr. Eugene Fisher, Dr. Michael Cook, Dr. Elaine Wainwright, R.S.M., Dr. Mary Margaret Pazdan, O.P., Dr. Barbara Reid, O.P., Dr. Carolyn Osiek, R.S.C.J., The Most Reverend Richard J. Sklba, Dr. Carey Newman, Michael Domeracki, Maria Mayo Robbins, Alan Sherouse, and Robert Aronson, Esq., I owe enormous thanks for encouragement and good humor. Eric Brandt, my editor at Harper San Francisco: you are splendid! Lisa Zuniga, for her patience and attention to detail. Appreciation is also due to the Catholic Biblical Association of America, the Maryknoll Sisters of Quezon City, the Philippines, and their colleagues in the Catholic Biblical Association of the Philippines, the faculty and students at the Baptist Theological School of Richmond, Brite Divinity School, Episcopal Divinity School (Cambridge), Aquinas Institute (St. Louis), General Theological Seminary, Eden Theological Seminary, St. John's University (Collegeville, Minnesota), Luther Seminary, Bangor Theological Seminary, the University of Judaism, Baylor University, Tulane University, Flagler College, Averett College, the University of Richmond, West Virginia University, Bucknell University, Clemson University, Furman University, Earlham College, Trinity Lutheran Seminary, University of California at San Diego, Union Theological Seminary (Virginia), Seton Hall University, Adrian College, the University of Alabama, the National Cathedral and Cathedral College (Washington, DC), and the Institute for Jewish-Christian Understanding of Muhlenberg College.

Congregations that model an interest in interfaith conversation include, in Nashville, West End United Methodist Church, Westminster

Presbyterian Church, Christ Cathedral, Greater Nashville Unitarian Universalist Congregation, the Temple (Congregation Ohabai Shalom), Brentwood United Methodist Church, and St. Paul's Episcopal Church (Franklin). Splendid work also continues with the interfaith group of Mobile, Alabama, Congregation Beth Israel (West Hartford, Connecticut), Charis Ecumenical Center (Concordia College), West Shore Committee for Jewish-Christian Dialogue (Muskegon), Temple Beth-El and Myers Park Baptist Church (Charlotte, North Carolina), the Everett Institutes of the 92d St. Y, Temple Jeremiah (Northfield, Illinois), Temple Beth-Am (Abingdon, Pennsylvania), the E.L.C.A. Northern Illinois and Northeastern Ohio Synods, Christ Church Cathedral and Christian Theological Seminary (Indianapolis), Pennsylvania State Pastors' Conference, Epworth United Methodist Church (Elizabeth, New Jersey), First United Methodist Church (Orlando), Greater Durham Ministers Conference (North Carolina), the Anderson School of Theology (Anderson, South Carolina), St. Luke's United Methodist Church and Mizpah Congregation (Chattanooga), Congregation B'nai Jeshurun/Church of St. Paul and St. Andrew (New York), the Dayton Jewish-Christian Dialogue group, the interfaith group of Fresno, the United Church of Christ, Missouri Mid-South Conference, Christian Church/Disciples of Christ of MidAmerica, the Joseph Cardinal Bernadin Center, Temple Beth Ha-Tephila (Asheville, North Carolina), Temple Israel (Memphis) and the Memphis Ministers Association, the Kansas Area Seminar on Professional Ministry, Stetson University Pastors' School, Palm Beach Fellowship of Christians and Jews, Lake Travis United Methodist Church (Austin, Texas), St. James Episcopal Church (Lenoir, North Carolina), Temple Sinai (New Orleans), the Cathedral of St. John (Providence, Rhode Island), St. John's Lutheran Church/Temple Sinai (Summit, New Jersey), Houston's Foundation for Contemporary Theology, Congregation Shaarai Zedek (Tampa), the Jewish Center of the Hamptons, St. Martin De Porres Shrine and Institute (Memphis), Park Synagogue/Anshe Ameth Beth Tefilo Congregation (Cleveland Heights), the Catholic-Jewish Conference of Milwaukee, the United Church of Christ of Ames, Iowa, First Congregational Church (San Jose), Grace United Methodist Church (Naperville, Illinois), Temple Sinai, Congregation Beth-El and Sixth Presbyterian Church (Pittsburgh), Larchmont Temple, Congregation Beth Emeth (Albany), Temple De Hirsch-Sinai and the

Shemanski Institute for Christian and Jewish Understanding (Seattle), First Presbyterian Church and Ohev Tzedek Congregation (Youngstown, Ohio), Grace–St. Luke's Episcopal Church (Memphis), Greater Carolinas Association of Rabbis, the Westminster Presbyterian Church and Community for Progressive Christianity (Wilmington, Delaware), and the Stephen Wise Free Synagogue (New York).

Notes

INTRODUCTION

1 For an exhaustive treatment of Mosaic motifs in Matthew's Gospel, see Dale C. Allison Jr., *The New Moses: A Matthean Typology* (Minneapolis: Fortress, 1993).

2 Krister Stendahl, "Can Christianity Shed Its Anti-Judaism?" *Brandeis Review* (Spring 1992): 27.

3 James Carroll, *Constantine's Sword: The Church and the Jews: A History* (New York: Houghton Mifflin, 2001); David Klinghoffer, *Why the Jews Rejected Jesus: The Turning Point in Western History* (New York: Doubleday, 2005).

4 See Simon Wiesenthal, *The Sunflower* (New York: Schocken, 1976).

ONE: JESUS AND JUDAISM

1 E.g., E. P. Sanders, *Jesus and Judaism* (Philadelphia: Fortress, 1987); Geza Vermes, *Jesus the Jew* (Philadelphia: Fortress, 1973); *The Gospel of Jesus the Jew* (Newcastle upon Tyne: University of Newcastle upon Tyne, 1983); *Jesus and the World of Judaism* (London: SCM, 1983); *The Religion of Jesus the Jew* (Philadelphia: Fortress, 1993); James H. Charlesworth, *Jesus Within Judaism* (New York: Doubleday, 1988); James H. Charlesworth, ed., *Jesus' Jewishness: Exploring the Place of Jesus in Early Judaism* (New York: Crossroad, 1991); John Meier, *A Marginal Jew*, vol. 1 (New York: Doubleday, 1991), vol. 2 (1994), vol. 3 (2001); Bernard Lee, *The Galilean Jewishness of Jesus* (New York: Paulist, 1988); Geza Vermes, *Jesus in His Jewish Context* (Minneapolis: Fortress, 2003); Donald A. Hagner, *The Jewish Reclamation of Jesus* (Grand Rapids: Zondervan, 1984).

2 David Klinghoffer, *Why the Jews Rejected Jesus: The Turning Point in Western History* (New York: Doubleday, 2005), p. 59.

3 David Stern, *Parables in Midrash: Narrative and Exegesis in Rabbinic Literature* (Cambridge, MA: Harvard University Press, 1991), p. 57.

4 Stern, *Parables in Midrash*, p. 57.

5 Robert Doran, "The Pharisee and the Tax Collector: An Agonistic Story" (unpublished paper).

6 Timothy A. Friedrichsen, "The Temple, a Pharisee, a Tax Collector, and the Kingdom of God: Rereading a Jesus Parable (Luke 18:10–14A)," *Journal of Biblical Literature* 124.1 (2005): 89–119 (94).

7 Doran, "The Pharisee and the Tax Collector."

8 Friedrichsen, "The Temple, a Pharisee, a Tax Collector, and the Kingdom of God," p. 118.

9 James Barr, "'Abba' Isn't 'Daddy,'" *Journal of Theological Studies* 39 (1988): 28–47.

10 John Ashton, "Abba," in D. N. Freedman, ed., *The Anchor Bible Dictionary*, vol. 1 (New York: Doubleday, 1992), p. 7, citing Joachim Jeremias, "Abba," in Joachim Jeremias, *The Prayers of Jesus*, trans. John Bowden (London: SCM, 1967), pp. 11–65.

11 See Vermes, *Jesus the Jew*, p. 211.

12 *Roman History* 18.2–3. See additional citations as well as discussion in Mary Rose D'Angelo, "*Abba* and Father: Imperial Theology in the Contexts of Jesus and the Gospels," in Amy-Jill Levine, Dale C. Allison Jr., and John Dominic Crossan, eds., *The Historical Jesus in Context* (Princeton, NJ: Princeton University Press, forthcoming).

13 *On Prayer* 27, 7; see the entry for *epiousion* in Frederick W. Danker, ed., *A Greek-English Lexicon of the New Testament and Other Early Christian Literature*, 3d ed. (Chicago and London: University of Chicago Press, 2000), pp. 376–77.

14 Translation by A. F. Klijn in James H. Charlesworth, ed., *The Old Testament Pseudepigrapha*, vol. 1 (New York: Doubleday, 1983), pp. 615–52. Rabbinic parallels on the banquet and the great monsters include the Palestinian Talmud *Sanhedrin* 10:5; *Genesis Rabbah* 19:4; and *Pesiqta de Rav Kahana* 6:8.

15 See *1 Enoch* 7–8, 69; 10; 21:7–10; 64–65; 69; *Jubilees* 5:16–11; 8:3.

TWO: FROM JEWISH SECT TO GENTILE CHURCH

1 For early statements concerning the general resurrection, see, e.g., Isaiah 26:19 ("Your dead shall live, their corpses shall rise") and Ezekiel 37:7–10 (the vision of the valley of the dry bones that "come together, bone to its bone").

2 Antiochus's abuses prompted what is known as the Maccabean revolt in 167 BCE. Defeating the Syrian forces, the Maccabees—so named for their general, Judah, nicknamed "Maccabee," the "Hammerer"—gained political independence; the holiday Hanukkah commemorates the Maccabees' rededication of the Temple in Jerusalem, which Antiochus had profaned.

3 This discussion is dependent on Judith M. Lieu, "Circumcision, Women and Salvation," *New Testament Studies* 40/3 (1994): 358–70, included in her *Neither Jew nor Greek?* SNTW (London: Clark, 2002), pp. 101–14.

4 See also Halvor Moxnes, *Putting Jesus in His Place: A Radical Vision of Household and Kingdom* (Louisville: Westminster John Knox, 2003).

5 The earliest references to these laws are in *Sanhedrin* 9:4 in the Tosefta (ca. 250); see also the Babylonian Talmud *Sanhedrin* 56a–b.

6 Citation from Hayim Nahman Bialik and Yehoshua Hana Ravnitzky, eds., *The Book of Legends: Sefer Ha-Aggadah*, trans. William Braude (New York: Schocken, 1992), p. 31.

7 See Daniel Boyarin, *Dying for God: Martyrdom and the Making of Christianity and Judaism* (Stanford, CA: Stanford University Press, 1999); *Borderlines: The Partition of Judaeo-Christianity* (Philadelphia: University of Pennsylvania Press, 2004).

THREE: THE NEW TESTAMENT AND ANTI-JUDAISM

1 See Elaine Pagels, *Beyond Belief: The Secret Gospel of Thomas* (New York: Random House, 2003).

2 Ben Witherington III, *Commentary on 1 and 2 Thessalonians* (forthcoming).

3 Beginning with "Guidelines and Suggestions for Implementing the Conciliar Declaration *Nostra Aetate*," No. 4, Vatican Commission for Religious Relations with the Jews (December 1, 1974), continuing with "Notes on the Correct Way to Present the Jews and Judaism in Preaching and Catechesis in the Roman Catholic Church," Vatican Commission for Religious Relations with the Jews (June 24, 1985), and including numerous documents not only

from American bishops, but also from the bishops of France (1973, 1997), Germany (1980, 1988 [with Austria], 1995), Poland (1991, 1995, 2000), Hungary (1994), the Netherlands (1995), Switzerland (1997), and Italy (1997). The churches of Asia, Africa, and Latin America are absent from this list, primarily because the events of the Shoah did not take place in their areas and also, I suspect, because they do not perceive a "Jewish problem." See http://www.bc.edu/research/cjl/resources/documents/catholic/.

4 Justin Martyr *Dialogue with Trypho* 16.4; see 96.2.

5 Epiphanius *Haereses* 29.9.

6 Jerome *Commentary on Isaiah* 2.18.

7 Boyarin, *Borderlines*, p. 69; the following discussion draws from this volume, esp. pp. 68–70.

8 Boyarin, *Borderlines*, p. 70.

9 Burton L. Visotzky, "Methodological Considerations in the Study of John's Interaction with First-Century Judaism," in John R. Donahue, ed., *Life in Abundance: Studies in John's Gospel in Tribute to Raymond E. Brown* (Collegeville, MN: Liturgical Press, 2005). See also the discussion in Boyarin, *Borderlines*, esp. pp. 222–25.

10 See Amy-Jill Levine, "Anti-Judaism and the Gospel of Matthew," in W. Farmer, ed., *Anti-Judaism and the Gospels* (Valley Forge, PA: Trinity Press International, 1999).

11 http://learn.jtsa.edu/topics/quote/archive/111201.shtml.

FOUR: STEREOTYPING JUDAISM

1 The material in this chapter was developed in two talks. The first, "Christians Say the Darndest Things," was given at Baylor University in Waco, TX (March 2005). The second, "Kinky Friedman, Jesus, and Judaism," was a plenary address to the Catholic Biblical Association of America at St. John's University in Collegeville, MN (August 2005). That a Baptist university and a society that promotes Catholic biblical scholarship would welcome a Jewish woman who belongs to an Orthodox synagogue to talk about the New Testament and anti-Judaism shows a generosity of spirit, an open mind, and the progress made in interfaith conversation.

2 Warren Carter, *Matthew and Empire: Initial Explorations* (Harrisburg, PA: Trinity Press International, 2001), p. 122.

3 Josephus *War* 2.117–18; *Antiquities* 18.1–10.

4 Josephus *War* 2.169–74; *Antiquities* 18.55–59.

5 Josephus *War* 2.175–77; *Antiquities* 18.60–62.

6 Josephus *Antiquities* 18.261–72, 305–9.

7 Justin Martyr *Apologia* 1.31.6.

8 Lester A. Grabbe, *Judaism from Cyrus to Hadrian*, 2 vols. (Minneapolis: Fortress, 1992), 2: 580–81.

9 A variant appears in *Lamentations Rabbah* 2.2.4.

10 Luke Timothy Johnson, *The Acts of the Apostles*, Sacra Pagina 5 (Collegeville, MN: Liturgical Press, 1992), p. 26.

11 "Psalms of Solomon," trans. R. B. Wright, in James H. Charlesworth, ed., *The Old Testament Pseudepigrapha*, 2 vols. (Garden City, NY: Doubleday, 1985), 2: 639–70 (667).

12 Joanna Dewey, "'Let them renounce themselves and take up their cross': A Feminist Reading of Mark 8.34 in Mark's Social and Narrative World," in Amy-Jill Levine, ed., *A Feminist Companion to Mark*, Feminist Companion to the New Testament and Early Christian Writings, 2 (Sheffield: Sheffield Academic Press, 2001), pp. 22–36 (24).

13 *On the Dress of Women* 1.1.2.

14 http://www.jhom.com/topics/topsyturvy/women.html, from Judith Hauptmann, *Re-reading the Rabbis: A Woman's Voice* (Boulder, CO: Westview Press, 1998).

15 Jerome H. Neyrey, "What's Wrong with This Picture? John 4, Cultural Stereotypes of Women, and Public and Private Space," in Amy-Jill Levine, ed., *A Feminist Companion to John*, vol. 1, Feminist Companion to the New Testament and Early Christian Writings, 4 (Sheffield: Sheffield Academic Press, 2003), pp. 98–125 (123–24). The article originally appeared in *Biblical Theology Bulletin* 24 (1994): 77–91.

16 Neyrey, "What's Wrong with This Picture?" p. 124.

17 See the several articles on the Samaritan woman in Amy-Jill Levine, ed., *A Feminist Companion to the Gospel of John*, 2 vols. (Sheffield: Sheffield University Press; New York: Continuum, 2002).

18 Charlotte Elisheva Fonrobert, "When Women Walk in the Ways of Their Fathers: On Gendering Rabbinic Claims for Authority," *Journal of the History of Sexuality* 10 (2001): 398–415 (404).

19 Walter A. Elwell and Robert W. Yarbrough, *Encountering the New Testament: A Historical and Theological Survey* (Grand Rapids, MI: Baker, 1998), p. 341.

20 Josephus *Antiquities* 15.259.

21 Josephus *Antiquities* 20.143–47.

22 Josephus *Antiquities* 18.110.

23 Josephus *Life* 415.

24 Marcus J. Borg, *Meeting Jesus Again for the First Time* (San Francisco: HarperSanFrancisco, 1994), p. 13.

25 Borg, *Meeting Jesus*, p. 51.

26 Borg, *Meeting Jesus*, p. 51.

27 Elizabeth Struthers Malbon, "The Poor Widow in Mark and Her Poor Rich Readers," *Catholic Biblical Quarterly* 53 (1991): 589–604 (see 600). See also Pheme Perkins, "The Gospel of Mark: Introduction, Commentary, and Reflections," in *The New Interpreter's Bible*, vol. 8 (Nashville: Abingdon, 1995), pp. 507–733 (quotation on p. 683).

28 *New Interpreter's Bible*, p. 683.

29 Obery M. Hendricks Jr., "John," in Michael D. Coogan et al., eds., *New Oxford Annotated Bible*, 3d ed. (New York: Oxford University Press, 2001), p. 150 (New Testament).

30 Richard Horsely, "Mark," in Coogan et al., eds., *New Oxford Annotated Bible*, p. 79 (New Testament).

31 Bruce Chilton, "Caiaphas," in David N. Freedman et al., eds., *Anchor Bible Dictionary*, vol. 1; *Rabbi Jesus: An Intimate Biography* (New York and London: Doubleday, 2000).

32 http://www.explorefaith.org/LentenHomily03.15.01.html.

33 Josephus *Antiquities* 18.261–309; *War* 2.184–203; Philo *On the Embassy to Gaius* 188, 198–348.

34 Frederick Danker, ed., *A Greek-English Lexicon of the New Testament and Other Early Christian Literature* [also known as the Bauer-Arndt-Gingrich Lexicon], 3d ed. (Chicago and London: University of Chicago Press, 2000), p. 478.

35 Philip F. Esler, *Conflict and Identity in Romans: The Social Setting of Paul's Letter* (Minneapolis: Fortress, 2003), p. 63, cited in a trenchant review by Margaret P. Aymer, *Review of Biblical Literature* 7 (2005).

36 John H. Elliott, "Jesus Was Neither a 'Jew' nor a 'Christian': Pitfalls of Inappropriate Nomenclature." I thank Professor Elliott for sharing with me a copy of this talk and for the numerous conversations we have had concerning it.

37　Robert Doran, *Commentary on 2 Maccabees* (forthcoming). Doran cites Elias Bickermann, "Beiträge zur antiken Urkundengeschichte," *Archiv für Papyrusforschung und verwandte Gebiete* 8 (1927): 223–25; Claire Préaux, "Les Étrangers à l'époque hellénistique (Égypte-Delos-Rhodes)," in *L'Étranger/Foreigner*, Recueils de la Société Jean Bodin pour l'histoire comparative des institutions 9 (Paris: Dessain et Tobra, 1984), pp. 189–93. See also Koen Goudriaan, *Ethnicity in Ptolemaic Egypt* (Amsterdam: Gieben, 1988); Per Bilde, Troels Engberg-Pedersen, et al., eds., *Ethnicity in Hellenistic Egypt* (Denmark: Aarhuis UP, 1992); Margaret H. Williams, "The Meaning and Function of *Ioudaios* in Graeco-Roman Inscriptions," *Zeitschrift für Papyrologie und Epigraphik* 116 (1997): 249–62; and Shaye J. D. Cohen, *The Beginnings of Jewishness: Boundaries, Varieties, Uncertainties* (Berkeley: University of California Press, 1999).

38　Cohen, *Beginnings of Jewishness*, p. 70.

39　Cohen, *Beginnings of Jewishness*, p. 106.

40　Elliott, "Jesus Was Neither a 'Jew' nor a 'Christian.'"

41　Bruce Malina and Richard Rohrbaugh, *Social-Scientific Commentary on the Gospel of John* (Minneapolis: Fortress, 1998), p. 44.

42　Malina and Rohrbaugh, *Social-Science Commentary on John*, p. 44.

43　http://www.spiritrestoration.org/Church/Research%20History%20and%20Great%20Links/Was%20Jesus%20a%20Jew.htm.

44　http://www.khazaria.com/genetics/abstracts-cohen-levite.html.

FIVE: WITH FRIENDS LIKE THESE . . .

1　See the discussion in Mary Boys, *Has God Only One Blessing? Judaism as a Source of Christian Self-Understanding* (New York: Paulist Press, 2000), esp. p. 79, as well as introductory remarks on liberation theology, pp. 13–14.

2　Gustavo Gutiérrez, *A Theology of Liberation* (Maryknoll, NY: Orbis Books, 1973), p. 161.

3　Leonardo Boff, *Passions of Christ, Passions of the World* (Maryknoll, NY: Orbis Books, 1987), pp. 16, 13.

4　For a helpful collection, see the International Council of Christians and Jews, *The New Relationship Between Christians and Jews: Documentation of Major Statements* (International Council of Christians and Jews, Martin Buber House, Heppenheim, Germany).

5　http://www.wcc-coe.org/wcc/what/interreligious/cd33-22.html (the date of the posting is 1999).

6　Jules Isaac, *The Teaching of Contempt* (New York: Holt, Rinehart and Winston, 1964).

7　Marguérite Fassinou, "Challenges for Feminist Theology in Francophone Africa," in Ofelia Ortega, ed., *Women's Visions: Theological Reflection, Celebration, Action* (Geneva: WCC, 1995), pp. 8–17 (8–10). Another essayist in this volume correctly notes the danger of Christian feminist anti-Semitism.

8　Ruth M. Besha, "A Life of Endless Struggle: The Position of Women in Africa," in Aruna Gnanadason, Musimbi Kanyoro, and Lucia Ann Mcspadden, eds., *Women, Violence and Nonviolent Change* (Geneva: WCC, 1996), pp. 56–65 (62); the citation (n. 11) is to *By Our Lives: Stories of Women Today and in the Bible* (Geneva: WCC, 1985).

9　Grace Eneme, "Living Stones," in John S. Pobee and Bärbel von Wartenberg-Potter, eds., *New Eyes for Reading: Biblical and Theological Reflections by Women from the Third World* (Geneva: WCC, 1986), pp. 28–32 (30).

10　Bette Ekeya, "Woman, for How Long Not?" in Pobee and von Wartenberg-Potter, eds., *New Eyes for Reading*, pp. 59–67 (64).

11 See Amy-Jill Levine, "Discharging Responsibility: Matthean Jesus, Biblical Law, and Hemorrhaging Woman," in *Treasures New and Old: Recent Contributions to Matthean Studies*, Society of Biblical Literature Symposium Series, no. 1, eds. David R. Bauer and Mark Allan Powell (Atlanta: Scholars Press, 1996), pp. 379–97, reprinted in Amy-Jill Levine, ed., *A Feminist Companion to Matthew*, Feminist Companion to the New Testament and Early Christian Writings, 1 (Sheffield: Sheffield Academic Press, 2001), pp. 70–87.

12 Teresa Okure, "Feminist Interpretations in Africa," in Elisabeth Schüssler Fiorenza, *Searching the Scriptures*, vol. 1 (New York: Crossroad, 1993), p. 82. See also Elizabeth Amoah, "The Woman Who Decided to Break the Rules (Reflection, Mk 5:25–29)," in Pobee and von Wartenberg-Potter, eds., *New Eyes for Reading*, p. 3.

13 Teresa Okure, "Women in the Bible," in Virginia Fabella and Mercy Amba Oduyoye, eds., *With Passion and Compassion: Third World Women Doing Theology* (Maryknoll, NY: Orbis Books, 1988), p. 55.

14 John Meier, "The Historical Jesus and Purity," paper prepared for the joint sessions of the "Historical Jesus" and "Jewish-Christian Relations" task forces, Catholic Biblical Association of America (St. John, MN: August 2005), p. 19.

15 Meier, "The Historical Jesus and Purity," p. 19.

16 Musimbi Kanyoro, *Turn to God: Rejoice in Hope* (Geneva: WCC, 1996), p. 13.

17 Deborah Malacky Belonick, "Love and Transformation: Women Who Met Jesus," in K. K. Fitzgerald, ed., *Orthodox Women Speak* (Geneva: WCC, 1999), pp. 56–68 (61).

18 Belonick, "Love and Transformation," p. 61.

19 Belonick, "Love and Transformation," p. 61.

20 Dimitra Koukoura, "Women in the Early Christian Church," in K. K. Fitzgerald, ed., *Orthodox Women Speak* (Geneva: WCC, 1999), pp. 69–74 (70).

21 S. Wesley Ariarajah, *Did I Betray the Gospel? The Letters of Paul and the Place of Women* (Geneva: WCC, 1996), p. 21.

22 Nirmala Vasanthakumar, "Rereading the Scripture: A Hermeneutical Approach," in Musimbi Kanyoro, ed., *In Search of a Roundtable: Gender, Theology and Church Leadership* (Geneva: WCC, 1997), p. 46. In the same volume, Datuk Thu En-Yu, Lutheran bishop of Basel Christian Church of Malaysia, Kota Kinabalu, Sabah, Malaysia, insists that those in the church who would deny ordination to women "had neither a firm biblical/theological basis nor a strong Asian cultural background. Their claims revolved around a certain interpretation of the Jewish patriarchal tradition, and an unholistic theological view which ignored the priesthood of all believers" (p. 140).

23 Wanda Deifelt, "Power, Authority and the Bible," in Kanyoro, ed., *In Search of a Roundtable*, pp. 48–56 (52).

24 Elisabeth Schüssler Fiorenza, "Reading the Bible as Equals," in Kanyoro, ed., *In Search of a Roundtable*, pp. 57–70 (58).

25 Bärbel von Wartenberg-Potter, *We Will Not Hang Our Harps on the Willows: Engagement and Spirituality*, trans. Fred Kaan, Risk Book Series 34 (Geneva: WCC Publications, 1987), pp. 55–56.

26 Fernando F. Segovia, "Reading the Bible as Hispanic Americans," in Leander Keck et al., eds. [none Jewish], *The New Interpreter's Bible*, vol. 1 (Nashville, TN: Abingdon, 1994), pp. 167–73 (169).

27 See Mark A. Chancey, *The Myth of a Gentile Galilee*, Society for New Testament Studies Monograph Series 118 (Cambridge: Cambridge University Press, 2002).

28 Chan-Hie Kim, "Reading the Cornelius Story from an Asian-Immigrant Perspective," in Fernando F. Segovia and Mary Ann Tolbert, eds., *Reading from this Place*, vol. 1, *Social Location*

and Biblical Interpretation in the United States (Minneapolis: Fortress, 1995), pp. 165–74 (172–73). This essay and several others mentioned in this chapter are also cited either in my "Lilies of the Field and Wandering Jews" or in my JFSR *Roundtable*.

29 Kwok Pui-lan, "God Weeps with Our Pain," in Pobee and von Wartenberg-Potter, eds., *New Eyes for Reading*, pp. 90–95 (92).

30 Louise Kumandjek Tappa, "God in Man's Image," in Pobee and von Wartenberg-Potter, eds., *New Eyes for Reading*, pp. 101–6 (102).

31 Virgilio Elizondo, *Galilean Journey: The Mexican-American Promise* (Maryknoll, NY: Orbis Books, 1990), p. 57.

32 John Bluck, *The Giveaway God: Ecumenical Studies on Divine Generosity*, Risk Book Series 93 (Geneva: WCC Publications, 2001), pp. 15, 36, 20.

33 Several of these examples come from Michael C. Kotzin's essay, "The Continuing Challenge of Anti-Semitism," presented at the meting of the International Council of Christians and Jews (Chicago, IL, July 26, 2005). I thank Mr. Kotzin for permission to quote from his essay.

34 http://www.episdivschool.edu/whatsnew/AteekAddress.html (accessed February 2002).

35 Naim Ateek, "Pentecost and the Intifada," in Fernando F. Segovia and Mary Ann Tolbert, eds., *Reading from this Place*, vol. 2, *Social Location and Biblical Interpretation in Global Perspective* (Minneapolis: Fortress, 1995), pp. 69–81 (69).

36 *The Tennessean*, Dec. 5, 2002, p. 2A.

37 James E. Dittes, *Pastoral Counseling: The Basics* (Louisville, KY: Westminster John Knox, 1999), pp. 149–50. My thanks to Kenneth M. Jackson, who brought this book to my attention.

38 Kwok Pui-lan, "Roundtable Discussion," *Journal of Feminist Studies in Religion* 20.1 (Spring 2004): 104.

39 Kwok Pui-lan, *Postcolonial Imagination and Feminist Theology* (Louisville, KY: Westminster John Knox, 2005), p. 96.

40 Amy-Jill Levine, "The Disease of Postcolonial New Testament Studies and the Hermeneutics of Healing," *Journal of Feminist Studies in Religion* 20.1 (Summer 2004): 91–99; that piece, to which Kanyoro responded, is based in part on my "Lilies of the Field and Wandering Jews: Biblical Scholarship, Women's Roles, and Social Location," in Ingrid-Rosa Kitzberger, ed., *Transformative Encounters: Jesus and Women Revisited* (Leiden: Brill, 2000), pp. 329–52.

41 Musimbi Kanyoro, "Roundtable Discussion," *Journal of Feminist Studies in Religion* 20.1 (Spring 2004): 107.

42 World Council of Churches, *The Theology of the Churches and the Jewish People: Statements by the World Council of Churches and Its Member Churches* (Geneva: WCC, 1998), p. viii.

SIX: DISTINCT CANONS, DISTINCT PRACTICES

1 Justin Martyr *Dialogue with Trypho* 43; cf. 67–68.

2 Justin Martyr *Dialogue with Trypho* 71.

3 www.christianseparatist.org/sixth/errancy.html (accessed 24 August 2005).

4 See Roger Brooks and John J. Collins, eds., *Hebrew Bible or Old Testament? Studying the Bible in Judaism and Christianity* (Notre Dame, IN: University of Notre Dame Press, 1990).

5 *On Marriage and Concupiscence.* 2.26.43.

6 From *Tanhuma, Bereshit* 6 (and see *Genesis Rabbah* 12); citation from Bialik and Ravnitzky, eds., *The Book of Legends*, p. 22.

7 From *Bet ha-Midrash* 2:118ff. (ed. A. Jellenik); citation from Bialik and Ravnitzky, eds., *Book of Legends*, p. 31.

8 *Bava Kama* 8:1; *B. Bava Kama* 84a; and Rashi's commentary. Concise discussion appears in Joseph Telushkin, *Jewish Literacy: The Most Important Things to Know About the Jewish Religion, Its People, and Its History* (New York: Morrow, 1991), pp. 500–501.

9 "Guidelines for Lutheran-Jewish Relations" (http://www.elca.org/ecumenical/interfaith relations/jewish/guidelines.html).

10 http://www.pcusa.org/interfaith/study/christiansjews.htm.

11 Original in French and Italian; in April 2002, the Vatican Web site posted an English translation.

12 See also, e.g., Isaiah 44:1–5; 45:4; 48:20; 49:3.

13 For additional commentary, see Amy-Jill Levine, "Roland Murphy, the Pontifical Biblical Commission, Jews, and the Bible," *Biblical Theology Bulletin* 33.3 (Fall 2003), 104–13; and "The Jewish People and Their Sacred Scriptures in the Christian Bible: A Jewish Reading of the Document," *The Bible Today* (May/June 2003), 167–72.

SEVEN: QUO VADIS?

1 The expression was coined by Clark Williamson in *A Guest in the House of Israel: Post-Holocaust Church Theology* (Louisville, KY: Westminster John Knox, 1993), pp. 3–5.

2 Letter to the Eighth Assembly of the World Council of Churches from the Women and Men of the Decade Festival of the Churches in Solidarity with Women," *Ministerial Formation* 85 (April 1999): 61–66 (64).

3 *Forward Day by Day* 71.2 (May/June/July 2005): 57.

4 Klinghoffer, *Why the Jews Rejected Jesus*, p. 43.

EPILOGUE

1 Megan McKenna, *Rites of Justice: The Sacraments and Liturgy as Ethical Imperatives* (Maryknoll, NY: Orbis Books, 1997), pp. 200–221.

Subject Index

Scripture Index